Supply Chain Management and Logistics in Construction

Supply Chain Management and Logistics in Construction

Delivering tomorrow's built environment

Edited by
Greger Lundesjö

LONDON   PHILADELPHIA   NEW DELHI

Publisher's note

Every possible effort has been made to ensure that the information contained in this book is accurate at the time of going to press, and the publishers and authors cannot accept responsibility for any errors or omissions, however caused. No responsibility for loss or damage occasioned to any person acting, or refraining from action, as a result of the material in this publication can be accepted by the editor, the publisher or the authors.

First published in Great Britain and the United States in 2015 by Kogan Page Limited

Apart from any fair dealing for the purposes of research or private study, or criticism or review, as permitted under the Copyright, Designs and Patents Act 1988, this publication may only be reproduced, stored or transmitted, in any form or by any means, with the prior permission in writing of the publishers, or in the case of reprographic reproduction in accordance with the terms and licences issued by the CLA. Enquiries concerning reproduction outside these terms should be sent to the publishers at the undermentioned addresses:

2nd Floor, 45 Gee Street	1518 Walnut Street, Suite 1100	4737/23 Ansari Road
London EC1V 3RS	Philadelphia PA 19102	Daryaganj
United Kingdom	USA	New Delhi 110002
www.koganpage.com		India

© Greger Lundesjö, 2015

The right of Greger Lundesjö to be identified as the author of this work has been asserted by him in accordance with the Copyright, Designs and Patents Act 1988.

ISBN 978 0 7494 7242 9
E-ISBN 978 0 7494 7243 6

British Library Cataloguing-in-Publication Data

A CIP record for this book is available from the British Library.

Library of Congress Cataloging-in-Publication Data

Lundesjö, Greger.
  Supply chain management and logistics in construction : delivering tomorrow's built environment / Greger Lundesjö.
    pages cm
  ISBN 978-0-7494-7242-9 (paperback) – ISBN 978-0-7494-7243-6 (ebk)   1. Construction industry–Management.   2. Construction industry–Materials management.   3. Business logistics.   I. Title.
  HD9715.A2L85 2015
  624.068'7–dc23
                                                                                          2015015895

Typeset by Graphicraft Limited, Hong Kong
Print production managed by Jellyfish
Printed and bound by CPI Group (UK) Ltd, Croydon, CR0 4YY

CONTENTS

Contributor biographies x

Introduction 1
Greger Lundesjö

The expanding role of logistics in construction 1
Perspectives and opinions 4
Outline of the book 4

PART ONE Strategic perspectives 7

01 The challenge of construction logistics 9
Michael Browne

Introduction 9
Factors that influence logistics activities 13
The role of logistics management within construction 16
The challenges of the urban environment 21
Conclusion 22
Note 23
References 23

02 Aggregating global products for just-in-time delivery to construction sites 25
Mark Franklin

Introduction 25
Global sourcing 26
Investment in procurement and centralized decision making 27
Environmental legislation, quality and good waste management 28
Lean supply onto site with plot-picked delivery 29
Who is best placed to deliver an aggregation and lean delivery capability? 32
Commercial and risk issues 33
Conclusion 34

03 Construction logistics – supply of bulk materials 35
Matthew Woodcock

Introduction 35
Logistics, customers and bulk materials 35
Logistics models in construction bulk materials 43
Supply chain maturity 55
Conclusion 61
References 61

04 Effective management of a construction project supply chain 62
Stephen Robbins

Introduction 62
A typical construction project supply chain 63
Construction logistics 64
Defining 'effective' management of a construction supply chain 67
Best practice – 2020 70
Improvement strategy 71
Conclusion 74
References 75

05 Construction supply chain management strategy 77
Brian Moone

Introduction 77
Supply chain risks 79
Framework agreements 84
Supply chain management of logistics in construction 84
Case study: Mace Business School 85
Conclusion 87
Reference 87

PART TWO The impact of BIM and new data management capabilities on supply chain management in construction 89

06 Data management for integrated supply chains in construction 91
Wes Beaumont and Jason Underwood

Introduction 91
Information management in construction 92
Big data and construction 102

Data and the integrated supply chain   111
Enterprise-level integration   115
Conclusion   117
References   118

PART THREE   Construction logistics and sustainability   121

07   The role of logistics in achieving sustainable construction: a Swedish perspective   123
Monika Bubholz, Camilla Einarsson and Lars-Göran Sporre

Introduction   123
Sustainable construction logistics   126
Practical considerations for efficient and sustainable construction logistics   130
Case studies: 134
   'The University Hospital of the future' – University Hospital in Linköping, Sweden   134
   Triangeln (the Triangle) – Malmö, Sweden   135
Conclusion   137
Reference   138

08   Resource efficiency benefits of effective construction logistics   139
Malcolm Waddell

Introduction   139
Construction sustainability impact   140
Supply chain influence on sustainable construction logistics   143
Construction logistics strategies and how they can influence resource efficiency   144
Material logistics planning   154
Conclusion   155
References   158

PART FOUR   Logistics operations   159

09   The role of the construction logistics manager   161
Andy Brown

Introduction   161
Logistics professional and service sourcing   163
Consulting logistics professionals   165
Construction logistics managers   169

Creating a construction logistics plan (CLP)   174
Conclusion   181

10 Third-party logistics operators in construction: the role they play and the role they could play   183
Pete Flinders

Introduction   183
3PL definition   184
Complicated and 'unstructured' supply chain   185
Impact of downturn   185
Supply chains with a dominant entity   188
Case studies: 189
   Aircraft Carrier Alliance   190
   B&Q   192
Omni-channel   194
Primary and secondary distribution networks   194
International construction supply chains   195
Final mile logistics – construction consolidation centres   196
Why doesn't the construction industry make better use of 3PL services?   197
Case study: London 2012 Olympics   199
Evolution of the 3PL role   200
What will trigger momentum of the 3PL role in construction logistics?   202
Conclusion   203
References   203

11 Managing construction logistics for confined sites in urban areas   205
Ruvinde Kooragamage

Introduction   205
Identifying current challenges in managing construction logistics   206
Developing a theoretical framework   211
Conclusion   218
References   221

12 Consolidation centres in construction logistics   225
Greger Lundesjö

Introduction   225
The resources, functionality and operation of a CCC   227
The benefits of using a CCC   233
Types of CCC   237

Locating a CCC   239
Conclusion   240
End note   241
References   242

13   Delivery management systems   243
Rick Ballard and Nick Hoare

Introduction   243
What is a delivery management system?   244
The features of computerized delivery management   246
The benefits of proper management of deliveries   247
Who is it for?   250
The future   251
Case studies: 252
   Royal Adelaide Hospital   252
   Media City UK, Salford   253
   M1 motorway widening   254
   MidKent College   256
Conclusion   256

Glossary   258
Index   262

CONTRIBUTOR BIOGRAPHIES

Rick Ballard has worked for many years on supply chain and logistics developments in the UK and other parts of Europe, covering a range of industry sectors. He has worked on government-funded research projects in construction and has written many articles and papers on various supply chain issues. In recent years he has developed a special interest in the construction industry and has been one of the UK's leading advocates of the need for good supply chain and logistics practice in construction. He was the founding chairman of the Construction Supply Chain Forum of the Chartered Institute of Logistics and Transport and he was a member of both the Integrated Supply Teams Working Group and the Task Group on Logistics set up by the Strategic Forum for Construction.

Wes Beaumont (MCIOB) is a chartered construction manager with experience of all stages of a project life cycle. During his career he has worked in contracting, in both pre-construction and construction, latterly as a BIM manager for Kier Group plc. He led the early implementation of BIM, forging partnerships with all aspects of the supply chain during a change management process. He now forms part of Turner & Townsend's BIM and Analytics team and focuses on assisting the public and private sector with optimizing their assets through design, procurement, construction and operations. He was a core team member of the CIC's BIM2050 group and co-authored the Built Environment 2050 report focusing on procurement, supply chain integration and modern project-delivery strategies. He has a first-class honours BSc in Construction Management and an MSc with distinction in BIM and Integrated Design. His research interests include the adoption of modern procurement and project-delivery strategies to facilitate collaborative working, behavioural economics, lean construction and the use of data to improve contract administration through objective decision making and data visualization.

Andy Brown (BEng (Hons) FCIOB FCILT, Operations Director, Mace Group) is a construction executive who has worked in the industry for 20 years. A Mace Group Operations Director, Andy's project experience includes the Emirates Air Line, Bank Station Capacity Upgrade, the Birmingham Bullring and Heathrow Terminal 5. Andy has planned the construction logistics of billions of pounds' worth of capital works in his career to date and his teams have delivered over £50 million as construction logistics subcontractors. Currently consulting at London Underground, Andy has a degree in Civil Engineering, is a Chartered Construction

Manager, a Fellow of the Chartered Institute of Building and a Fellow of the Chartered Institute of Logistics and Transport.

Michael Browne is Professor of Logistics and directs logistics and freight transport research at the University of Westminster. Recent projects include: research on improving city logistics strategies, forecasting future trends in logistics and freight transport and identifying best practice in logistics management. He leads the university's input to the Volvo Research and Educational Foundation's Centre of Excellence for Sustainable Urban Freight Systems. He has worked on studies for Transport for London, the European Commission, the UK Department for Transport, research councils and commercial organizations. He teaches on master's courses in logistics and supply chain management at the university and is also a visiting professor at the University of Gothenburg and the University Paris II. He represents the university of Westminster on many external committees and boards and chairs the Central London Freight Quality Partnership.

Monika Bubholz is a sustainability consultant at Sweco Industry AB. Monika has more than 10 years' experience within the fields of sustainability and energy efficiency related to industrial projects. She was one of the authors of Sweco's sustainability concept 'Sustainable Industry', a method aimed at providing industry with a practical and structured sustainability concept. During the last few years Monika has spoken at industrial conferences, focusing on improving sustainability across a number of industrial sectors. She is also working with green procurement projects where environmental, ethical and social issues are embedded in the demands of supply chains.

Camilla Einarsson is a logistics consultant at Sweco Management AB. Camilla has been engaged in many of the largest construction projects in the eastern parts of Sweden and she developed the logistics concept for the new University Hospital, Linköping, Sweden. Known as 'Hospital of the future' this is one of the largest hospital projects in recent years. Currently she is coordinating a number of the major contractors in Sweden in a joint new development, also in Linköping. She has authored a report on construction planning for Bomässan Bo2017. At Sweco Camilla works as Project Manager with a wide experience of large and small projects and, as such, she believes that effective communication and collaboration from the very outset of a project are the key to success.

Pete Flinders is Contract Manager for Wincanton, running its construction consolidation centres and the distribution of building materials. He is a member of the CILT Construction Supply Chain Forum and completed a BSc (Hons) in Logistics at Aston University, where he was awarded CILT Student of the Year. He has supply chain experience in a breadth of sectors including construction, general merchandise, fast-moving consumer goods, drinks, home shopping and international logistics. His career has involved a depth of supply chain functions from implementing and developing new supply chain solutions to running warehouse, transport and IT systems.

Mark Franklin was Service and Supply Chain Director at Travis Perkins. A manufacturing engineer, he studied for an MSc at Warwick University whilst starting his career at Land Rover. Having worked across multiple sectors, including retail, automotive aftermarket and production, electronics, telecoms and building materials, he is interested in the transfer of knowledge from one sector to another. He is a member of the Institute of Logistics and Transport and the Logistics Directors Forum. Having returned to the automotive industry in 2014, he is Global Parts and Supply Chain Director at Jaguar Land Rover.

Nick Hoare is a senior systems consultant with The Logistics Business Ltd and he was a founder member of the consultancy when it started in 1991. He has been involved in a wide variety of logistics and supply chain projects and has been responsible for developing a number of software tools targeting supply chain issues. He came into contact with the construction industry in the 1990s where he saw the synergy between Yard Management Systems commonly used for fast-moving consumer goods warehouse sites and the management of deliveries to construction sites. He has been heavily involved in the development of delivery management systems for construction sites ever since, including some work with the Building Research Establishment (BRE) and the Waste & Resources Action Programme (WRAP).

Ruvinde Kooragamage has been working as a planner with Vinci Construction since November 2013 and has been involved with a range of tender and construction projects in London. He completed a Master of Civil Engineering degree in 2008 at UCL and obtained a Master of Construction Economics and Management degree in 2009 at the Bartlett School of Construction and Project Management, UCL. Ruvinde is currently finalizing a Doctorate of Engineering degree at UCL, which includes the development of a logistics model to control material flow to confined construction sites in congested cities. His research has been presented at several international conferences including the USA (ICCEPM, 2013), Malaysia (REAAA, 2013) and Australia (CIB WBC, 2013). Ruvinde has an active interest in construction information technology, chiefly the integration of BIM and RFID to manage real-time material flow.

Greger Lundesjö (FCILT) having gained an MSc in Industrial Engineering worked for Swedish company BT Systems and later the Swiss company Swisslog in senior roles in Sweden and the UK. His focus was on logistics automation for clients in retail and manufacturing. In 2004 Greger became an independent consultant but also worked as an associate to the consultancy The Logistics Business. Here Greger developed an expertise in construction logistics, applying the logistics thinking from other sectors in the construction industry. A major part of his work has been with WRAP (the Waste & Resources Action Programme) focusing on reducing the industry's environmental impact through efficient logistics. For WRAP he has produced several reports, including 'Using Construction Consolidation Centres to Reduce Construction Waste and Carbon Emissions'.

Brian Moone (FCIOB, MRICS) is Director of Supply Chain Management and Development at Mace, a leading international construction and consultancy business. Brian has a strong background in best practice, having previously been a director of Construction Best Practice, an organization established to share best practice across the construction industry. The knowledge and experience gained from leading best practice has been combined with his practical experience as a practising chartered building surveyor and chartered builder to deliver innovative and robust supply chain management solutions. Brian has been responsible for establishing the highly respected Mace Business School, a unique solution to driving continuous improvement through the development of managers within the Mace supply chain.

Stephen Robbins has worked for Laing O'Rourke as Logistics Manager since 2005 and has been involved in the development and implementation of logistics and supply chain management strategies on a number of major projects, including the operation of a construction consolidation centre.

In 2004 Stephen authored the Department of Trade and Industry (DTI) sponsored report 'Construction Logistics Consolidation Centre' and went on to co-author *Managing Construction Logistics* in 2010. He is particularly interested in construction logistics models and third-party stakeholder management and is actively involved in research in this area.

Lars-Göran Sporre is Senior Vice President and is heading the industry division of COWI AB. Lars-Göran has 30 years' experience of industrial investment projects within the areas of production, warehousing and distribution. He has been managing projects, national and international, in all phases from early feasibility studies to start-up and operation of new installations. He has a special interest in the planning of efficient internal logistics operations. After heading Sweco's industrial division, Lars-Göran is now concentrating on development of consultant services related to industry and logistics.

Jason Underwood is currently a senior lecturer in Construction ICT and Civil Engineering Surveying along with Director of Postgraduate Research Admissions and Training and Programme Director of the MSc in Building Information Modelling programme within the School of the Built Environment at the University of Salford. He is also Director of Construct IT For Business, an industry-led non-profit making collaborative membership-based network, comprising leading edge organizations representative of the construction industry supply chain in addition to professional institutes and R&D/academic institutions, whose aim is to improve industry performance through the innovative application of IT and act as a catalyst for academic and industrial collaboration. Dr Underwood's background is a combination of civil/structural engineering and construction ICT with over eighteen years' research experience in the area of concurrent engineering, integrated and collaborative computing in construction, product and building information modelling, and organizational e-readiness towards delivering strategic value from ICT investment through involvement in both UK and EU funded research projects, on which he has published extensively. In relation to BIM particularly, his interest is focused towards BIM implementation and deployment together with education and training in the development of BIM capabilities, in particular bringing together the concept of organizational e-readiness with BIM. At a national level he is actively engaged in the Education & Training working group to deliver the UK Government BIM strategy, member of the Behaviours4Collaboration Group, and the present Chair of the UK BIM Academic Forum. He is also engaged at a local level including the Northwest BIM Hub of the UK Government BIM Strategy and the Northwest Construction Hub BIM Special Interest Group. Dr Underwood is Editor-in-Chief of the Journal of 3D Information Modelling (IJ3DIM) specifically focused on BIM along with 3D GIS and their integration.

Malcolm Waddell works for WRAP, whose vision is a world where resources are used sustainably. Malcolm has worked in the construction sector focusing on improving resource efficiency. He has led WRAP's work in construction logistics developing guidance, exemplars, tools and resources and material logistics planning. He has led WRAP's work supporting the construction products sector by developing product resource efficiency action plans including flooring, timber, plasterboard, windows, ceiling tiles and rigid insulation, clay bricks and blocks, precast concrete and ready-mix concrete. Previously Malcolm worked with key clients, contractors, suppliers and manufacturers in working towards halving waste to landfill and led on improving waste management throughout the utility sector.

Prior to joining WRAP, his background involved working in on-site logistics management, transport management and business development. This includes working as National Operations Manager for a major retailer's returns process, which involved the management of the operations, maximizing the value of returned items by liaising with vendors and secondary markets, providing bespoke product information and ensuring effective waste management.

Matthew Woodcock (FCILT) is Head of Group Logistics and Supply Chain, Lafarge Tarmac. Over the last eight years, Matthew has held senior logistics and supply chain roles across a number of the major building materials companies including Lafarge Tarmac, Aggregate Industries and CEMEX. A passionate advocate for the supply chain concept, his focus is on developing and delivering capability improvement in this area. Matthew is a chartered fellow of CILT and has been a committee member of CILT Construction Forum for over five years. Prior to entering the construction sector he held a number of logistics and supply chain roles in retail, airports, management consultancy and food service, working with or for blue-chip companies.

Introduction

GREGER LUNDESJÖ

The expanding role of logistics in construction

If you ask professionals from a range of industries to define the term logistics you might be told that it refers to the methods and systems whereby specified products and materials are delivered to the right location at the right time, in the right quantity and quality and at the lowest cost. Others would say that it relates to the transport, storage and handling of products through the supply chain from raw material through value-added processes to the end user.

The construction industry is different. In construction, at least traditionally, the answer would typically be that the logistics function has responsibility for site security, vertical lifts, cleaning, walkways, hoardings, signage, staff welfare, the canteen and possibly also accommodation for construction workers, health and safety, traffic management, gates etc. That is, the logistics function is responsible for all the various site services essential for a functioning construction project except for the actual construction work. Put another way, the logistics function is a supporting role to the primary activity of construction. When asked about the supply of materials to the point of use, the logistics manager on a construction project might state that this is the responsibility of the various trade subcontractors engaged in the project, who are contracted on a fixed-price basis including all materials, and not part of the logistics operation. When logistics has included materials handling it has related to site logistics with little concern about what happens in the supply chain. As Andy Brown of Mace remarked during discussions about this book: 'We are responsible for everything that does not get left behind when we leave the completed project.' (The responsibilities of the logistics manager are covered in depth in Chapter 9 by Andy Brown.)

During recent years however there has been a growing involvement by logistics in issues concerning the management and handling of materials both on construction sites and in the supply chain. Comparisons are frequently made with other sectors – mainly retailing and manufacturing – and attempts are made to apply the advanced logistics and supply chain management practices from those sectors in the construction industry. But progress in this area is difficult for many reasons: construction lacks the continuity of other industries – projects start, run for a limited period of time during which conditions change continually and then finish; projects consist of many different, often uncoordinated, supply chains operated by a range of subcontractors; construction projects are often large and the main contractor's first priority is to offload the risk by splitting the project into a number of fixed-price separate work packages; and cash flow management might lead to subcontracts being let as late as possible within the programme. All this makes collaboration in the supply chain extremely challenging and illustrates why logistics and supply chain management do not play (or at least have not played) the central and strategic role that they do in some other sectors. Another contributing factor to logistics being undervalued is that the necessary logistics tasks within work packages are often not explicitly identified; no cost is assigned and they are assumed to be included 'free'.

One of the objectives of this book is to develop the logistics concept within construction to encompass the complete, often global, supply chain. It should be emphasized at this point that the site services traditionally provided by the logistics function are essential and without them no project can be safely and efficiently completed. Indeed with a majority of projects being constructed in busy, high-density cities and urban areas those tasks are becoming ever more challenging. Nor should we imagine that logistics in construction will be just the same as in, say, retailing. The following chapters will demonstrate some of the ways in which a modern approach to logistics and supply chain management can enhance the performance of the industry.

Construction is logistics

Logistics plays a much greater role in construction than many people realize; it is simply taken for granted. This is why there is so much scope for efficiency improvements (cost reductions and programme certainty) through the application of a professional logistics approach. The extent to which construction is made up mainly of logistics activities is illustrated in Figure 0.1 by Stephen Robbins (the author of Chapter 4).

The diagram in Figure 0.1 is of course an extremely simplified example. In real projects there are many such supply chains, but that does not weaken the argument; in fact the opposite is true. The various supply chains often compete for scarce resources such as gate access, site storage space, forklifts and manual handling capacity. The supply chains are interrelated in time with often complex build programmes; the just-in-time (JIT) delivery of appropriate quantities of materials, the norm in manufacturing industries, is often not achieved on building sites. The result is all too often poor utilization of construction labour, and time and/or cost overruns. It follows from this that a stronger focus on all aspects of logistics and supply chain management does not just improve logistics efficiency – it can greatly improve overall construction project performance in terms of efficiency, cost and programme certainty.

FIGURE 0.1 Building a block wall

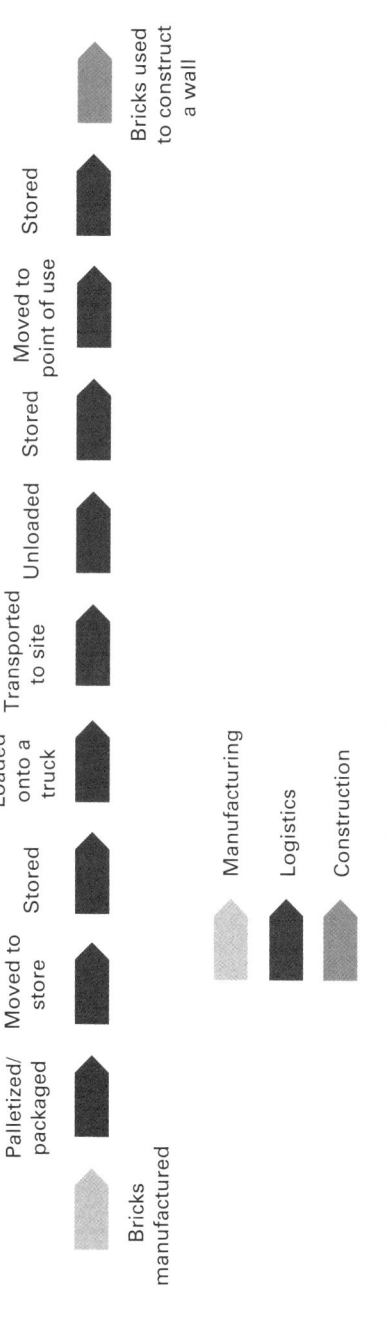

Perspectives and opinions

It is in the very nature of supply chains that they are made up of different actors fulfilling different but interrelated roles. In this book, rather than only taking a bird's-eye view of the supply chain, we also let the different actors speak. Chapters are provided by: academics specializing in logistics, supply chain management and the application of IT and building information modelling (BIM) in the construction industry; main contractors, including both supply chain management specialists and logistics specialists; the supply side of the industry with chapters from the heavy products sector (cement, asphalt etc) and from the builders' merchants; the third-party logistics industry; sustainability experts; and from consultants and system suppliers.

Not only does this wide variety of voices provide different perspectives on the topic, but the various contributors also share with the reader their opinions as to the state of the industry and the direction it should take with regard to logistics and supply chain management.

Outline of the book

The book has four parts:

- Part One: Strategic perspectives on supply chain management and logistics in the construction industry.
- Part Two: The impact of BIM and new data management capabilities on supply chain management in construction.
- Part Three: Construction logistics and sustainability.
- Part Four: Logistics operations in the construction industry.

It should be said that these are very broad areas and that many of the writers cut across all areas from strategy to operations; but the structure might help to steer the reader to his or her particular area of interest.

Part One looks at logistics and supply chain strategy from three different viewpoints. Michael Browne sets the scene in Chapter 1 by defining logistics and analysing the key factors that impact on logistics in construction. Under the chapter title 'The challenge of construction logistics', he shows how construction logistics must respond to the global trend of increased urbanization while at the same time conforming to ever higher demands for sustainability.

In Chapters 2 and 3 Mark Franklin and Matthew Woodcock apply the suppliers' perspective. Franklin in Chapter 2 looks at the builders' merchants sourcing a wide product range globally for delivery to construction sites on a JIT basis. The chapter discusses how to achieve a lean supply chain and also who is best placed to serve this market, including not only the traditional players but also new web-based retailers. By contrast Woodcock, in Chapter 3, analyses in depth the significant market of bulk materials. After analysing four key product areas (cement, aggregates, asphalt and ready-mixed concrete) the chapter assesses supply chain maturity in each area, how it can be improved and the benefits that will follow.

In Chapters 4 and 5 Stephen Robbins and Brian Moone respectively address supply chain management in construction from the main contractor's perspective. In Chapter 4, Robbins analyses the effective management of a construction project's supply chain. The chapter reviews existing theory and writing on the subject and then provides a structured overview of a number of strategic options for managing the logistics of the supply chain. In Chapter 5, also from a main contractor's point of view, Moone takes a corporate perspective and introduces the concept of supply chain management with a focus on the assessment of risk, how to select partners and how to develop partners through learning.

In Part Two, Chapter 6, Wes Beaumont and Jason Underwood take on the subject of information and data management in the construction industry. They look at how the structure of the industry has changed and how that has influenced the ways in which information is held and distributed among the supply chain participants. The introduction of BIM is analysed, as is the concept of big data and how it applies to the construction industry. The chapter envisions how an often fragmented industry, where information flows can be chaotic, can move towards effective, lean and integrated processes; and the old concept of master builder gets a revival.

Part Three deals with sustainability and construction logistics. In the current debate about climate change and how to create a sustainable society there are those who argue that sustainability carries a high cost and requires sacrifices, while others maintain that with the right approach a focus on resource efficiency in fact lowers costs. Whatever your view on the wider debate, logistics is one of the areas where resource efficiency, and reduced environmental impact, go hand-in-hand with cost efficiency. In Chapter 7, Lars-Göran Sporre, Camilla Einarsson and Monika Bubholz look at the role of logistics in achieving sustainable construction from a Swedish perspective. They present an eight-dimensional model of sustainability and a logistics strategy for construction. Two case studies illustrate the approach. From a UK perspective, in Chapter 8 Malcolm Waddell analyses the resource efficiency benefits of effective construction logistics. The chapter shows some of the environmental impacts of the construction industry, such as waste volumes and CO_2 emissions, and then expands on a set of logistics strategies with demonstrated positive impacts on resource efficiency and cost.

Part Four starts with Chapter 9 and the role of the logistics manager. While it is focused on site logistics rather than supply chain management aspects, this chapter sets out in great detail the far-reaching responsibilities of the logistics manager in a modern context. Whether you need to draw up a logistics manager's job description or want some input for developing a construction logistics plan (CLP), you will find the information here. Finally, Andy Brown also takes a critical look at how the role has been viewed traditionally and how it needs to develop.

In Chapter 10 Pete Flinders analyses the role of third-party logistics operators (3PLs) in the construction industry. 3PLs play a significant and often sophisticated role in other sectors and while they are active in construction their capabilities are not utilized to the extent they could be. Flinders analyses why that is the case and how they could provide much more value to the industry. A telling quote from the chapter is worth highlighting: 'It is fairly inconceivable to imagine a town centre convenience retail store being supplied along similar lines to that of a common construction supply chain. Instead of consolidated deliveries with "shelf ready" packs on flexible-wheeled handling units coordinated outside of peak trading periods, the common building site approach to the supply chain could involve store aisles being full of materials that were delivered three weeks early, but missing some key lines, multiple vehicles waiting to unload outside the store with goods being moved by hand and a lot of packaging waste.' Flinders then details how 3PLs can add value to the industry and illustrates the opportunities for improvement through case studies.

One of the fundamental trends identified in Chapter 1 is that of globally increased urbanization. This means managing construction logistics in high-density, inner-city areas with all that entails in terms of space restrictions, traffic conditions, rules laid down by local authorities etc. This is the topic of Chapter 11, 'Managing construction logistics for confined sites in urban areas'. Ruvinde Kooragamage provides an in-depth analysis of the topic with all its ramifications and suggests management strategies.

Several chapters mention construction consolidation centres (CCCs) as a useful logistics solution for construction logistics. In Chapter 12 Greger Lundesjö analyses consolidation and its role in construction. The chapter sets out the resources required and describes the functionality, operation and benefits of a CCC. Many of the examples and benefits are drawn from studies carried out focusing on the environmental benefits of better construction logistics, mirroring some of the conclusions of Part Three of this book.

Finally in Chapter 13 Rick Ballard and Nick Hoare focus on one critical aspect of construction logistics: delivery management. This again is an aspect of construction becoming ever more critical as a result of the pressures of construction in inner-city areas. When the logistics strategy depends on JIT deliveries, the logistics manager needs the tools to plan, control and monitor those deliveries. The principles are further demonstrated in case studies from the UK and Australia.

PART ONE
Strategic perspectives

The challenge of construction logistics

01

MICHAEL BROWNE

Introduction

Construction logistics is a very challenging area in which to manage the range of logistics activities, including inventory control, transport, recovery of waste, recycling and so on. Some of the features of construction are unique to that industry. However, there are often useful lessons that can be found in other sectors such as manufacturing and retail. The aim of this chapter is to provide a broad introduction to logistics management as a discipline and to explain some of the main features of logistics management that have emerged since the mid-1990s. The chapter starts by defining logistics and explaining something about the interactions with other areas such as purchasing and supply chain management. The second part of the chapter focuses in more depth on transport and storage activities within logistics. Third, the chapter reviews some of the issues that have emerged in the consideration of construction logistics. Many of these themes are discussed in detail in subsequent chapters. A great deal of construction activity is associated with urban areas and this spatial context is discussed in the fourth section of the chapter. Finally, a short conclusion draws out some of the key features of the challenge of managing logistics within the construction sector.

Definitions and the importance of logistics

Logistics is now a widely used and understood term throughout the business world, and refers essentially to the management of supply chains in commerce and industry. The box below contains several definitions of logistics and shows the scope of the discipline and some of the changes over time.

Definitions of logistics

The management of all activities which facilitate movement and the co-ordination of supply and demand in the creation of time and place utility.
(Hesket, Glaskowsky and Ivie, 1973)

The technology of control of the physical flow of materials and goods and related information that a firm sends, transfers and receives.
(Colin and Fabbe-Costes, 1994)

Logistics is an application-oriented scientific discipline. It analyses and models division-of-labour economic systems as time-based and location-based flows of objects (above all goods and people) in networks, supplying recommendations for action on the design and implementation of these networks.
(BVL, 2010)

Logistics management is that part of supply chain management that plans, implements, and controls the efficient, effective forward and reverse flow and storage of goods, services, and related information between the point of origin and the point of consumption in order to meet customers' requirements.
(CSCMP, 2013)

The Chartered Institute of Logistics and Transport defines logistics as 'the time-related positioning of resource'. This definition is interesting because it draws attention to the importance of time as a feature that has been significant in changing the way that managers think about planning and organizing their supply chain operations and logistics activities.

Logistics is also described as the 'five rights'. Essentially, it is the process of ensuring that a product or a service is:

- in the right place;
- at the right time;
- in the right quantity;
- at the right quality;
- at the right price.

Precise definitions can therefore be seen to vary, but the common thread is a concern for the movement and storage of goods, together with the associated information flows, from the beginning to the end of the supply chain (the supply chain being the entire system of supply from point of growth/production through to the point of use/consumption then beyond that to the point when products are recycled or enter the waste stream). So, for a manufacturing company, logistics management could include:

- the procurement and sourcing of raw materials or components;
- inwards transport;
- materials handling and storage and the link to production processes;
- the final distribution of finished products to customers;
- after-sales services, including return and ultimate disposal.

Therefore logistics costs include storage costs, together with the financial cost of holding stock or inventory, handling costs, transport costs, packaging and administration. Increasingly, with the growth in environmental pressures and legislation and the need therefore to reuse or recycle materials, the transport and handling costs incurred in these activities can also be considered in the total logistics costs for a product.

The costs of these activities (transport, storage, handling and so on) can be considerable. It is not unusual for them to amount to some 10 per cent of the total sales value of products produced by a manufacturing company. Of course their importance as a proportion of the final price of goods varies according to the product in question. For products with a low value to mass ratio the significance of logistics costs in their final price is likely to be considerable.

However, measuring logistics costs can be difficult. Definitions vary and the significant role of outsourcing can make it hard for companies to keep track of the true costs of their logistics operations. Managers often adopt a number of key performance indicators (KPIs) in order to track and monitor costs (Braithwaite, 2014). Understanding and controlling costs and anticipating trends is argued to be an essential part of remaining competitive.

Logistics management has been referred to as 'joined-up thinking' and indeed it is this aspect of considering the trade-offs and interrelationships between different activities taking place in a supply chain (transport and storage, for example) that lies at the heart of logistics planning.

Logistics and the supply chain

Logistics management is a discipline that spans boundaries within an organization – therefore it helps to ensure the coordination of activities including purchasing, production, inventory management, finance and marketing. Logistics management is also required when flows between companies are considered. Supply chain management can be seen as a broader management approach that includes a strong focus on the interaction of organizations that are working together in the supply chain. Much of this interaction will involve the management of logistics.

Logistics management is an integrating function, which coordinates and optimizes all logistics activities. Logistics management also integrates logistics activities with other functions including marketing, sales, manufacturing, finance and information technology. Mangan *et al* (2011) define supply chain management as 'the management across a network of upstream and downstream organisations of material, information and resource flows that lead to the creation of value in the form of products and/or services'.

Management decisions concerned with the construction supply chain need to encompass many factors including:

- Spatial aspects of the supply chain (issues such as where to source products and materials and where to locate distribution centres to best serve the downstream construction activity).
- Transport operations within the chain (for instance the mode of transport used, whether transport is operated in-house or contracted out, consideration of different stages of transport in the supply chain etc).
- Stockholding systems used in the chain (for instance the size and degree of automation of warehouses, the amount of stock that should be held).
- Materials handling systems used in the supply chain (ie the systems used to load and unload transport vehicles and convey products within a warehouse and at a construction site. This can involve examination of the equipment used and the appropriateness of the operation itself).
- Interaction between different logistics activities in the chain (for instance consideration of trade-offs between different logistics activities such as transport and stockholding – by reducing the total number of warehouses it is possible to reduce total stockholding costs but transport costs are likely to increase; supply chain analysis can help to examine the most appropriate solution within a given set of constraints).
- The role of, and interaction between, different supply chain parties (ie consideration of how those involved in the chain could perform their tasks in a more efficient manner and how different parties could work better together through planning and information exchange).

By considering the entire supply chain associated with moving a product to the end user in an integrated manner it is possible to gain a better understanding of logistics costs arising in the supply of a product, and to consider ways in which the supply chain can be efficiently organized and managed in order to reduce these costs.

Diversity of the construction industry

A challenge for construction logistics is that while the processes described above can be argued to be generic, the application of these processes in construction is extremely varied. Construction sites vary from the small-scale building of private houses to major areas of urban regeneration with multiple activities taking place in a city location at the same time. The nature of the construction industry means that organizations of many different sizes and levels of sophistication will often be involved in a project. This means that the coordination aspect of logistics management is complicated and can be hard to achieve.

Factors that influence logistics activities

When considering the logistics costs associated with a product a number of key factors about the characteristics need to be considered. The particular characteristics of any given product will have an impact upon the distribution system for that product. Product characteristics that will influence the distribution system can be classified in three categories: volume to weight ratio, value to weight ratio and special characteristics. Given the range of materials and products used in construction it is clear that there is tremendous variety in terms of these ratios and the special characteristics and storage, handling and transport requirements. It is also important to recognize that global issues also impact on construction logistics. For example the many political, regulatory and cultural differences that need to be taken into account when shipping materials internationally.

Volume to weight ratio

Both the volume and weight characteristics of a product are likely to have a significant impact upon transport costs. Distribution systems tend to deal with products with low volume to weight ratios more efficiently than products with high ratios (examples of products with low ratios include dense products such as steel and hard woods, whilst high-ratio products include many items such as insulation materials). This is because products with a low volume to weight ratio tend to fully utilize the carrying capacity of a road freight vehicle, handling equipment and storage space. Meanwhile high-ratio products occupy more space and result in the underutilization of vehicle/handling equipment weight constraints, and therefore raise transport and storage costs.

Value to weight ratio

The higher the value of the product, the greater the potential for absorbing the logistics costs (ie the smaller the proportion of the final cost of the product accounted for by logistics). By using the value to weight ratio it is possible to consider the distribution costs associated with a product in terms of the value per unit weight of that product.

Products with low value to weight ratios (such as sand, ore, coal and gravel) tend to be associated with higher transport costs (as a proportion of total delivered cost) than products with high ratios (for example, electronic equipment and computers). However, conversely, the storage costs for products with high value to weight ratios are greater than those for products with low ratios; this is explained by the level of capital tied up in the stock and the need for expensive, secure warehousing.

Special characteristics

There are a number of other characteristics of a product that affect the selection of an appropriate transport, storage and handling system. The fragility of a product will determine the packaging requirements to safeguard the product during transportation and handling. The perishability of a product will affect the conditions under which it must be moved and stored and the speed at which it must travel through the supply chain. Certain products possess hazardous characteristics and must therefore be moved, handled and stored in isolation from other products and within stringent regulations. The nature of construction logistics means that there are many products that exhibit special characteristics, leading to complicated and challenging logistics management requirements.

Time issues

Construction logistics has many varied time issues that influence the scope for efficiency. For a large project, planning will take place over a long time period and the time before construction (or initial demolition if the site is already built on) may easily be a period of several years. The construction phase itself will run into years for a large project and during that time the flows to and from the site will vary considerably in terms of the volume of materials, the number of vehicle movements and the nature of the items being moved on to and away from the site. In addition, during the construction phase managing the flow of materials becomes critical to efficient use of the resources of labour and equipment at the site itself. All this planning and then execution takes place against a background of uncertainty over weather and, in the case of construction in urban areas, the need to consider complex traffic patterns and congestion, which can all influence the timely arrival of materials to a site. Much attention in logistics has been focused on just-in-time (JIT) systems and construction projects are often argued to need to adopt the principles of JIT. But the complexity and challenges of doing this must be acknowledged. Later chapters in the book give many examples of how logistics management can be improved to deal with the time challenge for construction.

Key transport and storage considerations for products

Transport

Transport is an extremely important element in the supply of most products. It is the key link in the supply chain – for example, in the case of food supply it joins all the activities that have to take place between the point of production on-farm through to the point of sale (eg at a supermarket) and finally point of use (eg consumption by the customer at home). Transport links together all these activities in the supply chain, which can include growing the food, harvesting, manufacturing and processing, handling and storage and the locations in which they occur.

The same is true within the construction industry where transport is essential in the process of transforming raw materials into finished products and ensuring that these materials and products are delivered efficiently and safely to many different destinations.

As well as transport being significant in any consideration of product supply systems – because of the role it plays in making the product flow smoothly between the point of production and consumption – transport is also important as a result of the costs associated with it. Transport expressed as a proportion of total delivered cost will vary depending upon the product in question, but is likely to be relatively high in the case of low-value products that are transported over long distances (which will be true for some construction materials). It is therefore very important that the necessary attention is given to consideration of transportation issues when planning the supply of materials and products.

Storage

Storage costs are made up of three key elements:

- the physical costs of stockholding (ie the cost of building, equipping and operating warehouses) including labour costs;
- the opportunity cost of holding stock (ie the cost of having money tied up in stock) or the cost of borrowing money;
- the costs of 'goods loss' during storage: this can result from damage to the stock, theft and changes in taste that make the goods unusable (or means they cannot be sold).

Products can be stored at several points in the supply chain: the point of extraction/harvest, the manufacturing/processing point, the distribution centre and at the retail outlet. Each point of stockholding requires handling of the product – and the more times the product is handled the greater the total logistics costs (as handling requires both equipment and labour).

As well as raising issues about who will be responsible for storage, this also has implications for the point in the supply chain at which storage costs will arise and who will bear these costs (and the impact that money tied up in stock will have upon cash flow). The size of the storage facilities in the supply chain will also affect the transport arrangements. For example, a retail outlet with a relatively small on-site stock level (eg just what is displayed on the shelf – a few days' supply) will require more frequent, evenly spread deliveries than an outlet with a large storage capacity (eg with an attached warehouse).

Control of the supply chain

The issue of supply chain control has received considerable attention over the years. Within a supply chain there are often many different organizations and the relative power of these organizations within the chain can play an important part in affecting the scope for efficiency and coordination. Within the grocery retail supply chain in the UK a strong trend has been for the major retailers to control more of their upstream supply chains. Until the 1970s the pattern of control in the grocery supply chain was one of manufacture control until the point of delivery to store (shop). However, retailers realized that by adopting a system of regional distribution centres (RDCs) they could gain valuable efficiency benefits in terms of receiving products from suppliers and also when delivering in fewer and more consolidated vehicle loads to their stores. Having achieved a high degree of centralization in the period from 1980 to the mid-1990s retailers then went a stage further and in some cases sought to control the whole of the physical chain between the supplier and the store, instigating what became known as 'factory gate pricing'. This control enabled retailers to derive further efficiency gains and to improve service levels and reduce waste such as empty trips. A question that arises is whether this degree of control can be copied by other industries. It seems that in construction the scope for very tight upstream control may be more limited because the complexity of sourcing, the specialized nature of materials and handling requirements, the lack of a fixed infrastructure such as the RDCs all make it a more complicated logistics puzzle. Nevertheless the principle of control and visibility is an important one and it is evident that good construction logistics seeks high levels of transparency and visibility of the materials in the upstream chain.

The role of logistics management within construction

Clearly logistics is at the heart of construction activities and since the late 1990s it has received much more attention. The increased focus on logistics has been driven by a number of studies and working groups that identified the way in which logistics management in construction lagged behind other sectors such as retail and some manufacturing industries (for example the automotive sector).

The report 'Accelerating Change', published by the Strategic Forum for Construction in September 2002, highlighted that 'a considerable amount of waste is incurred in the industry as a result of poor logistics'. Evidence of poor logistics management affects transport, storage and coordination. The Strategic Forum for Construction Logistics Group (2005) noted the following:

- poorly loaded vehicles that often had to wait for access because scheduling was not well organized;
- materials being unavailable on site, leading to poor time utilization;
- excessive stockpiling of products with extra costs and the greater risk of deterioration and damage;
- lack of coordination between activities;
- high proportion of damaged and returned items.

More information about these problems is detailed in the following box.

The consequences of failing to manage construction logistics

Additional costs

All the evidence points to there being additional cost in the system that could be saved if the process operated more efficiently as a result of improved logistics. Research by BSRIA has shown that on average 10 per cent of the working day of site operatives in all trades is lost due to waiting for materials, or collecting materials, tools and equipment. Given that site operations account for about 30 per cent of construction costs, this would suggest that this inefficiency alone is adding about £3 billion to the annual cost of construction.

Poor image of the construction industry

Lorries parked in an inconsiderate way outside construction sites whilst waiting to unload do not give the image of an efficient industry. Disorganized sites with skilled craftspeople being used for unskilled jobs do not encourage quality people to join the industry. Vehicles driving around empty or with part-loads do not convey the image of an industry that has environmental concerns at the top of its agenda, nor do large amounts of waste being removed from site, 85 per cent of which go to landfill. None of this seems consistent with the growing attention that companies are expected to pay to corporate social responsibility.

Poor quality construction

Working in a disorganized environment will inevitably make the production of quality construction more difficult. Work interrupted whilst materials are sought from elsewhere on site, or delayed whilst products are delivered, will have an adverse effect on quality. Secondary working of products on site is also less likely to provide the same quality of product that could be manufactured in a factory environment.

Increased project time

Most of those features of construction projects that point to poor logistics will add to the time of construction projects. Delays whilst product is unloaded, subsequent movement of products around site and secondary working of product all add unnecessary time that would be eliminated in a well-organized project.

Added risks to health and safety

Unnecessary products stored on site inevitably bring with them additional potential hazards. Additional manual handling (either because product is in the wrong part of the site, or because the right equipment is not available) adds to the health risks to those on site. Secondary working of material also brings risks and research has shown that a number of accidents on site occur as a result of workers tripping over discarded material arising from secondary working.

SOURCE: Construction Logistics Group (2005)

Managing the logistics activities within construction has to take account of the way that many projects are developed and organized and the resulting implications for the supply chain structure. A recent report (BIS, 2013) identified very high levels of fragmentation in relatively simple packages of work – particularly at the Tier 2 and 3 levels of final transactions with suppliers.[1] Construction projects involve very high volumes of purchasing activity and supplier coordination. This has a major impact on the way in which logistics management needs to work.

There are many reasons for this structure and the BIS (2013) report referred to above stressed that developments in technology could encourage even higher levels of fragmentation in view of the increasing complexity of the technology used in construction products and services. The building services supply chain was noted to be an example of this.

Construction is heavily reliant on road freight transport with a typical construction site requiring many vehicle trips each day. The types of vehicles arriving and leaving sites will of course vary according to the type of project and the stage of development. In a number of recent large projects non-road modes have been used to a greater extent than was common in the past. Two UK examples are the construction of Terminal 5 at Heathrow Airport and the work on construction in connection with the 2012 Olympic Games in London (Lafarge, 2011; ODA, 2011). In both cases extensive use was made of rail transport and this was part of the commitment of the projects to achieving high levels of sustainability. Other examples have also been noted relating to the removal of waste materials from the Cologne metro and the Alter Mainzer Tunnel projects (DB Schenker, 2013). The pressure to increase levels of sustainability within construction supply chains places more requirements on logistics management, and the application of non-road alternatives will continue to receive attention.

One country that is often noted for its technological innovation is Japan; the scope for prefabrication in construction has been noted as one of the areas where innovation can be achieved. There are some activities that can be changed in terms of where the activity takes place. The scope to transform products off site through prefabrication has been noted (Linner and Bock, 2012):

> Japanese prefabrication industry acts rather like a 'production industry' than a 'construction industry'. Similar to many other high-tech industries, Japan's prefabrication industry incorporates the latest product and process technologies and combines automation, products and services into complex value-capturing systems.

There are many ways that the flow of materials to and from construction sites can be planned and organized in order to minimize environmental and other impacts. The boxes below contain summaries of two examples of UK initiatives that have received considerable attention: construction logistics plans (CLP) and construction consolidation centres (CCC).

Construction logistics plans

Freight vehicles play a key role in all construction projects by transporting equipment, delivering materials and removing waste. A construction logistics plan (CLP) provides a framework to better manage all types of freight vehicle movement to and from construction sites. Having a management plan will improve the safety and reliability of deliveries to a site, reduce congestion and minimize the environmental impact. There are a number of benefits and advantages:

- reduced delivery costs and improved security;
- more reliable deliveries, meaning less disruption to the business day;
- time saved as you identify unnecessary deliveries;
- less noise and intrusion.

In addition, the plan provides an opportunity to feed into a corporate social responsibility (CSR) programme and ensure operations comply with health and safety legislation. Freight operators also benefit:

- legal loading areas mean less risk of freight operators receiving penalty charge notices;
- fuel savings through reduced, re-timed or consolidated deliveries;
- more efficient use of vehicles as greater delivery reliability will help with planning;
- improved reputation.

A CLP should be developed as part of a transport assessment. Each CLP needs to be tailored to a site's requirements, but things to consider include:

- looking at where legal loading can take place;
- using freight operators who can demonstrate their commitment to best practice – for example, accreditation to the Fleet Operator Recognition Scheme (FORS);
- consolidating deliveries so that fewer journeys are needed;
- using more sustainable delivery methods;
- working with other construction sites in the area.

SOURCE: Transport for London (2014)

> ### Construction consolidation centres
>
> A construction consolidation centre (CCC) is a distribution facility through which material deliveries are channelled to construction sites. Specialist material handling, storage and consolidated delivery combine to improve the overall resource efficiency of a construction project.
>
> WRAP (2011) notes that while data varies from project to project, use of a CCC can:
>
> - reduce freight traffic to site by up to 70 per cent;
> - increase productivity of site labour by 30 minutes per day leading to a 6 per cent productivity gain;
> - cut waste reduction by 7–15 per cent through less material damage and shrinkage.

Other examples of innovation in construction management and logistics can also be identified and further chapters in the book feature these.

The challenges of the urban environment

A high proportion of construction activity takes place in cities. Given the scale of construction activity during periods of economic growth, and when there are many regeneration projects, it is not surprising that construction logistics faces some very demanding requirements in terms of operations in urban areas. Urbanization is already very pronounced in richer countries where over 70 per cent of the population is typically urban. However, globally the pattern is complicated and is changing rapidly. In 2013 the United Nations noted that overall the proportion of the population living in urban areas reached 50 per cent. Globally, urbanization is expected to rise to 70 per cent in 2050 and by then there will be 27 'megacities' with at least 10 million people. It is not just the large cities that face change – at least half the urban growth in the coming decades is predicted to be in the many smaller cities. This growth in cities will have implications for supply chains. Construction activities in many cities will grow in response to this. Yet at the same time the pressure for a sustainable way of dealing with urban logistics, and particularly freight transport activity, will put more pressure on everyone concerned with managing commercial supply chains. This will be very much the case for the construction industry.

Due to the high populations and extensive commercial activities of urban areas they require the delivery and collection of large quantities of goods and the provision of services for commercial and domestic use, resulting in considerable freight activity. Making better use of the capacity available for urban freight, and finding smarter solutions to sharing space in cities, is becoming ever more essential. Again this general trend will be very much applicable to construction. A consequence will be the rise in the requirement for even greater efficiency in the operation of construction logistics activities and tighter management of all aspects concerned with sustainability within logistics. This development includes aspects related to safety. For example, Construction Logistics and Cyclist Safety (CLOCS) is an initiative to increase the consideration of vulnerable road users. CLOCS has developed the CLOCS Standard for construction logistics: managing work-related road risk, a common standard for use by the construction logistics industry (CLOCS, 2014).

It has to be recognized that although the activities associated with construction logistics are essential to the well-being of cities they also contribute to social and environmental impacts, particularly to local air quality and noise. The problems experienced by those providing logistics services in urban areas are far less well understood. In many cases, urban freight activities result in conflicts between economic and social/environmental issues. Addressing such conflicts and trade-offs in urban freight transport requires change and innovation in the public and private sectors.

Interestingly the management consultancy firm PwC (2014) noted in their survey of chief executive officers (CEOs) that the CEOs of transport and logistics organizations considered urbanization to be one of the most important trends facing their industry. Awareness therefore appears to be high, which is a positive factor.

Conclusion

There are many challenges in construction logistics and among them are: 1) the challenge of place; 2) the challenge of complexity; 3) the challenge of achieving higher levels of sustainability. There are many others but these three challenges profoundly influence the need for excellent construction logistics management.

Construction activity most frequently takes place in urban areas. The locations change over time (unlike a factory location for production, or a retail store). In combination this makes each project to an extent unique, with specific local problems in logistics that need to be solved. The processes of coordinating the logistics activities of transport and storage – and ensuring the supply chain interaction such as purchasing and the provision of materials and finished products – are very hard to achieve. However, construction logistics management is improving all the time and the construction industry has devoted considerable efforts to devising solutions to these problems. The next few years are very promising in terms of the scope to apply new tools such as BIM to this field. Nevertheless the challenge of managing complex projects in major cities will become even more demanding as the need to pay ever higher levels of attention to aspects such as noise and safety will become even more prominent in future.

Multiple stakeholders and decision makers are typical of construction projects. In many cases there is a complex interaction between the public and private sectors as well. This leads to complexity within the supply chain and makes good logistics management more difficult. It is also typical for greater complexity to lead to higher logistics costs. Of course organization within construction logistics seeks to manage this complexity and prevent extra cost burdens. Construction logistics also covers a wide range in relation to the scale of activities from major sites to very small developments. Techniques that work for one will not necessarily work at a different scale, even if the principles are the same.

Balancing the economic, social and environmental requirements is always a challenge, and for construction logistics there are many dimensions to this. As discussed in this chapter, most movements to and from construction sites take place by road. The use of fossil fuels for transport continues to receive considerable attention. Within the EU the goal of achieving virtually CO_2-free city logistics by 2030 has received considerable attention. This will be very difficult for construction logistics because of the current reliance on large vehicles for many of the transport activities associated with this industry. While it is possible to see how smaller vehicles will be able to use alternative fuels and possibly to achieve zero emissions at the point of use, by means of electric vans for example, the picture is more complicated for the larger vehicles. As noted earlier in the chapter there are examples of using non-road modes (especially rail) for some large construction projects both in the UK and elsewhere. However, it will be a challenge to translate the lessons learned on these large projects to a wide range of construction projects that take place across a city.

Note

1 Tier 1 refers to designers and constructors that have a direct contract with the ultimate client. Tier 2 are those designers, constructors and suppliers with a subcontract with the Tier 1 contractor. Tier 3 are those with a subcontract with Tier 2. This pattern of contracts and subcontracts is common in construction. Examples from Tier 2 include: manufacturers and material distributors, suppliers of major plant and equipment such as tower cranes. From Tier 3: specialist subcontractors, manufacturers and material distributors, and plant and equipment supply and hire firms.

References

BIS (2013) Research Paper No. 145 (2013) Supply Chain Analysis into the Construction Industry: A report for the construction industrial strategy within the Department for Business Innovation and Skills

Braithwaite, A (2014) Performance measurement and management in the supply chain, in *Global Logistics: New directions in supply chain management*, 7th edition, ed D Waters and S Rinsler, Kogan Page, London

BVL (2010) Position paper on a basic understanding of logistics as a scientific discipline (prepared by Werner Delfmann, Wilhelm Dangelmaier, Willibald Günthner, Peter Klaus, Ludger Overmeyer, Werner Rothengatter, Jürgen Weber, Joachim Zentes), Working Group of the Scientific Advisory Board of German Logistics Association (Bundesvereinigung Logistik)

CLOCS (2014) Construction Logistics and Cyclist Safety [Online] http://www.clocs.org.uk/

Colin, J and Fabbe-Costes, N (1994) Formulating logistics strategy, in *Logistics and Distribution Planning: Strategies for management*, ed J Cooper, Kogan Page, London

Construction Logistics Group (2005) Improving Construction Logistics: Report of the Strategic Forum for Construction Logistics Group (August)

CSCMP (2013) Glossary terms prepared by the Council of Supply Chain Management Professionals (CSCMP)

DB Schenker (2013) Customized Logistics Solutions for Building Materials, Industrial and Consumer Goods, *DB Schenker, Mainz* [Online] https://www.rail.dbschenker.de/file/rail-deutschland-en/7961648/ZWaWOl-x9_fP6sIzzpyz73Ruo40/2382650/data/individually_conceived_logistics.pdf [accessed 17 February 2015]

Heskett, JL, Glaskowsky, NA Jr and Ivie, RM (1973) *Business Logistics*, 2nd edn, The Ronald Press, New York

Lafarge (2011) Heathrow Terminal 5: Supplying the Construction of the Largest Free-Standing Structure in the United Kingdom [Online] http://www.lafargetarmac.com/media/108680/heathrow-terminal-5-portland-cement-case-study.pdf [accessed 13 February 2015]

Linner, T and Bock, T (2012) Evolution of large-scale industrialisation and service innovation in Japanese prefabrication industry, *Construction Innovation*, 12 (2), pp 156–78

Mangan, J et al (2011) *Global Logistics and Supply Chain Management*, 2nd edn, Wiley, Chichester

ODA (2011) Transport of Construction Materials by Sustainable Means [Online] http://learninglegacy.independent.gov.uk/documents/pdfs/sustainability/149-transport-of-construction-materials-sust.pdf [accessed 13 February 2015]

PwC (2014) 17th Annual Global CEO Survey: Key findings in the transportation & logistics industry (February)

Strategic Forum for Construction (2002) Accelerating Change: A report by the Strategic Forum for Construction Chaired by Sir John Egan, *Strategic Forum* [Online] www.strategicforum.org.uk/pdf/report_sept02.pdf [accessed 27 April 2015]

Transport for London (2014) Preparing Construction Logistics Plans. Documents and guidance available [Online] https://www.tfl.gov.uk/corporate/publications-and-reports/freight [accessed 6 May 2015]

WRAP (2011) Using Construction Consolidation Centres to Reduce Construction Waste and Carbon Emissions, *Waste and Resources Action Programme (WRAP)* [Online] http://www.wrap.org.uk/content/construction-consolidation-centres [accessed 6 May 2015]

Aggregating global products for just-in-time delivery to construction sites

02

MARK FRANKLIN

Introduction

Many industries have fundamentally changed and improved their supply chain approach since the mid-1990s (eg automotive line-side sequencing of material and retail just-in-time (JIT) delivery to eliminate backstore stocks). The same cannot be said of the construction industry, where delivery of products to sites has remained fundamentally unchanged for the past 30 years or more. Some isolated examples of new processes can be found, for example construction consolidation centres (CCCs). These have not become the norm however as they have predominantly only been justified on the basis of a specific issue such as security (Olympics, Heathrow developments) or access/city-centre constraints (the London Construction Consolidation Centre).

Aggregation of products can occur anywhere along the supply chain and benefits can be gained at both the supplier end and at the demand end of the process. At the supply end, for example, merchants and retailers who are sourcing multiple products from a number of factories benefit from investing in regional hubs to consolidate products for onward shipping to the demand market, eg the UK. Whilst there is a cost benefit in doing this the real value is in being able to consolidate small quantities of individual items and still be able to transport them at a sensible economic rate, thus allowing global sourcing of relatively low volume items.

This chapter, however, looks at the opportunity to aggregate at the demand end of the chain, presenting kits of products, at the appropriate time, to individual building site locations – convenient to the site and in support of their build schedule. This allows the workforce to focus purely on adding value to the construction and removes waste from the current processes, which push larger quantities of individual items at the site.

Whilst the benefits of better planning, control and process improvement should be reason enough for the industry to innovate in this area, there are a number of other factors that have evolved recently that will accelerate the need for change. These include:

- global sourcing;
- investment in procurement and an intent to centralize decision making in the larger construction and housebuilding businesses;
- environmental legislation, quality and the importance of good waste management.

Once these factors are combined with the improved control and reliability of lean logistics, seen in other industries, the need for change becomes overwhelming.

This chapter will explore each of the three factors, along with the mechanisms and benefits of such an approach and who is best placed to provide the services needed.

Global sourcing

The globalization of manufacturing is old news and many construction products are now sourced in Asia, Eastern Europe, Turkey etc. Despite this, the processes on site for receipt of materials have changed little over the years.

Whilst products with a high logistics cost to value ratio continue to be produced locally, close to the demand, higher-value items arrive in the UK from further afield. Thus a brick manufacturer can deal directly with a specific site and often deliver in full loads, but what is the best process to supply, say, taps and bathroom fittings from three Chinese factories to a five-house site in Manchester?

A standard three-bedroom house comprises around £30,000 to £40,000 of materials and products, sourced either directly from the manufacturers or from general builders' merchants (eg Travis Perkins, Jewsons etc) or specialist distributors (eg PTS, Wolseley).

Around one-third of this value is in heavy locally-sourced items, such as bricks, blocks and lintels, leaving a significant spend on items that originate from around the globe. That might include timber from Scandinavia, sanitary ware and radiators from Turkey, electrical products from Poland, taps and fixings from different areas of China and doors from the UK and mainland Europe.

Faced with similar issues and to control these product streams and ensure availability whilst minimizing inventory and waste, other sectors have evolved a consolidation step in the process. By aggregating the products it is possible to decouple the lead times of the manufacturers and the delivery requirements of the sites. By adding value off site, and picking 'plot lots', labour efficiency and achievement of timelines can be greatly improved in the on-site construction process.

Off-site manufacturing, involving manufacture of pods or modules for on-site assembly, is a growing part of the sector with numerous reports forecasting major growth in this approach. The efficiency benefits are often claimed to be around 40 per cent in added value, derived from greater process management and focused work adding value rather than chasing materials, managing variability etc. A proportion of this efficiency can be realized on all sites, by controlling the availability of product and presenting it to the builder/craftsperson at the appropriate time, in a planned and efficient way. The physical logistics approaches and alternatives will be covered in other chapters, but the interrelationship with other elements is key to this approach.

With increasing labour rates in China, pressure on transport costs and lead times, re-shoring of manufacturing has become a potential trend. I would argue that this will not materially affect the need for consolidation. Wherever a product is made it still needs to arrive on time at a specific build plot, for example anywhere in the UK. Once an aggregation capability exists, products from near or far are drawn through the operation(s). Indeed during any resourcing from one supplier to another the added complexity and issues of scaling down one supply route and ramping up another cry out for the control and process of a consolidation operation. Therefore potential re-shoring is no reason to delay the cultural and physical changes needed in the industry.

Investment in procurement and centralized decision making

Whilst maintaining customer choice and value any procurement organization will seek to maximize its purchasing power.

One key requirement within construction is more standardization of specifications. This does not necessarily mean less customer choice – but why would the radiator specification of a similar house type in Leicester be different from one in Birmingham? The relative power of central and regional procurement and operations teams is a key factor here, though it seems likely that more standardization will develop. This enables the possibility of off-site plot picking, where kits for specific job schedules are pre-sorted, picked and carefully packaged for onward distribution to specific plots at an appropriate time.

For example, a site in the Midlands could aggregate the seven radiator types, valves, pipework, boiler and controller for a particular house type, pick standard packs on a kanban basis and supply Leicester and Birmingham sites direct to the plot just in time. The kanbans can be set for the high-volume specifications and prepared ahead of time, with the low-volume kits being prepped to order.

UK housebuilders have delivered around 100,000 units for each of the past four years, with the largest, Barratts and Taylor Wimpey, achieving around 10,000 each. Is this enough to generate enough volume of a specific item, when differentiation and various house types are taken into account? It is in many product areas -- and the housebuilders are attempting to standardize and consolidate demand to improve their buying power. The more successful they are, the more likely that the physical consolidation and logistics will be required.

For many items, however, even the largest housebuilders, with 10,000 units per year, do not have a huge purchasing power in some product areas. Perhaps physical aggregation for multiple construction businesses could bring additional value in procurement, by aggregating demand and hence purchasing power. Furthermore, the volumes of certain items in the repair and maintenance market dwarf the new-build requirements, eg thermostatic radiator valves (TRVs).

This is an opportunity for general merchants or multichannel aggregators (eg Amazon) to offer real value by enabling a greater volume negotiation on key products, bringing together the demand requirements for both new build and repair and maintenance.

Environmental legislation, quality and good waste management

The sustainability agenda is strong and growing, with increasing obligations affecting construction businesses. Greater attention to planning and scheduling site deliveries and synchronizing this with the build programme and labour plans delivers a number of environmental benefits. For example, efficiency and transport improvements, reducing CO_2 and also enabling other improved processes such as waste removal and de-trashing of products off-site.

Stand outside any building site and you will observe multiple deliveries from numerous suppliers, merchants, specialists and parcel carriers, every hour. Even within the same group of companies different brands and product specialists will deliver independently. This is clearly wasteful, inefficient and adds to congestion and dangers on site. UK car plants had similar congestion and inefficient delivery processes to the assembly lines in the 1980s. This is no longer the case as the processes have been re-engineered and a lean approach has been applied in many circumstances.

A key issue for any business wanting to source internationally is to ensure the corporate social responsibility (CSR) compliance of its suppliers. The consequences of poor compliance can be devastating for supplier employees and for the UK brand using the outputs of the factories. Consider, for example, the Rana Plaza building collapse in Bangladesh in 2013 and the subsequent actions taken by the likes of Walmart to learn from this disaster. To ensure compliance and safety the facilities, not just the sales offices, must be audited on a regular basis and plans proposed and monitored to address any failures to comply with a rigorous and in-depth set of criteria.

Where the demand for a specific set of products in a particular factory is small this can be costly – and when the factory is in a remote part of China it may be prohibitively so. Again, being able to consolidate enough demand to enable the investment and buying power required is critical.

Therefore, with the pressure building in the construction sector there are significant reasons to change. The next sections explore how the approach might work and who is best placed to provide the change necessary.

Lean supply onto site with plot-picked delivery

By applying basic lean principles to the building products supply chain, waste and inefficiencies can be eliminated. The most basic principle is working back from the customer, in this case the bricklayer, carpenter, electrician or plumber who is adding value to the property. The supply chain process should support this as simply and reliably as possible.

Characteristics of a lean aggregated supply chain model would include those shown in Table 2.1, compared with the traditional process outcomes. This capability radically changes the site environment, moving the materials fulfilment from the traditional multi-delivery unplanned culture to a much more planned and controlled process. However, will any project ever be fully planned, with no unforeseen shortages or requirements? It is likely that an emergency/back-up process will also be required to cover damages, poor quality or unforeseen demand. Hence any solution needs to be able to provide this service either directly or through partners. Potentially an agreed 'emergency' range might always be available at a guaranteed lead time.

In UK construction, work prior to plastering is differentiated from the fixing of electrical sockets, timber and plumbing fittings afterwards. This is termed first and second fix and typically second-fix products will derive more benefit from this approach, though numerous first-fix items will also benefit. The following product areas lend themselves to consolidation and plot-pick JIT delivery to site:

- first- and second-fix timber;
- lintels;

TABLE 2.1 Comparison between lean and conventional processes

Lean Aggregated Supply Chain Characteristics	Traditional Process Outcomes, Seen Today on Many Construction Sites
Scheduled delivery slots, convenient to the construction operation and in line with their build plan.	Unspecified deliveries arrive throughout the day, convenient to the supplier delivery routing.
Build pack supply, tailored to actual requirement.	Excess materials received in full or part loads.
Designed stockholding, reducing inventory and minimizing waiting/collection time.	Skilled construction workers spend time chasing, collecting and sorting materials.
Standardized build specifications and costs.	Non-standard approach across regions and sites drives complexity and dilutes volume and spend.
Ordering and processing of 'solutions', rather than individual products (Bills of Material), driving simplification.	Individual components are ordered and managed throughout the chain, with increased chance of error and waste.
Control and clear invoicing, eg heating system installation.	Whole system costs sometimes difficult to identify. Orders and proof of delivery often manually input at line level, with associated administration costs.
Waste management services on return transport.	Significant improvement across the industry, though often with inefficient logistics.
Clear reporting and measures form a basis for continuous improvement.	Minimal process performance measurement and limited culture of improvement.

- doors and ironmongery;
- sundries and metalwork;
- plasterboard;
- tiling;
- insulation;
- external doors;
- first- and second-fix plumbing and heating;
- roofing;
- first- and second-fix electrical.

These products account for around one-third (at least £10,000) of materials for a typical three-bedroom house in the UK.

A good example of the benefits to the approach is the internal doors and ironmongery. Fitted towards the end of the build, for obvious reasons, imagine a process whereby the full specification of doors, fixings and ironmongery arrives at the specific plot, at the planned time. The products have been picked and inspected to ensure quality and carefully packaged onto pallet(s) for delivery. The fitment process starts in a predetermined way on the first floor and works down the building. Hence the doors are picked with door one on top; the handles etc are sequenced in returnable containers in the same order. Outer packaging, crates etc have been separated and recycled at the off-site warehouse and delivery packaging (much of which is reusable) is returned on the next delivery vehicle to the plot/site.

Product groups that may not suit this approach are:

- bricks;
- blocks;
- aggregates;
- manholes and groundwork products, which cannot be standardized;
- kitchens: though the principles apply, this product may not suit a shared consolidation approach.

Other considerations

- Subcontractors: one of the reasons that construction has not progressed as quickly in this area as in some other industries is the broad number of interested parties. In thinking about the buying power of housebuilders in the above, it was assumed that all procurement is direct with the manufacturers. In some areas this is not the case and subcontractors will provide work packages, including labour and materials pricing, to complete a number of properties. Hence a strategy will be required to capture or control material spend and distribution through subcontractors.

- Concern around exclusivity/reliance on the other.
- Commercial approach to ensure fair value/benchmarking and ability to reflect future cost increases, eg fuel inflation.

Who is best placed to deliver an aggregation and lean delivery capability?

There are a number of alternative groups who might be able to best provide the services detailed above:

- in-house provision by the construction business;
- established builders merchants, such as Travis Perkins, Wolseley and Jewson;
- third-party logistics (3PL) specialist warehousing and logistics operators: for example TNT, DHL and Wilson James (a construction specialist);
- multichannel providers such as Screwfix or Amazon.

Some of the larger construction businesses may be able to provide the services themselves, though even for them the costs and distributed nature of the requirement will make it difficult.

Additionally, for the reasons outlined above a key aspect will be accessing sufficient demand to allow for increased purchasing power and to justify the investments required to access global suppliers to drive down total costs. Hence I suggest that the in-house and 3PL service options are not viable in their own right and could only add value as a partner business, for example in providing the physical logistics solution.

This leaves two groups of potential providers: 1) general merchanting groups; 2) emerging web-based retailers. In assessing which group can offer the best solution, let's assume that they would be interested in providing such a service and that the additional volume is attractive for these businesses.

Key requirements to assess are:

1 a central distribution capability able to receive product from the various global manufacturing facilities, store, pick and distribute;
2 a regional distribution capability for bulkier items;
3 an existing or planned global sourcing capability, with volume, partners and reliable quality/CSR auditing capability;
4 lean supply chain expertise and understanding of the end-to-end supply chain;
5 owned or arranged ability to provide emergency backup for damaged items or other unexpected demand issues.

Considering the capabilities of the two groups in the above areas, each is assessed in Table 2.2 against high, medium or low expertise:

Aggregating Global Products for Just-In-Time Delivery to Construction Sites

TABLE 2.2 Analysis of general merchants versus emerging web retailers

	1	2	3	4	5
General Merchants	H^^	M<<	M	M	H
Emerging Web Retailers	H	L	H**	M	L

NOTES
^^ Travis Perkins are strong in this area, whereas Jewsons have limited capability, relying more on their suppliers.
<< No one can provide this regional capability today, though Travis Perkins are able to in certain geographies.
** The CSR audit capabilities of the emerging web retailers would need to be carefully assessed, though clearly Screwfix have experience in this area.

As of mid-2014, no single business can provide a full UK-wide aggregation and lean delivery capability for all product groups. Specifically the infrastructure to provide capability for regional distribution for bulkier items does not exist across all areas of the UK.

However, many of the major product groups that are likely to be globally sourced, and which lend themselves to plot-pick JIT deliveries, are received and distributed through a central national delivery centre (NDC) in a number of businesses. Therefore, companies that operate a central NDC and professionally source product from around the world are well placed to provide this service to the construction industry.

Going forward, any business that can additionally aggregate large bulky items, such as timber and sheet materials, and merge this product with plot-picked kits from a central NDC will have a strategic advantage in this area. Overall both groups could provide solutions to the construction industry, with opportunities to increase the geographical and product breadth as and when further investment is made in regional distribution capability.

Commercial and risk issues

The fact that this type of approach has not stuck in the sector to date suggests that the obvious logistical control benefits have not been seen to outweigh the costs and barriers to change, so far. With the additional three pressures covered in the first section, and in particular the aggregation of purchasing spend, the total benefits will clearly increase and initiate change in the more progressive businesses. How will these businesses manage the commercial risks involved?

As with any strategic outsourcing arrangement a key question will be reliance on one or more partners. If purchasing demand has been aggregated, contractual terms would need to be agreed and are likely to be for a number of years, perhaps two or three years minimum. Are housebuilders or construction businesses willing to make this commitment and is there a risk in committing to these terms with a single provider? From a service provider perspective the additional potential volumes are attractive, though the added complexity and historical lower margins are certainly a hurdle to be overcome.

The web marketplace engineered and provided by Amazon, for example, could be configured to serve this requirement. The plot-pick and configuration capability could be developed in their distribution centres (DCs), allowing access for Amazon to this sector of the market. Alternatively the Amazon business model and IT/physical infrastructure could be utilized by global manufacturers themselves, perhaps cooperating together to create a new and efficient route to market that allows them direct access to new-build markets.

Conclusion

The supply of products to the UK construction market has recently started to change, particularly in response to specific needs, eg to support the large construction businesses engaged in the Heathrow upgrade projects. However, these ways of working have not spread throughout the UK or across the different parts of the industry. The sector can learn more from other industries and accelerate the rate of change, continuing to respond to specific challenges such as city-centre congestion and expanding the application, making aggregation and JIT delivery the favoured approach across the market.

An increasing number of providers could now perform the role of aggregator, consolidating products from multiple global suppliers, plot picking and delivering to site. The basic starting requirement is a central consolidation capability, buying power linked to global manufacturing centres and the ability to control and audit these suppliers. Existing merchant businesses who have a central distribution capability can service a number of product groups, in many areas of the UK. There is an opportunity for operators in the web marketplace to move into this business to business (B2B) space, leveraging their systems processes and expertise developed in business to consumer (B2C).

Whilst no one organization can currently cover all products (notably not heavy and bulky items) in all areas of the UK, solutions are emerging and new players and multi-business cooperation may break through in the next few years.

The construction industry may still be able to catch up with other sectors such as automotive and retail, delivering an aggregated, lean supply route to the UK's building sites. The key will be in combining a number of elements – commercial, logistical and cultural – to deliver a compelling business case.

Construction logistics – supply of bulk materials

03

MATTHEW WOODCOCK

Introduction

The construction industry covers a massive range of projects from small builders to multibillion strategic infrastructure development. The range of products involved is equally wide ranging from the supply of hundreds of millions of tonnes of bulk materials (such as aggregates) to individual fit-out components (such as a light switch).

Within such a diverse industry the scale and scope of 'logistics' clearly can vary immensely. This chapter focuses on the supply of bulk materials and the associated physical transport operations and planning. After introducing the products and operations covered within this area, it moves on to a view of the current maturity of this area and the next steps required to move it forward in order to realize the benefits achievable through a truly integrated supply chain.

Due to the range and scale of even this sub-segment of the wider industry, this chapter focuses on four key product areas: cement, aggregates, asphalt and ready-mix concrete. The chapter initially looks at each product area separately, before then considering the potential developments needed to improve supply chain collaboration and maturity for these areas.

Logistics, customers and bulk materials

In this section we focus on introducing the four key product areas – cement, aggregates, asphalt and ready-mix concrete – the nature of their supply, common modes of transport and their customer base.

Together accounting for an industry turnover of around £9 billion per year and employing 70,000 people, these products form the largest element of the construction supply chain. Around 200 million tonnes of these products are used within the construction industry each year, the largest material flow in the UK economy (MPA, 2014).

Cement

Product

Cement is a binder that can bond materials such as blocks and bricks, or bond aggregate to form concrete (the most consumed man-made material in the world). The familiar grey powder is made by heating a mixture of limestone or chalk with clay or shales at high temperatures to produce a mixture of calcium silicates known as clinker. The clinker is then ground with gypsum into a fine powder called cement. Varying the size of the powder or the addition of other materials such as ground granular blast furnace slag (GGBS) or pulverized fly ash (PFA) produces cements with a range of strengths, colours and chemical properties.

Demand in the UK market varies with the wider construction market, with around 10 million tonnes sold in 2012 (down from pre-recessionary levels of around 15 million tonnes). Nearly 90 per cent of this volume is provided by four key suppliers: Lafarge Tarmac, CEMEX UK, Hanson and Hope Construction Materials.

Supply

Production of cement is a heavily capital-intensive process requiring significant investment, with plants costing in excess of £100 million. Access to required raw materials and fuels, coupled with the environmental considerations of carbon-intensive production, community impact and the requirements for free and easy access to the national road/rail network, all serve to limit the number and location of production facilities.

These factors have resulted in a market where 11 cement production plants, grinding stations and a small number of import terminals service all of the UK demand. Customer demand across the UK is supplied from plants commonly over 100 miles away, either directly or via a network of supply terminals that act as stockholding points or modal interchanges (ie rail to road, or sea to road).

Bulk cement

Supplied in loose powder form, bulk cement is usually moved utilizing road- or rail-based pressurized tankers and then blown into customer silos.

Road tankers, a common sight on UK roads, tend to be articulated vehicles with payloads in the region of 30 tonnes. These are loaded through hatches on the top of the tank, then subsequently unloaded via onboard pressure systems, used at the destination point to fluidize the powder and enable it to be blown into a customer silo.

Rail tank wagons of a variety of capacities are also utilized for supply from production sites to terminals or major projects. These can take the form of dedicated tank wagons or, for specific projects, demountable ISO-Veyor container tanks. These tanks are usually unloaded using pressure systems at the destination site.

In the UK the majority of bulk cement is delivered by the company that produced it, whereas in Europe and the wider world it is common for customers or distributors to collect directly from the production site.

Bagged cement

Bagged cement in the form of 25 kilogramme bags is the next most common form for the product. Bulk cement is bagged into paper or plastic bags, before being palletized and distributed via curtain-sided trailer. Payloads of 27 tonnes plus are the norm, with a single layer of pallets hitting the vehicle's weight limit.

Customer

Typical customers for bulk cement are ready-mix concrete plants (55 per cent of UK demand) and building materials production sites (precast concrete, building blocks, paving slabs etc) accounting for a further 23 per cent of UK demand. Both of these customer types tend to be fixed delivery points taking relatively regular repeat volume.

Bagged cement is more commonly supplied to either builders' merchants or DIY centres (between them accounting for 19 per cent of UK demand), for onward sale to builders and the public. Again, these tend to be fixed outlets taking regular supply. However, demand for this product is highly seasonal, with peaks at Easter and during the summer months.

Aggregates

Product

Aggregate is the general term for any crystalline or granular material that is extracted and used in the construction industry. Aggregates are used widely both in their own right as a base material under foundations, roads and rail tracks; as well as an ingredient in materials such as concrete and asphalt, where the aggregate adds strength to the overall composite material.

'Primary aggregate' is material such as sand, gravel and crushed stone, taken from natural sources specifically for use as aggregate. 'Recycled aggregate' is material produced by the processing of selected inorganic material previously used in construction. 'Secondary aggregates' are generally by-products of mining, quarrying or industrial processes.

Demand in the UK market varies with the wider construction market, with around 200 million tonnes sold in 2012 (down from pre-recessionary levels of around 275 million tonnes). Nearly 75 per cent of this volume is provided by four key suppliers: Lafarge Tarmac, CEMEX UK, Hanson and Aggregate Industries.

Supply

As a high-density, relatively low-value product, the local supply of aggregate is determined by the underlying geology of the UK. The average delivery distance is 30 miles, with longer journeys reserved for specific high-value or specialist-use materials (such as stone with a high-polished stone value used in surface layer asphalt for road construction in order to minimize skidding).

Aggregates are primarily supplied loose in bulk form, distributed either by road, rail or barge. Road-based delivery is made on 'tipper' vehicles where the body of the vehicle forms a box, which is tipped by means of a hydraulic ram, allowing the box to be lifted and the contents to be discharged via a tailgate. These vehicles come in a variety of sizes with the most common being eight-wheel rigid vehicles (capacity around 20 tonnes) and articulated tippers (capacity around 30 tonnes). Use of rail allows greater volumes to be moved increased distances more cost-effectively, with trains commonly ranging in capacity from 1,000 to 1,800 tonnes. Aggregate rail wagons tend to comprise box wagons (discharged by unloading from above using a grab) or hopper wagons where bottom-opening doors discharge the product.

Aggregates are primarily sourced from three main segments: land won (crushed rock or sand and gravel), marine dredged (sand and gravel) and recycled/secondary materials (including construction and demolition waste, iron and steel slag, waste glass etc).

Land won

A network of around 1,000 quarries produce two-thirds of the overall supply of aggregates in the UK.

Crushed rock quarries account for 44 per cent of overall aggregate supply; these quarries reflect the traditional view of a quarry with rock blasted from deposits, before being crushed into a range of size profiles for specific uses. Although distributed quite widely around the UK, specific areas of the country such as the south-east and east of England do not tend to have these deposits, and rely heavily on materials brought in from the East Midlands, south-west England and Scotland, often utilizing rail or short-sea to minimize cost and environmental impact. These quarries tend to require fixed plant to crush and process the stone and hence are larger in size in order to facilitate suitable returns on capital invested, producing anywhere from 500,000 tonnes to many millions of tonnes of aggregates per year.

Land-won sand and gravel deposits make up a further 22 per cent of overall aggregate supply in the UK; these quarries are usually much shorter-term, shallower quarries. At a sand and gravel quarry, the topsoil is removed, the aggregate dug from the ground and taken to a processing plant where the clay and silt is removed, and the sand and gravel is separated into different grades. The deposit is usually worked and restored in progressive phases. These quarries vary significantly in scale and equipment requirements, ranging from small mobile screening units with a loading shovel, to large fixed washing plants with many miles of conveyors to bring the material back from the deposit.

Marine dredged
Marine-dredged aggregates make up around 5 per cent of overall aggregate supply in the UK. Sand and gravel deposited by outflowing rivers originally during glacial times now lie on the seabed. These sand and gravel materials are dredged from 70 licensed deposits around the coast by a dedicated fleet of around 30 ships, which take the resulting materials back to a network of 35 wharves for processing. Each dredger typically carries a load of 5,000 tonnes.

Although representing a relatively low percentage of the overall aggregate supply in the UK, marine-dredged aggregates are geographically far more significant in London and the south-east (accounting for around one-third of all primary aggregate used in that area) and in South Wales (up to 90 per cent of the sand consumed in the area). The majority of the material dredged is subsequently used in the manufacture of concrete.

Recycled and secondary
Two growing sources of aggregates are recycled and secondary aggregates, generally grouped together to focus on the fitness for purpose of these materials as a replacement for primary aggregates. They currently account for just under 30 per cent of overall aggregate supply in the UK and are likely to grow significantly in usage with the ever increasing focus on sustainable construction.

Recycled aggregates can be sourced from a variety of materials arising from construction and demolition, highway maintenance and utility operations. Materials such as recycled aggregate, recycled concrete aggregate, recycled asphalt planings and spent rail ballast are carefully processed and separated before reuse.

Secondary aggregates can be derived from a very wide range of waste or by-products of other industrial processes. Manufactured secondary aggregates include blast furnace slag, pulverized fuel ash (PFA) and furnace bottom ash (FBA), arising from steel and power production. Natural secondary aggregates such as china clay sand are by-products of the extraction of the principal product.

Recycled aggregates are available nationally; however, secondary aggregates tend to be more localized to their site of original production (china clay in south-west England, metallurgical slag in South Wales, Yorkshire and Humberside).

Customers
Typical customers for aggregates fall into two main types: fixed sites accounting for around 75 per cent of volume and the general market accounting for the remaining 25 per cent.

Fixed sites generally use aggregates as a raw material for a subsequent production process, most commonly to make concrete, asphalt or precast-concrete building materials. These customers take relatively regular repeat volume, often utilizing (where practical) the larger-capacity articulated tippers for delivery.

General market customers are significantly more variable, ranging from single deliveries for a domestic gravel driveway to multiple thousands of tonnes for large fill jobs. The nature of these customers and the project work makes the delivery locations and demand levels variable.

Asphalt

Product

Asphalt, also known as tarmacadam or more simply the brand name tarmac, is a construction material formed from heating and combining a blend of aggregates of different sizes (a fine component and a coarse component) and an asphaltic binder (usually bitumen, a thick tar-like material refined from crude oil). Laid hot onto a surface, it is compacted and then sets to form the familiar (usually) black, flat, durable surface.

The primary use of asphalt is for surfacing, ranging from roads to runways and from car parks to driveways. The asphalt acts to spread the load on the surface to the substrate, through a series of layers or 'courses' each made with progressively smaller aggregates.

Modern tarmac/asphalt pavements are made up of these layers:

- The lowermost layer is a 'sub-base' of compacted aggregate fill materials.
- This is followed by a relatively thick layer of 'base' course using a larger aggregate size and a medium size 'binder' course.
- This is topped with a 'surface' (or 'wearing' course) of finer aggregate, with materials appropriate for the role of the pavement (eg high-polish resistant aggregate for high-speed roads in order to avoid skidding, or coloured stones and binders for a coloured pavement section).

Demand in the UK market varies considerably with the government's road-building and repair programmes, with around 20 million tonnes sold in 2012 (down from pre-recessionary levels of around 23 million tonnes per annum). Around 70 per cent of this volume is provided by four key suppliers: Lafarge Tarmac, Aggregate Industries, Hanson and CEMEX UK.

Supply

Asphalt plants are usually constructed on quarry locations or next to a virtual quarry (such as an aggregate railhead) in order to reduce double handling of aggregate raw materials. Where plants are located on quarries, the range of types of asphalt needed often requires further materials to be imported into that quarry (eg high-polished stone-value aggregate for surface courses for a limestone quarry) or a trade-off made to use over-specified materials in base courses at a hardstone quarry.

Usually produced in batches on demand (or, less commonly, popular products can be batched in advance and stored in hot storage silos), aggregate and asphalt sand is heated before being mixed with bitumen. This product is then dropped into the body of the delivery vehicle, which for most delivered products will be an eight-wheel tipper with an insulated body and some form of sheeting system to cover the top of the body. Smaller tipper vehicles are still sometimes used where access constraints are present. Use of larger artic vehicles with their higher payloads has been slow to take off, due to safety concerns around these vehicles tipping over. These concerns, which can be overcome through the use of appropriate types of trailer and surface conditions, unfortunately are hard to move past.

Most orders of any scale are for supply into pavers, where the tipper vehicle is pushed along slowly by the paver as it slowly discharges into a hopper on the front of the paver, which then lays the asphalt as a semi-compacted layer of the desired thickness, ready for further compaction by a roller. Small orders, however, are often still offloaded on site directly onto the ground, or through chutes into wheelbarrows.

Demand for materials for road building brings a number of supply challenges:

- Significant quantities are often required in small time-windows requiring coordinated supply from multiple plants and consistency of raw materials.
- Roads are often only available for 'possession' at night for small windows of time, with significant compensation payable where the window is exceeded.
- For maximum durability of the finished product, and efficiency of laying, a constant supply of asphalt to the destination site is required. Lack of trust in the supply side can lead to road workers building queues of 10 plus vehicles in order to ensure continuity, thus tying up disproportionate numbers of vehicles and causing demand spikes on production facilities.

Customers

Asphalt is mainly used for road maintenance and construction, with large contracting companies consuming significant quantities when building new roads or resurfacing existing ones. The scale of each job can vary significantly from 100 tonnes for a small section of road resurfacing to many thousands of tonnes for a new road or major resurfacing scheme. Delivery points by the very nature of the work are constantly moving.

Another key customer base is the specialist area, with airport runways, car and lorry parks, pavements and sports surfaces taking specific product mixes to meet the individual needs of the job. These value-added products have specific properties such as withstanding extra wear, being permeable to water or being coloured. However, the logistics solutions required are very similar to other demand.

Finally there exists a sizeable market for smaller customers who supply a myriad of end customers, ranging from pothole repair to domestic or small industrial driveways. As well as the traditional delivered approach, these customers often collect small quantities directly from the plant.

Ready-mix concrete

Product

Concrete is a highly mouldable construction material formed from a blend of aggregates of different particle sizes (usually sand and gravel or crushed rock) and paste consisting of a hydraulic binder such as Portland cement and water. The paste coats the fine and coarse aggregates and, through a process called hydration, hardens and gains strength to form a dense semi-homogenous mass.

Ready-mix concrete is 'batched' at a concrete plant, from a 'mix' of roughly 15 per cent cement, 40 per cent coarse aggregate, 30 per cent fine aggregate and 15 per cent water. Through varying the ratio of this mix, the use of chemical admixtures or the addition of other materials, many hundreds of different recipes can be created to meet specific usage requirements or placing locations. It is then transported as a flowable material ready for placing and compacting into any desired shape and size on construction sites.

Demand in the UK market varies with the wider construction market, with around 15 million cubic metres sold in 2012 (down from pre-recessionary levels of around 23 million cubic metres). Over 50 per cent of this volume is provided by five key suppliers: Aggregate Industries, Lafarge Tarmac, CEMEX UK, Hanson and Hope Construction Materials.

Supply

As a perishable product ready-mix concrete is produced locally and delivered just-in-time to construction sites. Establishing a ready-mix concrete plant is relatively low cost when compared to the other bulk material production facilities; around 800 plants are currently being operated in the UK by major and medium-sized companies, with a number of other plants operated by smaller companies.

Plants range from ultra-mobile truck-based plants, which can be set up in less than 24 hours directly at a production site for a single shorter-term contract, to large fixed units producing hundreds of thousands of cubic metres per year.

Delivery distances for ready-mix concrete average at around six miles, although these vary depending on the location of the plant (rural, urban or project-based) and the nature of the product (standard concrete versus more specialized value-added products). The delivery usually needs to be made within two hours of the load being batched in order to maintain workability of the concrete. Large concrete pours can see three or more concrete plants coordinating their production and delivering to a single site.

Ready-mix concrete is almost always delivered using truck mixers. These mixers are usually rigid trucks fitted with an inclined rotating drum fitted with a screw mechanism, which agitates and mixes the product during transport and is subsequently reversed at delivery site to allow discharge. Sizes of these trucks vary with market, with 6- and 8-cubic-metre capacity trucks serving most jobs and 4-cubic-metre mini-mix vehicles reserved for the smaller deliveries. In the United States and other major countries, articulated lorry-based systems carrying 11 cubic metres are also utilized.

In the UK the majority of concrete is bought delivered from the manufacturing company. However, a number of companies exist that will collect and onwards sell the concrete.

Customers

With the wide range of applications for ready-mix concrete and the significant role it plays in the built environment, customers are extremely varied.

Big pours and large construction sites can account for huge volumes, especially major projects such as power station developments, civil engineering projects and large skyscrapers. The primary contractors leading these schemes may directly contract with the concrete provider or nominate a preferred supplier to their supply chain. Although provided on a project basis, the demand can last several years as the scheme develops.

There then exists a very large list of customers covering every type of construction project, from concrete pads for large warehouses at one end of the spectrum, to domestic customers requiring a few cubic metres for a pathway, or footings for an extension at the other.

Logistics models in construction bulk materials

Logistics as a discipline is a relative newcomer to the construction bulk materials industry. In fact in many companies it is an area still struggling to be recognized as a value-adding area of focus, as opposed to a traditional 'necessary evil' last step of the production process that simply adds cost and often issues. True supply chain thinking (as will be discussed later in this chapter) is still a long way from being a reality in all but the most forward-thinking companies in this sector.

The geographic scale and local focus of aggregates, asphalt and concrete materials in particular has led to major companies organizing themselves on a product and geographic basis, limiting the development of new disciplines outside the traditional sales and operations areas. Even in cement manufacture where the focus on a few key production assets, supplying product regionally or nationally, lends itself to a more functional set up, it is still a relatively undeveloped area when compared to the sophistication of other industries such as retail and automotive.

Order-to-cash processes for these products often run as very linear processes, jumping from one functional silo to the next. The lack or unsophisticated nature of feedback loops in order taking (eg availability to promise feedback from logistics planning to the sales team) and limited focus on the true costs of common customer behaviours, such as short lead time and volatile demand focused in narrow windows at the start of the day, are symptoms of this relative lack of development.

At this relative level of functional immaturity, logistics as an area is split into two main areas that for simplicity are called planning and transport.

The logistics planning area is one that across organizations in this sector has a multitude of names and a wide scope range. At its widest, it encompasses: order taking, customer services, complaint management, production allocation, transport planning, vehicle scheduling and allocation. On occasion it includes the addition of the more medium-term integrated sales and operational planning (S&OP) concept. At its narrowest it is a person in a weighbridge handing a delivery ticket to the next driver in the queue. Typical models range in complexity from plant-based to sector/area planning to larger regional or national planning centres.

The logistics transport area is more homogenous, and the relative concentration of the bulk materials supply market into a small number of often highly vertically integrated large organizations has led to the existence of only a few dominant logistics models.

For the products requiring specialist vehicles (concrete mixers, cement powder tankers, insulated asphalt tippers) the approach is a dedicated fleet for the majority of the volume, although the ownership model for that fleet varies. Own-fleet operations are common, although capex constraints and investment priorities have led to a reduction in the relative proportion of these fleets in recent years, especially amongst the bigger suppliers. Third-party logistics providers operate in the cement powder tanker area, but have yet to target to any great success the mixer and insulated tipper areas, where the low margins and volatile nature of the demand leave them struggling to demonstrate value.

A different approach taken by most of the major suppliers is the use of independent contract hauliers to build fleets of concrete mixers and/or insulated tippers. These contract hauliers are a form of owner–driver, usually operating in the livery of the supplier and running between one and five vehicles. Although not exclusively dedicated to operating for that single supplier, they do primarily provide their services to that one company. Schemes vary between companies and usually involve a level of business support beyond that which a traditional subcontractor might expect. This can take the form of access to corporate rates for vehicle finance, fuel, insurance and vehicles; or truck parking, training, self-billing invoices and VAT services in order to reduce barriers to entry and cost of operation. The use of independent contract hauliers moves the fleet capital costs off balance sheet, provides a semi-dedicated resource on a variable cost basis (at least in the short term) and the entrepreneurial nature of these hauliers is intended to drive productivity benefits due to a perceived hunger for them to maximize earnings.

Other products such as bulk aggregates and bagged cement do not require such specialized transport (bulk tippers and curtain-sided vehicles respectively) and as such can access pre-existing markets for haulage of this type, rather than having to rely solely on dedicated fleets. This leads to a far greater use of spot or subcontract haulage, in addition to the approaches already mentioned.

As mentioned previously, rail and ship-based transport is utilized for the non-perishable products of cement and aggregates. Of these two modes of transport, rail is by far the more common with around 3,500 million tonne/miles of movement in 2013 (ie the equivalent of moving 35 million tonnes across a distance of 100 miles). These rail movements utilize locomotives provided by the small number of freight operating companies such as DB Schenker Rail and a mixture of owned, leased and supplier-provided rail wagons. Ship-based transport within and around the UK is far more limited and is normally restricted to specific short-sea or barging operations.

Concrete

Planning

The planning, order management and scheduling of concrete production and delivery are difficult processes, with demand tending to fall into two key types, either associated with large continuous pours for major developments or the far more variable ad hoc demand of small-scale pours. Each type of demand comes with its own challenges.

Large pours, although defined and known about in advance, are still subject to the impact of weather – with temperature, wind and rain all impacting build programmes. These pours often require the resources of multiple concrete plants and need a consistent flow of mixer vehicles to the destination site at regular intervals. This puts strain on the inbound supply chain of cement and aggregates, which need to be coordinated with the production of the concrete, as many sites do not hold sufficient depth of raw material stocks to cover even one day's production. The last-minute postponement of one of these pours (be it due to wind levels preventing crane use, or temperatures too low to allow the concrete to be laid effectively) can cause significant disruption to planned operations. The peaks of demand caused by these pours have a knock-on impact to vehicle requirements and the ability of the plant to service its more usual ad hoc demand.

The smaller ad hoc demand for concrete suffers from different planning challenges: lead times are typically short (less than 24 hours) and customer behaviour is reactive. Extreme peaks and troughs occur at an individual plant level, both within the day (early morning being a favoured delivery time), across the week (such as Tuesday, Wednesday, Thursday peaks) and across the month (deliveries timed to maximize credit terms). Supply levels within an area drive both price and service-led ordering by customers.

The specialist nature of the concrete mixers provides an inelastic supply of vehicles, leading to extremely variable levels of utilization for the vehicles depending on the peak or trough nature of demand on the day. Planning for this demand, and scheduling the work to plants and vehicles, varies in approach between the major companies. Some favour the local, responsive and flexible nature of 'plant-based shipping', where each plant operates independently with a 'shipper' both taking the order and scheduling the vehicle. This provides simplicity of operation and a direct connection to the plant, but limits economies of scale and cross-plant coordination. The second common approach is the regional or national planning centre, where call-centre-style teams receive orders and a secondary team allocates demand to plants and sometimes vehicles. This adds economies of scale and a joined-up approach to resource balancing, but with the ad hoc nature of the demand the connection with the local site, local conditions and the ability to squeeze in an additional order into the schedule can be lost. The third hybrid approach groups a small number of plants into a cluster or sector in a tight geographic area, attempting to capitalize on the benefits of both of the first two approaches.

The nature of the demand described above does not lend itself to systemized planning, so use of transport management software is rare, with shippers instead tending to rely either on paper-based or system-driven manual white-board/Gantt chart-style plans, built as the day's order bank is built and changes, with spreadsheet models built in regional centres to manage more tactical fleet-level planning. Track-and-trace systems are relatively prevalent; however, these are often utilized as reactive tools to answer questions such as 'where is my load?' and to review incidents, as opposed to the more proactive utilization measurement.

Transport operations

The management of transport within the concrete industry is often seen as an extension of the manufacturing function, as opposed to a separate discipline in its own right. The number of plants and low levels of vehicles associated with each plant, coupled with the short there-and-back deliveries of time-sensitive materials, can see the vehicles considered as mobile plant equipment, no different to a loading shovel.

Ongoing management of vehicles, be they own-fleet or owner–driver, is often picked up by 'production and transport' managers as one of their many responsibilities, except in larger plants where the fleet size covers the overhead of a dedicated transport manager. In larger companies, the scale drives a requirement for specialist roles to provide the focus to join up requirements between plants, sectors or areas – managing vehicle specification, group commercial deals, transport model and other related areas. These roles usually operate in a matrix approach outside of the operational line management structure as an advisory or support function.

With all but the largest plants only requiring a handful of mixer vehicles on a day-to-day basis, and the criticality of having a high level of control around the operation of those vehicles with short lead times, dedicated fleet is a necessity. The two usual approaches are the use of an own fleet or owner–driver contract hauliers to invest in the specialist vehicles required. These dedicated fleets are supplemented by the use of vehicles (and drivers) hired for the day or week, when volume peaks demand extra capacity. Although multi-vehicle contract hauliers and haulage companies exist, a concern around the level of control they could exert on a company where they operate as the sole supplier of haulage, and the difficulty in sourcing an alternative provider should the relationship sour, tend to keep demand low for these bigger providers.

Operationally, managing the vehicles requires a focus on the usual areas of payload and utilization, as well as the driver impact on the quality of product. Payload is critical in an area with tight margins and, in the delivery of concrete, keeping vehicle tare weights down is a continuing challenge. At the design stage, 8-cubic-metre mixers struggle to carry their full capacity, with the weight of the chassis, drum and associated equipment all eating into the carrying capacity. With varying densities of stone and concrete mixes that vary in the proportion of water added, a full load can either put a vehicle over weight or risk concrete splashing out of the end of the drum on an incline. In daily use, build-up of concrete on mixer blades and the inside of the drum further lessens this capacity, and requires the regular chipping out of the vehicles.

As in all logistics, utilization is another key area, with vehicles delayed on site, held up in queues to load or unavailable due to maintenance and other issues having a significant impact on transport capacity. Vehicle delays on site are common, with large jobs queuing vehicles as they either pump the concrete to where it is required, or require it fed into extruding machines at relatively slow and consistent rates. For the smaller jobs, time can be lost as product is discharged in small quantities into wheelbarrows or while waiting for the product to be manually spread.

Unusually for most delivery operations, the driver can have a significant impact on the quality and consistency of the product. This is most significantly through the addition of water, with either the driver's experience or demands from site to 'wet up' the mix through use of the onboard water tank potentially leading to issues with the strength of the concrete as it hardens.

Concrete mixers typically have a planned lifespan of eight years, although many are operated for much longer – either sold on to mixer hire companies or operated until they can no longer be repaired. As can be expected, the profitability of the operation often drives the likelihood of the vehicle to be replaced, with high demand areas such as London operating modern fleets and lower demand areas such as East Anglia operating older vehicles.

Aggregates and asphalt

With both aggregates and asphalt being delivered by tipper truck, and most asphalt operations sited at a quarry or aggregate stockholding unit, the planning and transport operations of the two products are most commonly combined into a single operation. Asphalt delivery requires the use of insulated tipper trucks, whereas aggregates may be delivered in either an insulated or non-insulated tipper. This crossover allows the specialized asphalt delivery vehicles to be further utilized for aggregate deliveries when demand patterns allow. The trade-off for this enhanced utilization is the lower payload of the usually smaller insulated vehicles.

This combined operation tends to split itself by the nature of the demand rather than the product type, with the replenishment of aggregates to fixed sites handled separately to the aggregate general market and asphalt demand, except where cross-working benefits can be found.

Planning (asphalt and general market aggregates)

The planning, order management and scheduling of asphalt and general market aggregates is also a difficult process. Demand at a product level is highly volatile (although overall demand tends to be smoother) with short lead times, due to low levels of customer (and supplier) supply chain maturity with heavily siloed processes, limited forward planning and an exposure to weather-driven changes and delays.

A number of major companies have implemented basic S&OP processes, which aim to forecast demand for one to three months into the future, translate the demand into operational requirements and enable the appropriate trade-off decisions to be made. However these are still struggling to gain traction in the traditional world of asphalt and aggregates, with its strong functional silos and production-led approach.

In a similar manner to concrete, large projects demanding asphalt or aggregates are usually known about well in advance and with it the overall levels of expected demand. However it is common for these programmes to move, as parts of the scheme progress at different speeds due to unexpected problems, weather impacts and other issues that challenge the plan. Deliveries tend to be called off against the plan on the day before the job, although penalties for changes are rare, so customers can often make last-minute changes in volumes, product type or even destination.

On the day of the delivery, outside of specific night deliveries, the asphalt market is heavily weighted towards deliveries in the morning (especially at 8 am), which causes a spike in demand across the morning. On top of this daily demand spike, planning is further complicated by the changing geographical destinations of the demand, varying reliability levels of production plants requiring demand to be relocated after plant breakdowns, and high levels of waiting time experienced at the customer site.

The usual buffer for managing short-term volatile demand in other industries is via the use of inventory but the small raw material bins, perishable nature of the product and JIT production of asphalt makes this a challenge. A common trade-off in companies is the use of trucks effectively as mobile storage in order to minimize production costs, sacrificing delivery capacity and utilization as a result.

With actual quantities required and timings uncertain for a lot of customers, it is usual for an internal or external sales team to raise a quote for a particular piece of work. When actually required the call-off of demand against these quotes can be a commercial or logistics responsibility, utilizing usually regionally-based offices to receive these call-offs by phone. At the present time, very few of these call-offs are electronic, other than perhaps as a simple e-mail.

The responsibility for then planning the fulfilment of these call-offs falls to planning teams, which vary significantly in sophistication and set-up across companies. Essentially, though, the key tasks remain the same whatever the set-up:

- Capacity and network planning: maximizing the use of the production plants in the network, looking at the most economic source of supply for jobs and linking back to the order-take teams to avoid over-commitment.
- Fleet planning: taking the overall network plan and resourcing sufficient fleet at each plant to meet the demand.
- Production planning: where possible planning the order of production for the plant on the day, minimizing changeovers and clean-outs between products.
- Scheduling and allocation: allocating individual deliveries to vehicles.

The location of the planning activity is mainly driven by company structure, plant density and systems maturity. Most usually the capacity, network and fleet planning will take place at a regional or national level depending on the organizational structure (geographic or functional). Production planning and scheduling can take place either at plant levels for more geographically isolated plants, or in area or regional centres where the density of the plant network provides benefits in planning the sites together. Scheduling and allocation tends to be a local weighbridge job unless a company has invested in a transport management system (TMS).

System usage within asphalt and aggregates (both the general market and replenishment work) remains generally relatively limited. As mentioned previously, supply chain planning tools and S&OP systems, where they do exist, tend to be spreadsheet driven. Track-and-trace systems are common for own and owner–driver fleets (albeit often used in a reactive manner in the same fashion as the ready-mix concrete track-and-trace systems) – however, visibility of the location of subcontracted vehicles is low.

The low-utilization levels of the core vehicles, coupled with the relatively dense plant networks, should provide a significant opportunity for the use of TMS to plan and optimize the utilization of vehicles. Indeed a number of the major companies have attempted implementation of these tools with varying degrees of success. The short lead-time, dynamic, changing nature of the demand, linked with highly variable waiting time on site and the generally low prevalence of supply chain thinking amongst customers and suppliers, however, have prevented their true potential from being realized.

Planning (aggregate replenishment work)

The planning, order management and scheduling of aggregate replenishment work to fixed sites is a relatively simple process. With repeatable, relatively forecastable demand for consistent products, these fixed sites tend to operate with large bulk orders covering up to a year, from which individual loads with short lead times are called off as required.

The call-off process operates in a number of ways across different plants, customers and companies, ranging from an informal relationship with a haulier to keep an aggregate bay at a site constantly topped up, to formal schedules provided to planning offices integrated with other demand. Larger sites will often be supplied on a turnaround basis, where a dedicated haulier constantly travels back and forth between the supplying and receiving plant delivering product all day.

A common challenge to planning teams in this area is often that of small stockholding areas at receiving plants and the wish of that receiving plant to start the day with full stock bays, which leads to a spike in demand early in the operating day. A second challenge is the shortage of demand management systems in the downstream activities and often the lack of collaborative planning, so sudden changes in demand levels can occur with very short notice. A site with large stock bays, simply waiting until they are nearly empty and then calling off enough volume to fill them back up, or a large job changing historic demand levels, both cause these changes to demand level. The vertically integrated nature of the industry tends to generate rather than solve these challenges, with internal business unit demand often the most challenging to manage, with the shortest lead times.

One simple system that can provide high benefit levels to these vertically integrated companies is 'auto-replenishment', where low stock levels at the downstream ready-mix concrete, asphalt or building materials plant generates a demand in the aggregates order system. This cuts administration and if planned well provides less time-sensitive demand, which can be used to up the utilization levels.

Where more developed relationships exist, these two challenges are starting to be addressed through approaches such as vendor-managed inventory (VMI), out-of-hours deliveries and collaborative planning. Currently these approaches tend to be few and far between and provide a source for significant future improvement.

Transport operations (asphalt and general market aggregates)

The management of transport operations within the asphalt and aggregates industry as a specific function of the business has a relatively long history (indeed it is the part that most people think of within the businesses when logistics is referred to). However, historically it is rarely seen as a value-adding area, more often being associated instead with all that can go wrong in the area, which, being the last link in the value chain, can be many things.

With asphalt and aggregates operations usually being organized into geographical structures of areas and regions, it is common to have a transport manager role in each area/region (dependent on their size) operating in a matrix role outside of the remainder of the operational/manufacturing team. Where scale demands it, the regional transport manager has a number of direct reports to allow sufficient coverage of the fleet, with the size of this team depending on the nature of the fleet (own-fleet or owner–driver) as well as the spread and relative size of the plants. Larger companies can also tend to justify specialist central roles, which can manage vehicle specification, the transport model and other related areas, coordinating the overall approach and direction of the transport team.

The specialist nature of the insulated tippers required for asphalt work leads to dedicated fleets being utilized by the majority of companies to service this work. Be they own-fleet or owner–driver the fleet is typically sized based on this asphalt demand (taking into account the high percentage of the demand in this area that occurs in the morning); the balance of the day is then filled up with either general market aggregates or aggregate replenishment work in order to spread the costs of the vehicle.

Unusually in the logistics world, payload is not a particular issue for these operations, with vehicles leaving full, unless a smaller load has been specifically ordered. Utilization of the vehicles is key, however, and makes a significant difference to the cost base. The spread of work through the day, the amount of time lost waiting to load or discharge and average delivery distance all have an impact – typically measured in loads per day – with an ongoing challenge for the transport teams to educate the wider businesses to the cost impact of each of these areas.

Despite the focus on utilization, double shifting of vehicles (operating them day and night) is still relatively rare for a mix of reasons including demand patterns, customer/site resistance or restrictions around night deliveries and the allocation of individual vehicles to individual drivers.

Transport operations (aggregate replenishment work)

As previously mentioned, aggregate replenishment work can be carried out on asphalt delivery vehicles or by making use of non-insulated bulk tippers, with the decision being driven by the trade-off between enhanced payload plus backhaul potential of the articulated bulk tippers and the overall cost-effectiveness of the often poorly utilized asphalt delivery vehicles.

Companies tend to build most of their fleet around the specialized insulated tippers, leaving provision of bulk tippers to external suppliers. In this section we focus on the bulk tippers. Transportation management structures vary between companies; however, in the major companies it is common to see elements of the logistics team focusing on the supply and management of these tippers, due to the higher focus on the commercial element of the relationship with the providers rather than the more technical and support nature of own-fleet and owner–driver relationship.

A number of possible models exist for the supply of these bulk tippers, although three main models cover the majority of set-ups:

- Ad hoc or spot: as demand arises it is offered out to or requested by a list of local suppliers, with rates varying depending on demand, seasonality and nature of the relationship. This approach is flexible and can be very cost effective during troughs in demand. However, it is subject to cost rises and service issues when demand rises unexpectedly, without any contractual fallback.
- Lead-haulier: a single haulier takes on responsibility for all or a significant proportion of the *outbound volume from a plant*, able to subcontract elements of the volume where required. This approach – as long as it is well managed – provides a good service level for deliveries, but can be limited in its flexibility during demand up- and downswings. It can also lead to cosy relationships, where costs become bloated over time and miss out on maximizing the potential of backhaul.
- Lanes: a single haulier takes on responsibility for all or a significant proportion of the *inbound volume to a plant from a specific source (or replenishment lanes)*. This haulier may have one or many of these lanes, which are awarded through competitive tender processes (or in some cases historical relationships). This approach allows hauliers to cherry-pick lanes that fit with their other volume and backhaul opportunities, producing cost-effectiveness while maintaining contractually backed service levels. The disadvantages are the increased management overhead of multiple providers and the potential for unwanted lanes that no provider can operate profitably.

The bulk tipper market is relatively well developed and a plethora of providers exists, although as relatively small-sized operations. The large 3PLs are only just starting to operate in this arena, albeit tending towards the agricultural side of the tipper market. Some providers specialize in the aggregate market, whereas others cover any of the bulk markets and their seasonal peaks (grain, sugar beet etc).

Transport operations (rail)

Aggregate rail operations are a specialist area that we only quickly touch upon. Rail can add significant cost advantages when large volumes or distances are involved, but often at the cost of high set-up/infrastructure costs and limited flexibility.

It tends to work best and most effectively where both the originating plant and destination point are on the rail network (removing the need for intermediary rail-handling sites) and volumes are large and consistently repeatable. Where these conditions are not met, it can still offer service or practical operational benefits, but they become more marginal.

Rail freight (the poor cousin of passenger traffic on the UK rail network) is provided by a number of freight-operating companies (FOCs), although two major aggregate companies have formed a joint venture that acts as an FOC to bring aggregates from south-west England into London. Factors such as this relatively small supplier base, constraints around access to drivers plus wagons, the high entry cost into these operations and the relatively low capacity available on the rail network all serve to hamper this strategically important area.

The specialist knowledge and approach required to run these rail operations often sees the creation of small dedicated teams within companies to manage them.

Cement

Planning

The planning, order management and scheduling of bulk and packed cement is closer to that of other industrial chemical process industries than it is to the other bulk construction materials. Demand for both areas tends to be less volatile and more readily forecasted, providing a different type of challenge where it is often the supply side that provides the greater level of difficulty.

The challenges that arise on the supply side, each causing disruption in the supply chain, include:

- a multi-stage production process (clinker production, grinding and, where appropriate, packaging);
- reliance on a small number of capacity-constrained physical operations (kilns, mills, packaging plants), with limited back-up capacity;
- a continuous production process for the clinker with limited ability to change the rate of production in the short term;
- finite limits to storage at each stage of the process, leading to low stock depth of what is a volume product (cement plant capacities vary, however 1 million tonnes per annum is common);
- finite limits to transportation capacity due to the use of specialized pressurized powder tankers and cross-contamination issues with other powder tankers;
- a need to shut down the kilns and other elements of the production process regularly for maintenance and replacement of wear parts, both through planned (often annual) shutdowns and unplanned breakdowns.

These challenges have led to a much higher prevalence of supply chain planning and/or S&OP processes amongst the cement producers, with these processes playing a key part in the execution and profitability of the business.

Demand for cement is almost exclusively to fixed sites and reasonably long-lifetime project plants. This, coupled with the buffering effect of stock held at the fixed sites, helps to remove a lot of the volatility experienced by the other bulk construction materials. However, on both the packed and bulk side, stockholding capacity at the destination can be low (30-tonne cement silos at ready-mixed plants are still quite common, providing capacity for roughly 100 cubic metres of concrete production).

Excluding the recession triggered in 2008, demand for cement usually exceeds the domestic production capacity of the UK. Although offset by an amount of cement importing from other countries, this high level of demand (especially when coupled with a production outage) requires customer supply trade-offs to be made on a regular basis.

Deliveries of bulk cement are normally full load and, as previously mentioned, are to fixed sites, providing opportunities for the use of scheduling and transport management systems to maximize efficiency, although full automated optimization is still rare. An uneven demand pattern across the day (with peaks first thing and then late morning) can cause delays in loading and a squeeze on transport resource. Additionally, discharge times on site can vary significantly, especially for sites with small silos (roughly the same capacity as the delivery vehicle) where the load will be ordered and on the road based on unsophisticated demand planning by the customer, often resulting in the delivery tanker waiting to offload until demand has been sufficient to empty the delivery silo enough to allow the load to be discharged.

Deliveries of packed cement can be full-load or part-load multi-drops dependent on the customer, usually made direct to store. The planning and scheduling of these loads is very similar to any other supply to retailers or builders' merchants, with high levels of annual seasonality both causing problems (such as at Easter when demand peaks) and providing opportunities (low demand during the pre-Christmas peak for other industries).

The structure of the teams for the planning, order management and scheduling of cement tends to be focused on national teams bringing the efficiency of operation, focus, consistency and network overview that this approach can provide.

Transport operations

As with the planning operations, management of transport operations within cement supply is usually far more developed than the other bulk materials and is seen as an integrated part of the logistics function and structured accordingly.

For bulk cement supply the specialized nature of the pressurized cement tankers and their operation requires the use of dedicated fleets of vehicles. The most common models are own-fleet operations, 3PL dedicated operations or a combination of the two, with the choice and balance between the models being driven by the company's approach to capital expenditure, resource control and business focus. There also exists a degree of tanker hire and a relatively small subcontract tanker market, which can be utilized for peak management.

Rail freight is also utilized by a number of cement-producing companies as a method of moving bulk volumes to stockholding depots. This tends to prove a cost-effective way of providing a national operation from a small number of production plants, with the cost benefit of using rail balancing the costs of double handling, as well as providing service and responsiveness benefits. A secondary benefit of these stockholding depots is during periods of supply chain disruption, where they can provide a buffer. As with the aggregates rail operations, this type of transport is a specialist area requiring its own focus and management.

Packed cement is usually delivered palletized on tautliner/curtain-sided vehicles, and other than being a relatively high-weight and -density product, requires no special handling. This lack of specialism opens up a wealth of possible transport models ranging from own-fleet to 3PL and general spot haulage, with each company choosing an approach to fit its own circumstances and wider strategy.

Supply chain maturity

The relative immaturity of the logistics function and the concept of supply chain thinking in the bulk construction materials industry provides many opportunities for improvement and enhanced value creation.

Research in this area is limited, specifically around the potential improvements possible for the construction industry and the bulk materials element of it. However, many studies by companies such as Gartner and the major management consultancies exist for other analogous industries. The 2013 global supply chain survey carried out by PwC (2013) showed for the chemicals and process industry that leaders in supply chain achieve a 29 plus per cent EBIT margin and a 22 plus per cent delivery performance versus laggards in that sector. Gartner research points at similar numbers and includes significant improvements in cash flow levels on top of the profit and service performance mentioned by PwC.

The potential improvements available in the bulk materials element of the construction industry are certainly significant, perhaps greater than those referred to in the chemicals industry due to the low starting point that many companies are coming from. Achievement of these improvements, though, will require a sizeable shift in mindset and approach, by both the material suppliers and the entire downstream demand chain.

The fragmented nature of construction supply chains, with multiple tiers of client, architect, specifier, main contractor, subcontractor and materials supplier, does not lend itself easily to the collaboration required to achieve an integrated and efficient supply chain. However, there are a number of stages of supply chain maturity and most companies can at least move forward through these stages, gaining benefit as they do so. Whether the entire construction supply chain can ever become truly integrated remains to be seen.

Most models of supply chain maturity see the ultimate end goal as being one where demand, supply and product considerations all overlap, producing an ecosystem where:

- end-customer demand drives the supply chain, as opposed to manufacturers pushing product up the chain;
- value is maximized across the chain, realizing that to achieve this some links in the chain may need to operate in a perceived inefficient fashion;
- demand is sensed in advance and shaped to drive value, rather than links in the chain reacting to today's demand;
- the response to the demand is managed at a supply chain level holistically, rather than by each link in the chain responding to the immediate demand from its predecessor in the chain;
- the demand is visible across the chain as quickly as possible, not held up by each link;
- all this is achieved across multiple company functions and layers of suppliers.

Few companies and industries have achieved this end goal, other than in specific discrete supply chains, but the journey towards it has been started by most leading companies either by necessity or a desire to improve. Industries such as high-tech, fast-moving consumer goods, retail and complex manufacturing are leading the way (stand-out companies include Intel, Apple and Unilever).

Stages of supply chain maturity

Looking at an individual company's journey towards increasing supply chain maturity, they will be at one of a number of steps or stages of development:

1. Business silos reacting: dominated by misaligned or siloed goals between business units and geographies, often led by sales or manufacturing and focusing on revenue, with different processes in each business unit; reacting to demand and fire fighting to stay on top on demand volatility; low levels of visibility and business-unit-specific KPIs. The individual business units may be very profitable, however their ability to scale and their cost efficiency are severely constrained.

2. Scaling and cost-efficiency: as companies look to scale their operations and focus on cost reduction, logistics functional leaders start to emerge within geographies or business units. A focus on lowest cost of physical delivery emerges with a focus on standardization to achieve this. Basic demand forecasting and planning capabilities develop, focused on internal utilization of assets. KPIs tend to be functionally focused and often are competing between functions.

3 Integrated decision making: functional barriers start to break down as decisions are made cross-functionally based on the implications across the internal supply chain. Supply chain considerations become an early input into the sales process and the focus is on trading off the balance between cost, working capital and service. S&OP becomes a key integrating process in the business. KPIs look across the integrated supply chain, with demand forecast accuracy a key measure.

4 Supply chain collaboration: at this stage the focus switches from internal within the company to looking at it as part of an external supply chain. Revenue becomes secondary to value creation. Collaboration with customers and suppliers becomes key, with the aim to ensure the demand is profitably fulfilled by the end-to-end supply chain. Processes are integrated across this extended supply chain, and real-time visibility and performance data cover the whole chain. Supply chain solutions are segmented to meet the needs of differing customer groups.

Clearly companies may exhibit some of the behaviours of a more advanced stage, or be further developed in some business units than others. However, to gain the full benefits of supply chain maturity the whole enterprise needs to be at a similar level.

It is worth noting that the movement between these stages is very much a journey, and companies wishing to improve in this area need to develop in a linear fashion from stage one to stage four. Attempting to skip a stage is very unlikely to be successful, as stakeholders will struggle to make the conceptual change and the enabling processes and technology, as well as run the risk that the customers and suppliers will be left behind.

The level of difficulty in moving between the stages is heavily influenced by factors such as organizational structure, customer maturity and the wider culture of the business. This creates an extra challenge for the large, often traditional, slow-to-change companies in the bulk materials industry.

Current maturity

The current level of supply chain maturity of companies within the bulk materials industry varies between the large and small enterprises, as well as between the product streams. There may well be many examples of smaller companies that are showing many aspects of the more advanced stages; however they will be constrained by the readiness of their customers to work in such a collaborative way.

The vertically integrated nature of many large suppliers of bulk materials for construction should, in theory, simplify the journey towards supply chain maturity. However, amongst the large 'majors' (CEMEX UK, Lafarge Tarmac, Hanson/Heidelberg, Aggregate Industries/Holcim and Hope Construction Materials) that make up most of the supply in the UK of the products covered in this chapter, maturity levels tend to be relatively low and certainly are not consistent across product streams.

It therefore becomes relevant to look at the product business units in isolation (as opposed to as part of the wider company's overall maturity level), even though this to some extent automatically restricts the maximum maturity level of that area.

For the major suppliers, this is as set out below.

Ready-mix concrete

Ready-mix concrete is at the lower end of the maturity scale, varying between stages one and two. The normal set-up with individual plants or small sectors helps to remove functional barriers, through small teams and employees with multiple responsibilities. However, demand planning and supporting systems tend to be basic. Additionally, the coordination between these geographical clusters is limited and significant portions of the customer base are not advanced enough to provide demand data or work collaboratively. Even the significant-scale major customers and projects can struggle with providing accurate demand information and collaborative working.

Aggregates and asphalt

Aggregates and asphalt operations tend to be organized into geographic regions and most individual regions are around the stage two level, although not in all aspects and certainly not at a national level.

With the larger scale of these operations, more functional roles emerge in each region, raising the challenge of competing misaligned functional goals. A strong focus on the physical manufacturing process and linear sales processes with limited early involvement of logistics can also hold them back. This physical manufacturing focus, coupled with limited focus on inventory levels, often leads to a decoupling between demand and supply, with plants focusing almost solely on production levels to maximize asset utilization, rather than availability and inventory.

The use and level of embedding of S&OP, as well as levels of business visibility and performance management, can vary significantly. Even in the majors, a number of companies see logistics/supply chain as simply dispatch and transport, limiting its influence as a function. Demand forecasting can be quite basic, with limited ability to shape demand and thus increase utilization levels.

The usual geographical organization structure can also limit levels of standardization, although most of the majors have some degree of centralized 'Centre of Excellence' to enhance this standardization.

Cement

Cement operations are the most advanced on average of the bulk materials, achieving stage two and some aspects of stage three maturity.

The national structure and understanding of the need for supply chain planning are big contributors to this maturity level. Historical profit levels have helped to support systems investment and the requirement to carefully manage inventory levels at each stage of the process, bringing credibility to the logistics/supply chain team. Early stages of demand shaping (ie flattening the daily demand) and the beginning of the use of vendor-managed inventory (VMI) and auto-replenishment systems also support this maturity.

Where next for bulk materials?

A general focus on building value, coupled with rising demand for the products that bulk materials suppliers provide, and an increasingly complex level of construction projects, all point towards the need to accelerate supply chain maturity.

As companies look towards providing solutions rather than commodity products, this will help to introduce the concept and benefits of this increased supply chain maturity. However, most companies in this area have not yet bought into this development area. Recruitment within the industry tends to be largely from the industry and new approaches can be slow to develop. The significant business, mindset and organizational change required to reach the advanced stages will be a large blocking factor.

Yet this challenge also provides an opportunity, as there are numerous small, practical steps that can be taken relatively easily, each improving step by step the overall maturity and benefit of the supply chain.

Assuming a company is at stage one or two, first they can leverage its scale to provide efficiency and cost reduction, then look to internally integrate across and align its supply chain functions, before finally coordinating across the external supply chain.

The exact steps would depend on the actual company; however a number of indicative focus areas are:

- Leveraging scale for efficiency and cost reduction: build the focus around geography as the primary factor, focusing on rationalizing the internal logistics processes, with simple and quick cost reductions.
- Performance management: driving the use of KPIs and increasing the visibility of both spend and performance, ensuring service delivery is measured and managed.
- Process: building structured and documented approaches to order-to-cash processes and using these to drive standardization; introduction of basic S&OP and demand planning, driving the concepts of demand-driven and cross-functional working.
- Organization: mapping existing talent in the supply chain, building succession plans for key roles and introducing career pathways and development routes.
- Technology: standardization of the use of existing systems, with small-scale developments where required to introduce elements such as capacity planning.

Integrating and aligning supply chain functions

For this step the focus moves to product flowing through the chain, moving past the geographic reporting lines of the organization, enabling improvements in efficiency:

- Performance management: actively trade off KPI performance (eg making conscious choices around utilization levels and their impact on service); leverage the S&OP process to drive cross-functional decision making, ensuring that data supports decision making and that products rather than geographies are measured.
- Process: structure decision making; introduce early segmentation of supply chains to fit differential service offers, focusing on the flow of product rather than the geography itself. Ensure that cost levers driving logistics costs are understood within the business and that cost-adding services are charged to the customer.
- Organization: invest in expertise and capability enhancement of supply chain talent; increase the scope and presence of the supply chain organization.
- Technology: create end-to-end efficiency through targeted systems investment, moving from manual and spreadsheet-based systems to enterprise resource planning (ERP) linked solutions (such as planning and forecasting tools, transport management systems etc).

Coordinating across the external supply chain

Finally, with geographic approaches in place and product moving efficiently through the supply chain the focus moves to creating profitable value for customers:

- Performance management: build real-time visibility capability both internally and along the supply chain. Measure the supply chain using the customer's measures of success. Forecast accuracy becomes the key internal KPI.
- Process: create processes that shape and sense demand; utilize S&OP to drive the business planning process and drive executive level trade-off decisions; segment the supply chain capability to match market channel needs.
- Organization: organization structure should be linked to the end-to-end supply chain approach, ensuring that high performers and rising talent spend time in the supply chain function.
- Technology: invest in collaboration systems allowing rapid real-time visibility cross-enterprise and across the end-to-end supply chain. Build systems responsiveness and demand-shaping capabilities through dynamic planning and auto-replenishment systems.

Conclusion

The supply of bulk materials is a wide-ranging and varied area, covering very different product areas. The scale of the logistics operation to plan and move these materials is massive, covering wide geographies and operations.

Logistics and supply chain maturity are still at relatively early stages of development, providing significant opportunities for improvement. The journey to higher levels of maturity, however, will not be an easy one, but it has the potential to generate significant value.

The significant steps for most companies at these relatively low stages of supply chain maturity are to consolidate the basics, move to cross-functional alignment and finally to cross-enterprise alignment – transitioning through a focus on geography, to product and then on to customer.

As construction projects continue to become ever more complex and multi-tiered, the impact of getting the supply chain right for these bulk materials can have significant cost, value and programme efficiency benefits for the entire chain. This moves these products from being mere commodities to being critical elements in an end-to-end integrated supply chain.

References

MPA (2014) Mineral Product Industry at a Glance [Online] http://www.mineralproducts.org/documents/mpa_facts_at_a_glance_2014.pdf [accessed 23 February 2015]

PricewaterhouseCoopers (2013) Global Supply Chain Survey 2013, *PwC* [Online] www.pwc.com/en_UA/ua/services/consulting/assets/global-supply-chain-survey-2013-eng.pdf [accessed 28 April 2015]

Effective management of a construction project supply chain

04

STEPHEN ROBBINS

Introduction

This chapter tracks some of the developments in construction logistics over recent years and explores the operational challenges associated with a construction project along with the organizational and cultural matters that influence both current and future practice. Considering the principal contractor's current approach to supply chain and logistics management, the chapter speculates how this might change over the next five years to 2020 and reveals significant opportunity to improve the supply chain and logistics performance on major construction projects. It goes on to propose a number of changes that are needed to facilitate this. It also demonstrates the viability of a logistics method that could revolutionize supply chain management within the industry.

Construction and the built environment have a significant effect on our everyday lives. An increasing population and the need to maintain, extend, adapt, renew and replace buildings makes construction one of the largest contributors to the UK economy. In 2011 it was directly responsible for 7.4 per cent of gross domestic product (GDP) or 14 per cent when considering the 'entire value chain' (UK Contractors Group, 2012). It employs over 2.5 million workers and was worth £69 billion gross value added (GVA) to the UK economy in 2010 (Department for Business Innovation and Skills, 2012).

'Managing a construction project supply chain effectively and efficiently is extremely difficult' (Abu Hassan, Ballal and Omar, 2013). The report by the Construction Task Force, Rethinking Construction (DETR, 1998) had a considerable effect on the industry. Its recommendations received widespread endorsement throughout construction and over the past 15 years considerable attention has been paid to improving performance and making the industry more efficient.

Increasingly strict legislation, the economic downturn triggered in 2008 and a fiercely competitive market have also instigated change and placed unprecedented pressure on building contractors and their supply chain to improve performance and reduce costs. Logistics affects many key performance areas of a project and has a particular influence on operational efficiency and cost. It is seen as a discipline that can help construction to improve standards, in the same way as other industries have (Robbins, 2005).

A major construction project places huge demand on its logistics function; planning and organizing people, materials, equipment and waste on large scales is a significant undertaking. A fragmented supply chain with multiple stakeholders makes coordination difficult and, to add further pressure, projects are often built in constrained environments where the building contractor has to complete the construction within strict time parameters (Robbins and Thomas, 2013). When the logistics function is managed correctly it can contribute enormously, by influencing critical areas including time, cost, quality, safety and environmental performance (Mossman, 2008). Yet dedicated logistics management is in its infancy within construction and lags well behind other industries (Barthorpe, Robbins and Sullivan, 2010).

This is a topical subject with government bodies such as Transport for London, Croydon Council (2012) and influential clients including BAA (Robbins, 2004) instigating further advancement of logistics techniques within construction.

This chapter examines the current supply chain and logistics practice of a major contractor that operates globally and has been responsible for some of the largest and most prestigious construction projects in the UK, including logistically challenging city-centre locations, security-sensitive sites and where construction activity has been carried out in live operational environments such as hospitals, airports, Ministry of Defence (MoD) facilities and sporting venues.

The company will remain anonymous throughout this chapter and no reference will be made to specific sites, subcontractors or individual employees who took part in the research.

A typical construction project supply chain

The construction of a major project is undertaken by a 'principal contractor', an organization that employs specialist subcontractors to construct elements of the building on their behalf. The principal contractor maintains responsibility for managing the site, coordinating the work and assuming overall responsibility for the project.

A project places a unique demand on its supply chain, requiring large volumes of materials and producing large volumes of waste. It depends on a global supply chain to provide a vastly diverse range of components.

Modern methods of construction (MMC) place further demands on construction logistics. One of the benefits of modularization and prefabrication is that the construction of the building can proceed far more quickly than would be possible using more traditional methods. However, this means that large components are made in advance, creating a need to store them (off site) and deliver them in a defined sequence. This requires more planning, coordination, resource and management.

A principal contractor's supply chain is enormous and its diversity spans across the industry and reflects the range of both current and previous projects. It is typically made up of companies that specialize in a particular trade or discipline and are employed on a project to carry out a 'works package' on behalf of the principal contractor. Regional procurement frameworks are established to ensure competitive rates and sustainable business opportunities, and to promote confidence and familiarity between organizations. Subcontractors are appointed on a project following a competitive tendering process; they may have responsibility for the design, supply, installation and maintenance of their package.

The role of the principal contractor involves managing subcontractors to ensure that they understand the project requirements and that whilst working on site they must comply with any rules or procedures that are implemented, including management of deliveries, storage and distribution of materials and managing waste. However, each subcontractor is responsible for their own supply chain (Figure 4.1). Logistically, this places a great deal of pressure on the principal contractor to manage project resources efficiently.

Construction logistics

Logistics is a discipline that has few parameters in its application; spanning a diverse range of industries from health care to Formula 1 motorcar racing. It has become a frequently used buzz word in business and is even referred to in people's everyday lives when planning the practical detail of an event or activity (Robbins and Thomas, 2013).

Robbins (2005) explains that construction logistics is different to logistics in other industries. Whilst its primary purpose is to ensure the efficient management relating to transportation, storage and distribution of materials and equipment on site, construction logistics also provides a 'support role' for the site, which includes security, cleaning, safety, welfare (site accommodation), community relations, emergency evacuation and first aid (Barthorpe, Robbins and Sullivan, 2010).

The fact that construction logistics has a secondary purpose causes obscurity in its application and detracts from its core value. Industry reviews by Latham (1994), Egan, Bourn and Accelerating Change (cited in

FIGURE 4.1 This illustrates the function of 'logistics' within the 'supply chain'

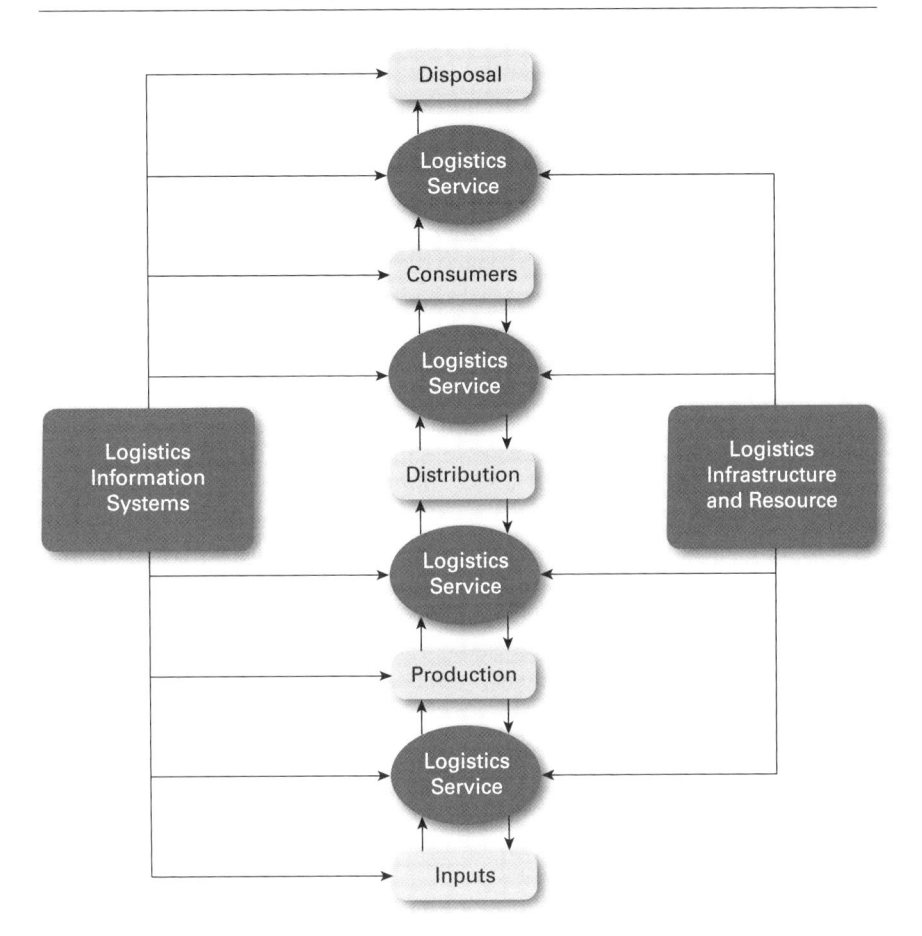

[Figure showing a flow diagram with the following elements arranged vertically from top to bottom: Disposal → Logistics Service → Consumers → Logistics Service → Distribution → Logistics Service → Production → Logistics Service → Inputs. On the left side is a box labeled "Logistics Information Systems" and on the right side is a box labeled "Logistics Infrastructure and Resource", both connected to the central flow.]

SOURCE: Taylor, Tseng and Yue (2005)

Barthorpe, Robbins and Sullivan, 2010) have all criticized construction for being uncoordinated, disruptive and wasteful and it is widely acknowledged that logistics is less advanced in construction than in other industries (Barthorpe, Robbins and Sullivan, 2010). This is an alarming insight given its significance to a project. Planning and organizing people, materials and equipment on the scale required for a major project places a huge strain on the project team, site resource, the supply chain and the people living and working in the surrounding area. Its impact on critical matters such as cost, safety, productivity, the environment and social impact means that it also has a considerable bearing on project performance and, as a consequence, it is essential that a reliable and robust logistics plan is developed for each project. A lack of clarity over its definition only serves as a hindrance both in its application on site and to its development within industry.

This problem is compounded when you consider other operational difficulties including the fragmented supply chain (Strategic Forum for Construction Logistics, 2005) and physical constraints associated with the location and layout of the site. These problems are unique to construction and put greater emphasis on the need to improve supply chain performance and logistics techniques within the industry.

In direct contrast to techniques applied in the manufacturing industry, materials are often ordered in larger volumes than required, '*just in case*' (Mossman, 2008), and delivered to site before they are needed. As a consequence, 'construction products are often stored on site for long periods of time and have to be moved to other parts of the site where they are eventually needed', which is extremely wasteful in terms of both time and damaged products that are disposed of (Strategic Forum for Construction Logistics, 2005). Furthermore, many logistical constraints emanate from the location and the physical characteristics of the site (Mossman, 2008), something that is normally determined by the client with little or no consideration made to either 'construction' or 'logistics'. Consequently, major projects are often built in a congested city centre where the site boundary does not extend beyond the footprint of the building or in a live operational environment such as an airport, hospital or MoD base where construction activities are coordinated around the business needs of the client (Robbins, 2005). This means that the site has a major interface with neighbours and third-party stakeholders such as airport passengers or hospital patients and staff, which places enormous pressure on the area immediately surrounding a project in terms of the number of people that work on site and the volume of materials required in the construction process. This has contributed to the poor image of the industry and is a source of major concern (Strategic Forum for Construction Logistics, 2005).

Cultural barriers also contribute to the problem and hinder the advancement of logistics management, including:

- A lack of clarity on the costs associated with construction logistics (Robbins, 2004).
- Dependence on subcontracting.
- Each project is unique, with a unique set of constraints relating to the location of the site, the size and physical layout of the project and the construction methodology.
- There is no benchmarking within the industry to measure performance in this area.

Inspired by Latham (1994), the 'Considerate Constructor Scheme' was established to 'improve the image of construction' and combat the common perception that construction causes disruption and inconvenience. This was achieved by promoting corporate responsibility and encouraging contractors to consider the impact on the community surrounding a project through its 'Considerate Code of Practice'. More recently, Transport for London has supported the use of 'construction logistics plans' (CLPs) for major schemes in an attempt to reduce congestion, air pollution and the number of road traffic accidents involving construction traffic (Steele, 2013).

These are significant developments that indicate both the impact that logistics has and the current level of inadequacy in its application. Many elements of the 'Considerate Constructor Scheme' code of conduct focus on logistics-related matters, which affect the image of both a site and the industry (Robbins and Thomas, 2013). Furthermore, CLPs consider the constraints associated with the location and physical layout of the site and define the most efficient method of managing the logistics function. It seems astonishing – given the impact that logistics has – that a document defining its function is not commonplace, with every site utilizing them to plan resources and communicate with the supply chain.

Defining 'effective' management of a construction supply chain

It is difficult to define 'effective' logistics and supply chain management of a construction project, due to the number of variables that significantly affect its management including the location of the site, the access and egress, construction methodology, storage and distribution of materials etc. A fast programme only serves to exaggerate these issues and add pressure to the project management team.

Equally, it is difficult to define true 'world class' best practice for construction logistics as there are few companies that have a global presence – and there is little in the way of global collaboration or knowledge sharing between contractors.

However, buildings all over the world are constructed using similar techniques, and contractors face the same challenges, with city-centre projects being particularly demanding. A large number of deliveries and vertical distribution cause a major challenge, particularly in large-value, small-footprint buildings. Many of the constraints on a project in London, for example, relate to its location and are the same constraints as those encountered in New York, Sydney, Tokyo etc. It is also difficult to define 'best practice' on a national level as construction logistics is a relatively new discipline and there are no significant industry-leading companies or defining methods to illustrate how a company should approach the management of a project. Published examples of 'best practice' promote the concept and advertise the benefits of good logistics, but lack the scope and clarity to address the subject holistically and identify which model of logistics management suits different types of project.

Logistics management and current best practice

It is clear that logistics has become more important to the construction industry over recent years. Clients are much more enlightened to the issues of poor logistics management both in terms of adjacent neighbours or their own operations, and contractors are more aware of the effects that good and bad organization can have on costs and performance. According to Robbins and Thomas (2013), a number of techniques have emerged over the past two decades that can be considered 'best practice'. The most prominent include:

- Vehicle holding areas: off-site parking areas to assist suppliers and subcontractors to meet allocated delivery times.
- 'Hub' construction consolidation centres (CCCs): off-site distribution centres used to store materials and deliver them to site in a more controlled and efficient manner.
- Dedicated logistics team (on site): responsible for receiving deliveries, distributing materials and managing waste, and can lead to improved safety standards (Robbins, 2004) and productivity of the skilled workforce, which currently spend up to 50 per cent of their time on logistics-related tasks (Mossman, 2008).
- Construction logistics plan (CLP): a document that considers site constraints and defines the logistics methodology for the project.

Whilst all of these methods are considered good practice within industry, they are far from commonplace.

The majority of sites manage logistics in the traditional way, by coordinating proceedings on site. However, this is ad hoc and not effectively managed: it completely ignores off-site logistics and resource efficiency within the supply chain, it relies on short-term planning and is highly dependent on collaboration between parties on site. Projects that adopt this approach continue to endure the problems identified by Latham (1994), Egan, Bourn and Accelerating Change (cited in Barthorpe, Robbins and Sullivan, 2010), which criticized logistical performance and suggested that significant improvements are possible.

An emphasis on control

The fragmented supply chain, along with the location of many projects, means that the emphasis of a project's logistics function is to increase the level of control, unlike other industries where logistics and supply chain management has been developed extensively in order to improve efficiency, reduce cost and gain competitive advantage.

A lack of coordination between parties can also lead to inefficiencies and a disjointed approach, with the procurement department responsible for supply chain management and the site responsible for logistics management. Procurement does not connect the supply chain effectively, information is of a poor quality and there is a lack of end-to-end planning. Procurement focuses on the quantum purchase rather than the detail of how things are to be manufactured, stored, called-off and delivered. Associated with this, logistics is normally considered in more detail on the most challenging of sites (Mossman, 2008), where awkward site conditions demand better planning and increased level of resource; they are also more likely to use the 'best practice' techniques discussed above.

In the most part, projects adopt a rather selfish viewpoint when implementing a logistics management plan, where the emphasis is focused on optimizing the use of resources on site and minimizing the impact of the site on the neighbours immediately adjacent to the site, often to the detriment of the stakeholders in the supply chain and the wider community. The focus of a project logistics strategy is to ensure timely deliveries to meet the production programme whilst maintaining the minimum amount of materials on site in order to reduce storage space. It is commonplace for projects to implement a booking-in procedure and allocate times for deliveries to arrive (highlighting the point above). The emphasis of a logistics strategy is regulating access of vehicles to site, and whilst this is an *acceptable* method, it is difficult for the supply chain to meet the times, due to the considerable number of off-site variables (as sites do not normally provide the infrastructure to assist, eg a vehicle holding area). Similar methodologies may be deployed effectively in other industries such as manufacturing, which typically offers a less constrained environment and operating conditions than are present on a construction site. The critical factor that determines the success of this in either construction or any other industry is the location of the site, warehouse or factory. If there is sufficient space to park vehicles, or the road network surrounding the facility permits easy access for large vehicles, then implementing a booking-in procedure to promote the efficient use of resources makes sense. If, however, the supply chain has difficulty accessing the site, then it can cause significant inefficiencies. Robbins (2004) states that in an effort to meet allocated delivery times, hauliers often circulate the roads surrounding a project for up to two hours before, adding to the cost of logistics and increasing congestion and air pollution in the area surrounding the site.

Furthermore, this problem is compounded by the site imposing restrictions on the volume of materials that can be delivered. Space-constrained sites often mean that there is a lack of available storage space, which results in limited volumes of materials being delivered. This means that there are inefficiencies relating to underutilized vehicles, which in turn means that vehicles have to visit the sites more frequently, placing more strain on resources and creating even more inefficiency throughout the supply chain.

Prefabrication and off-site production

The increase in off-site fabrication has increased the importance of planning and coordination, and created further pressure on the construction supply chain and logistics.

The benefits of prefabrication are that buildings can be constructed more quickly with less resource. However, it relies on a radical change in the approach to logistics and supply chain management.

To meet an accelerated programme, the factory has to manufacture the majority (sometimes all) of the components in advance. With limited storage provision on site, this places an enormous strain on the factory, which has to store the components until they are required and can lead to a situation whereby an interim storage location is required.

Traditionally, there is a reluctance to spend money or increase prelims or overheads. People often do not associate any costs with storage and transportation, they assume it is free and the common approach adopted on site is to just 'make do'.

Best practice – 2020

It is apparent that interest in this subject has increased and it is likely that its current impetus will continue and inspire change throughout the industry.

The literature review suggests that good logistics does not have to be expensive and should not be confined to the largest, highest value or the most complex or physically constrained projects. However, the interviews suggest that, whilst the contribution of logistics and supply chain management is increasingly recognized, consideration of the logistics function varies from site to site and is considered in more detail on certain projects. It is important that the industry adopts a more consistent and structured approach to this and CLPs will play an important part in achieving this.

A CLP is a document produced by the principal contractor that considers project constraints, identifies opportunities and defines a management strategy for the logistics function. The CLP should avoid the distractions associated with the peripheral issues identified previously within this chapter and focus on core 'logistics' matters relating to receiving, storing and distributing materials and managing waste. It will provide a holistic overview of the management plan; it will be a communicative tool that can be used to engage the supply chain; and it is an opportunity to implement the examples of 'best practice' identified above by prescribing the use of the techniques, such as an off-site holding area or CCC.

The CLP will consider the challenges associated with the project, along with opportunities to collaborate with other contractors engaged in adjacent projects – or their supply chains. It will also embrace other stakeholder interests by changing the focus from 'control' and 'resource efficiency on site' to 'collaboration' and 'resource efficiency off site'.

Every project should monitor and report on performance, including costs, vehicle utilization, turnaround times, productivity of skilled workforce, safety, environment and impact on the community surrounding a project.

Improvement strategy

It is generally accepted that construction logistics will never be as advanced as other industries due to cultural barriers and the unique challenges relating to the location and physical constraints of the site. However, current methods of best practice including vehicle holding areas, CCCs, dedicated logistics teams and, most importantly, CLPs are not widely used, and the standard practice of coordinating proceedings on site leaves significant scope for improvement.

To improve performance a more holistic view of 'good practice' should be adopted, where the emphasis is on multiple stakeholder benefits as opposed to increasing the level of control and resource efficiency on site.

It is apparent that a number of different techniques have been developed to manage logistics (Robbins and Thomas, 2013) although this seems to have happened subconsciously. There needs to be more research, the development of 'logistics models' and better understanding of how they can be suited to different types of projects.

Improving the performance of projects will mean both strategic and operational change. Strategically this will involve:

- more analysis of historical data relating to previous projects in order to understand the number of deliveries a project requires at each stage of the construction process;
- more integration between the procurement function and logistics function on site, with the aim of improving planning and collaboration throughout the supply chain;
- better understanding of the financial aspects of logistics and more transparency on cost throughout the supply chain;
- regional collaboration between principal contractors to share resources such as vehicle holding areas or CCCs;
- incentivized collaboration throughout the supply chain to make better use of resources.

Operationally, this will include:

- each project having a CLP;
- better communication and coordination with stakeholders, particularly the supply chain and community surrounding the project;
- greater levels of client involvement at the start of a project, particularly for 'sensitive' or live environments.

Demonstrating CCC as a sustainable proposition

The CCC is the most advanced method of managing the flow of materials to site as it provides multiple stakeholder benefits. However, it is also the most resource intensive and expensive option. Demonstrating this as a sustainable solution could revolutionize the industry's approach to logistics and make way for other techniques.

To determine whether the CCC could have been a sustainable proposition in the past, given the frequency and timing of major projects within a defined area, a review of historical data relating to a principal contractor's involvement in projects within the M25 over the period 2000–14 was carried out. The locations of these projects are illustrated on the map shown in Figure 4.2.

Figure 4.2 illustrates the relative locality between projects over the 14-year period 2000–14 and shows that the majority are situated in central London, where managing the supply chain and logistics function is most challenging.

Although the projects in the centre of London are clustered in a small area and are ideal for a CCC, their durations vary, which means that we must also consider continuity between projects in order to demonstrate the CCC as a sustainable proposition.

FIGURE 4.2 A sample of major projects considered in central London, 2000–14

FIGURE 4.3 Project durations

Major Projects in Central London

Project	Value	Postcode	2001	2002	2003	2004	2005	2006	2007	2008	2009	2010	2011	2012	2013	2014	2015
Project 1	£4.5bn	TW6															
Project 2	£200m	NW1															
Project 3	£45m	SE1															
Project 4	£480m	SW1															
Project 5	£195m	EC4															
Project 6	£390m	E20															
Project 7	£300m	W2															
Project 8	£240m	EC3															
Project 9	£81m	EC1															
Project 10	£95m	E12															
Project 11	£800m	TW6															
Project 12	£300m	W1															
Project 13	£390m	EC3															
Project 14	£420m	WC1															

Figure 4.3 depicts the durations of each of the projects identified above. It is clear that there is sufficient overlap between their commencement and completion dates to warrant a permanent CCC and that such a facility could be continuously used.

Using historical data as an indication of future projects, Figures 4.2 and 4.3 demonstrate that a 'hub' CCC that serves multiple, single contractor projects is a sustainable proposition. This could lead to significant, multiple stakeholder benefits, as it is widely accepted that the CCC methodology increases the level of control, improves safety and productivity on site and is more efficient for the supply chain (Robbins, 2004; Barthorpe, Robbins and Sullivan, 2010).

Whilst this example relates to projects in London there are variations to the CCC methodology, which means that it can be applied to other projects to overcome other constraints and continue to offer the same benefits to the project (Robbins, 2005).

Conclusion

This chapter outlines the construction industry's approach to logistics and supply chain management in 2014 and considers how this might change by 2020. It identifies that there is significant scope to improve performance and sets out the measures needed to facilitate a more holistic approach.

It is clear that the construction industry has changed over recent years and the logistics function has become more important, a factor that is due to a combination of the following:

- increased client awareness;
- influential organizations such as TFL (Transport for London) promoting the benefits of good logistics;
- industry publications acknowledging that logistics can improve performance by influencing critical areas;
- challenging projects where dedicated logistics management is a necessity.

However, this research has uncovered a number of problems in the way that logistics is managed:

- There is a disjointed approach with the procurement function responsible for supply chain management and the site team responsible for logistics.
- The level of consideration made to logistics varies between projects and there is a correlation between the size and complexity of a project and the level of consideration made to its logistics function.
- The standard approach of coordinating proceedings on site is most common but it is inefficient for the supply chain and leaves significant scope for improvement.

The construction industry has developed a number of 'best practice' techniques. These include:

- vehicle holding areas;
- dedicated logistics teams;
- construction consolidation centres (CCCs).

Although it has been demonstrated that these examples improve performance (Robbins, 2004; Barthorpe, Robbins and Sullivan, 2010), their application is extremely limited.

The implementation of CLPs as a mandatory feature of every project is crucial in enabling change and to move away from the standard approach and promote better logistics and supply chain management, including the best practice models identified. The aim should be to move from the current position of promoting 'control' and 'resource efficiency on site' to 'collaboration' and 'resource efficiency off site'.

Finally, this chapter has demonstrated the CCC as a sustainable method of managing the logistics function and has proved that a major contractor could invest in the operation of a 'hub' CCC that could serve multiple projects.

This is a significant development, as the CCC is the most resource-intensive method of the best practice models identified and would revolutionize the logistics function by offering multiple stakeholder benefits. If adopted, it would make way for other best practice models discussed in this chapter.

References

Abu Hassan, S, Ballal, T and Omar, B (2013) Exploring Context-Awareness in the Construction Logistics Services Delivery [Online] http://www.irbnet.de/daten/iconda/CIB21744.pdf [accessed 23 February 2015]

Barthorpe, S, Robbins, S and Sullivan, G (2010) *Managing Construction Logistics*, Blackwells Publishing, London

Croydon Council (2012) *Construction Logistics Handbook*

Department for Business Innovation and Skills (2012) Industry Strategy: UK Sector Analysis, BIS Economic paper 18, September

DETR (1998) Rethinking Construction: The Report of the Construction Task Force, *Constructing Excellence* [Online] http://www.constructingexcellence.org.uk/pdf/rethinking construction/rethinking_construction_report.pdf [accessed 23 February 2015]

Latham, M (1994) Constructing the Team: Final report of the government/industry review of procurement and contractual arrangements in the UK construction industry, HMSO [Online] http://www.cewales.org.uk/cew/wp-content/uploads/Constructing-the-team-The-Latham-Report.pdf [accessed 23 February 2015]

Mossman, A (2008) More Than Materials: Managing what's needed to create value in construction', paper for the 2nd European Conference on Construction Logistics, ECCL, Dortmund, May

Robbins, S (2004) Construction Logistics Consolidation Centres, Partners in Innovation, DTI

Robbins, S (2005) Revolutionising Construction Logistics by Implementing the Consolidation Centre Methodology, MPhil Thesis, University of Glamorgan, February

Robbins, S and Thomas, A (2013) Construction Logistics: Delivering an effective strategy, Chartered Institute of Logistics and Transport, *Focus* magazine

Strategic Forum for Construction Logistics (2005) Improving Construction Logistics: Report for the Strategic Forum for Construction Logistics Group [Online] www.strategicforum.org.uk/pdf/Logistics Report August 2005.pdf [accessed 23 February 2015]

Steele, S (2013) Interview with Transport for London Freight and Fleet Programme Manager, 21 February 2013

Taylor, A, Tseng, Y and Yue, W (2005) The Role of Transportation in the Logistics Chain, *Proceedings of the Eastern Asia Society for Transportation Studies*, 5, pp 1657–72

UK Contractors Group (2012) Construction in the UK Economy: The benefits of investment [Online] www.wates.co.uk/sites/all/modules/filemanager/files/PDF/L.E.K_Construction_in_the_UK_economy.pdf [accessed 23 February 2015]

Construction supply chain management strategy

05

BRIAN MOONE

Introduction

In this chapter we discuss how, as a result of changing working practices, the role of the supply chain has grown in the construction industry. With the increased involvement by large numbers of supply chain participants comes the need to assess supply chain risk. Risk is not one single, simple concept; many different categories of risk must be considered. We describe the main types of risk and how they should be assessed in the construction industry context.

Taking a main contractor's point of view, we then look at the critically important task of selecting supply chain partners. We conclude the chapter by describing how the quality and long-term stability of the supply chain is developed by the unique approach offered by the Mace Business School. (Mace is an international consultancy and construction company, expert in programme and project management, construction delivery, cost consultancy and facilities management.)

The concept of supply chain management

Historically construction companies employed their own labour and plant to carry out the majority of the construction process, with very little undertaken by third parties. This has gradually shifted to the current situation where a high percentage, and in many cases all, of the work on a project is carried out by third-party companies or, as it has become known, the 'supply chain'. There are a number of reasons for this change but a key factor is the specialist nature of the work and the need to invest in large items of plant or equipment.

This shift has meant that construction companies have had to develop skills to effectively manage the process of using supply chain companies undertaking the work. Done well, the use of supply chain companies brings technical superiority and innovation to the project, and their specialist knowledge and experience brings enhanced efficiency, quality and consistency of delivery. However, there can also be increased risk if the strengths and weaknesses of the third-party companies are not fully understood and managed.

Many industries including automotive, manufacturing and retail formalized supply chain management many years before the construction industry started to adopt this approach. It was from these industries that the construction industry learned the importance of understanding how the third-party companies form a continuous chain, from the extraction of raw materials through to the production and assembly of components to create the finished product. For most finished products that chain (which would perhaps have been better described as a pyramid, due to the exponential nature of each component being itself made up of a number of components) can encompass hundreds or thousands of links. It soon becomes obvious that the success of the final product is only as good as the weakest link in that supply chain.

For industries that manufacture on a large scale, investment in the effective management of the supply chain was an obvious development due to the high level of risk. Failure of a single link for a manufacturing company that produces thousands or millions of a single product can be catastrophic. Most people will be aware of instances of cars or electrical goods being re-called due to a single faulty component, a component that was most likely manufactured by a company in the supply chain. Whilst construction is fundamentally different, as it is often about producing a single unique building, the consequences of the failure of one part of the supply chain can still be as significant, particularly if it affects the safety of the building either during construction or once complete. Failure in the supply chain will also affect the construction programme in projects where time is critical, such as the London 2012 Olympic and Paralympic Games, where careful management of the supply chain can be equally important.

The intent when appointing a supply chain company to undertake the work is that they have been selected for their ability to succeed. Whilst contractual conditions will state the consequences and penalties for failure to deliver, for the finished product to be successful it is essential that all businesses manage to ensure that everyone succeeds, rather than focus on failure. The cost of failure can go far beyond the immediate costs that can be mitigated, and can include reputational damage to a business, which can be difficult to recover. As a result, the more advanced companies realized that it makes sense to manage these risks from the outset, and where possible to work with third-party companies that are known to their business and have a proven track record of delivering the specified requirements. It has been the development of a systematic approach to minimizing risk through this approach that has become known as 'supply chain management'.

Supply chain risks

There are a wide range of uncertainties when engaging with third-party companies, some of which are common to, and others very distinct from, self-delivery. For example, using new companies for the first time may bring new innovative solutions but they will also bring greater levels of uncertainty and therefore higher potential risks. As with any risk management there needs to be a balance between the benefits, the potential impact of the risk and the cost of mitigation. It is only possible to reduce or eliminate the risks that are within your control, all other risks have to be managed through mitigation. Working with third parties means that more of the risks are outside of your direct control and therefore require greater mitigation to manage them. Understanding these risks and how to efficiently manage them is key to the process of supply chain management.

A company within the supply chain will have failed if it is unable to deliver, in a compliant manner, the agreed service or goods to the specified quality in the agreed time. There are many reasons for failure, the ultimate being the company ceasing trading but it can conversely be due to the company being too busy. A company may also not have the knowledge, experience or skills required to deliver to the standards required in an efficient manner. Failure to adhere to legislation and other areas of compliance can also create risk, particularly where non-ethical processes are used, for example underage labour, or use of timber from unsustainable sources.

In summary, the risks described above can be categorized as follows:

- financially unstable;
- insufficient capacity;
- insufficient capability/skills/experience;
- non-compliant;
- incompetent – they do not apply the skills.

Understanding the company through prequalification

Understanding the risk to be managed begins by gaining an understanding of the company. This is normally done through a questionnaire to capture enough information about the company to enable the risks to be assessed. The questionnaire is known as the 'prequalification questionnaire' or 'PQQ'. The level of information captured within the PQQ varies and has grown over the years. Initially it began with capturing the key contact information and capabilities of the companies. It also captured information on basic compliance and therefore focused on statutory requirements such as insurance, tax registration, health and safety and employment legislation. In addition to an increase in the amount of legislation, the level of information captured has grown due to companies raising the bar on the level of compliance required to include codes of practice, ISO standards, best practice guidance or other standards set by the purchaser. The questionnaire is also increasingly used to poll the supply chain to generate statistical information, for example providing the client with information about the level of local labour used within the supply chain companies to meet local planning requirements.

Sections of a PQQ:

- general information: names, addresses, skills;
- compliance: can be assessed against a specified standard, which can be split into:
  - statutory;
  - best practice, COPs, ISO and other standards;
- references:
  - financial: filed accounts, credit score;
  - experience: previous work;
- poll: statistical data, ie breakdown of labour.

Assessing the risk

Before supply chain management was formally introduced the process of assessing the risks was undertaken in an ad hoc fashion, normally based on the previous experience of the person undertaking the procurement. While this can be adequate for smaller businesses, where the relationship is close and frequent, larger businesses need to formalize this to ensure that knowledge gained about a company in one part of the business is efficiently shared with another. Also, as standards and legislation continue to increase, it is essential that people with the relevant knowledge and experience assess a company for compliance. As a result it will often be necessary for the assessment process to involve teams of experts including health and safety, sustainability, legal, financial, industrial relations, HR as well as supply chain managers.

Assessing compliance

The PQQ is the most efficient means of capturing the information required. In some cases this is still paper-based but more frequently an online system is used, which allows the efficient capture of the responses and any supporting documentation and easy distribution to the relevant experts for assessment. There is a continual increase in the number of questions asked within the PQQ as clients strive to keep up with their legislative requirements, as well as having the statistics to respond to the ever increasing amount of data that has to be captured to provide statistical evidence to clients. This can range from knowing the percentage spend with companies that are small and medium-sized enterprises (SMEs) to the percentage of companies in the supply chain that source materials from outside of the European Union (EU).

As the PQQ has become longer and more complex, the time taken to provide and assess the information has become an increasing burden on the industry. Numerous studies by trade associations, government and academia have tried to quantify the impact. The problem is multiplied by the fact that companies in the supply chain work for several clients and each of those clients requires the supply chain company to complete very similar PQQs, creating unnecessary duplication of effort in the production and assessment of information. Unfortunately there has not been a standard questionnaire set, so while the gist of the PQQ is the same, the questions and the evidence required to support the answers can be different, which is inefficient. The UK Government has recognized this as a problem and has put in place PAS 91, which is a standard PQQ for construction. The government first required it on their contracts but unfortunately did not make it mandatory; however despite this, it is steadily becoming the base standard for the industry, although at the current rate it will be some time before it becomes the norm.

Assessing financial risk

There are a number of organizations that provide financial risk analysis, the more readily recognized include Dun & Bradstreet, Experian and Bureau Van Dyjk. These organizations have their own scorecards for assessing financial risk; typically these scorecards will review filed accounts, with consideration of turnover, profit, loans and assets. They will also obtain information from suppliers to assess the payment beyond term and factor in any county court judgments etc. From this analysis they provide a score, usually as a percentage, as an indicator of the financial risk. Obviously none of these companies are able to predict the future; however their trend analysis does provide a good indication. To be effective, larger organizations place their key supply chain companies on financial monitoring and receive daily reports on any significant changes in the financial risk profile of the company; they will use this to analyse trends to provide an indication of the future position. The risk reports provide not only changes to their risk rating, but also information about any material changes, for example to the registered directors or address, late filing of accounts, county court judgments etc. It is essential that the information provided by these organizations is only part of the method of assessing risk; it should also include real-time intelligence captured from the projects. Quite often the projects will pick up early signs of a company getting into financial difficulty as they struggle to obtain materials or labour. However, care must be taken to avoid basing decisions on rumours as these may have been created by unscrupulous competitors, and can also cause the downfall of otherwise healthy companies. The skill of a supply chain manager is in the assessment of the available data and industry intelligence to provide informed decisions about the financial risk associated with a company.

Assessing performance risk

The performance of a contractor must be continually assessed to provide real-time information about them. This is very much like taking the 'pulse' of the company; to a trained supply chain manager, poor performance can be symptomatic of wider issues, including financial difficulties or capacity issues. The measure of performance needs to pick up on the key elements, normally referred to as key performance indicators (KPIs). These indicators will vary depending upon what the company doing the measurement considers key, but all will generally include health and safety. Other areas may include design, on-site and off-site management, quality management, environmental management and close-out. Measures are usually a combination of qualitative and quantitative, and sophisticated scorecards may include weighting for some elements. It is important that there is sufficient data to allow the analysis of trends and to sift out any subjective scoring, which may not be truly representative.

At Mace we have a KPI scorecard made up of 17 KPIs. Every package on every project has to be measured against all applicable KPIs every month. At the time of writing, this equates to over 750 packages rated every month. This information is analysed and fed back as a rolling 12-month average across all 17 KPIs to inform future procurement. Analysing trends across all or selected KPIs is used to provide early warning of emerging issues, especially when compared with other data such as spend and financial risk analysis.

Third-party accreditation

A number of independent organizations and one government-funded organization have been set up to provide either a standard PQQ and online capture system, or a full third-party assessment and accreditation. At the time of writing these organizations include Constructionline (originally government funded), BuildingConfidence and Builders Profile. The theory behind this is that companies will be required to prequalify only once with one of these organizations, and that prequalification will be recognized by many of the supply chain clients. Unfortunately, with so many schemes there is no single simple route for the subcontractor to follow, so potentially this has just added an additional layer of bureaucracy. The supply chain now has to obtain assessment from a number of third-party accreditation bodies as well as the clients' own PQQs if they are not part of one of the schemes. Also, until a single standard accreditation is recognized or these schemes are all aligned and equally recognized, the supply chain company also has the additional cost that these third-party accreditation companies levy. There are also a number of organizations that are set up to assess just the health and safety criteria – most of these work to a common agreed standard, which is Safety Schemes in Procurement (SSIP), and include CHAS, Exor and Safemark. These schemes can provide exemption from the health and safety element of the PQQ but, again, not all PQQs recognize the SSIP scheme, creating further duplication of effort.

Assessing capacity risk

While it is easy to gather information about the level of current and future spend your company has with any company in its supply chain, the value and quantity of secured work and future order book with their other clients is difficult to obtain and keep up to date. Combine this with the detailed constitution of the work, and any changes in the company's labour, material stocks and ever changing work programmes and project variations, and it can be difficult for the company to be able to predict its own capacity. This can make it almost impossible for a supply chain manager who at best through regular meetings can obtain a snapshot of the current position, particularly if the supply chain company decides that being economical with the facts will portray their company in the best possible position to secure future work. A good supply chain manager will be aware of the other projects in the market, and understand the approximate value of key packages, and the contractors that are likely to be in the frame for the work or have secured it. This, combined with regular meetings with supply chain companies, which will include both the companies that secured the work as well as other bidders that were not successful, will allow a more accurate understanding of the position to be built up.

Many supply chain managers share capacity information with their counterparts from other companies, thus providing very useful cross-check information to help make more informed decisions. However, care has to be taken to ensure that any information shared will not enable a company to obtain a competitive advantage in contravention of competition law.

Assessing capability risk of new supply chain companies

Whilst company literature and websites will provide a certain level of information about a company, this should be evidenced by obtaining references or, better still, by personally witnessing work being undertaken and or factories/workshops if applicable. Site visits should be organized to visit projects that are as similar as possible to the type of work proposed. It is also important to investigate whether the capabilities are new to the company, as during declining markets companies may attempt to diversify to fill their order books, and take on work outside of their recognized capabilities – with variable results. These companies may also subcontract the works, bringing an additional level of uncertainty and variability.

Assessing second- and third-tier risk

The supply chain can consist of many tiers of subcontracted packages, labour or material supplies, with each tier able to affect the overall outcome of the project. Many contracts stipulate that any subcontracting of works must be notified or approved, although this is very often not monitored. Most prequalification assessments content themselves on this point by requesting evidence that the first-tier contractor or supplier has processes in place to manage their supply chain. Whilst this does provide a certain element of control it does not provide a continuous flow of control and alignment with the requirements and values of the main contractor or client.

There is a growing recognition of the need to extend supply chain management beyond first-tier contractors and suppliers, and on many recent industry-leading projects – such as the London 2012 Olympic and Paralympic Games and Crossrail – there has been significant investment in managing the entire chain to deliver higher levels of certainty.

Framework agreements

Good supply chain management is based on identifying the right long-term partners to help take your business forward. If both parties to a subcontract agreement continually deliver what is required and expected of them, then a long and healthy partnership will be built upon trust. The client can choose to formally recognize this type of relationship through a framework agreement. Typically this will give a subcontractor/supplier or a small number of companies exclusive rights to deliver their area of work. This gives some certainty to the subcontractor/supplier in terms of forward order book and the margins received, whilst reducing the burden, risk and cost of bidding for both parties. The increased certainty allows the subcontractor/supplier to invest in plant, equipment and labour etc to meet demand, and the client is able to standardize what is procured in order to drive economies of scale and obtain volume discounts. It is important that the supply chain manager manages this relationship carefully. To be successful, volume discounts must only come from savings that the subcontractor/supplier is able to obtain and pass on as a result of savings generated by the volume of work.

Framework agreements also allow the subcontractor to become fully conversant with the processes and procedures of their client. As a result, they can often become a natural extension of the client's company, helping to enforce standards and procedures beyond the work they are contracted to deliver.

Supply chain management of logistics in construction

The concept of logistics in the construction industry is broader than in many other industries, where it is largely seen as the management of the flow of goods and materials from source to the point of use. In construction, logistics will include transport and storage including the management and scheduling of lorry deliveries to site. More complex projects, particularly those on confined sites or with restricted or controlled access such as airports, may require specialist control points, consolidation centres and marshalling yards to allow accurately timed deliveries. Once product is delivered to site the logistics teams are responsible for storage and distribution on site. In most buildings this will require vertical as well as horizontal transport; therefore the logistics provider can also be responsible for providing and/or managing hoists and cranes, including scheduling of hook times for the cranes. As a result of controlling flow and deliveries through the site the logistics package generally includes site security, which may just be security personnel but may also include managing and monitoring security passes and, on more sophisticated sites, biometric scanning. Most logistics packages also include 'reverse logistics', which is the removal of waste or recyclable material from site, and ensuring the site is clean and tidy. In many cases the logistics team may also handle soft strip of existing buildings, the set-up of temporary office accommodation and any other general small builders work necessary which does not warrant a separate specialist package.

These functions are key to the smooth running of the site. Logistics is seen as core to the implementation of modern manufacturing and construction techniques such as 'lean' and 'just-in-time' delivery. Therefore, selecting the right logistics partner is central to a successful project. For a project to be successful the logistics contractor must be able to do more than simply provide labour and material when instructed. They must be able and willing to add value to the construction process by managing the smooth flow of materials and components onto the site and to the place of work, allowing the construction process to continue uninterrupted. They should also be capable of effectively scheduling deliveries to minimize multiple handling of materials, to be able to manage general labour resources and temporary access equipment across multiple trades to drive efficiency.

The scope of works undertaken is often seen as key to the project and so by being flexible it lends itself to frameworks or schedules of rates for many of the key items, including hoisting, office accommodation and security provision. This approach allows for the flexibility to adapt to uncertainties in the project whilst maintaining a level of financial control and trust between the parties, which is key to supply chain management.

CASE STUDY   Mace Business School

Since its inception in 1990 Mace has built a long-term relationship with its supply chain. Right from the outset Mace established 17 key performance areas for its supply chain companies, and measured every package delivered, so ensuring that the performance of the supply chain was fully understood at all times. The creation of an online system, accessible via the Mace intranet, allowed real-time sharing of information, meaning that all procurement decisions could be based on the most up-to-date status of the business whether financial, compliance, capacity or performance.

By 2006 Mace had established its own business school, a first of its kind in the industry, which focuses solely on improving performance of construction businesses in its supply chain through learning and knowledge sharing. The Mace Business School was a product of the growing complexity of projects requiring increasingly high levels of management throughout the supply chain. While most companies in the supply chain are highly competent in their specialist areas, analysis undertaken in 2006, using performance feedback, indicated that some were lacking when required to undertake more complex management of the programme and particularly in coordination and collaboration with other trades. One option would have been to try to source new contractors, but this went against the Mace ethos of developing long-term partnerships with its supply chain. The decision was therefore made to share Mace's expertise in management with its supply chain through formal training. The Mace Business School was created, with training delivered to the supply chain by Mace senior managers and directors with the relevant expertise.

The resulting programme of courses became the Mace Supply Chain Passport and the target audience was any staff member, from senior site supervisor and above. Mace analysed which companies should be trained in order to provide maximum impact from the training and in 2006, based on the analysis, 20 companies were selected to join the business school. Since then the membership has grown to 56, covering 20 of the key trades and representing approximately 75 per cent of Mace spend in the supply chain.

This approach has been unique in construction and in 2010 received the accolade of *Building* magazine Supply Chain Management of the Year Award. As well as winning awards, the Mace Business School has been referenced in *Construction Management Strategies: A theory of construction management* (2012) by Milan Radosavljevic and John Bennett. Independent research on the impact of the Mace Business School was undertaken by Jonathan Gosling of Cardiff Business School; his findings reported at an academic conference demonstrated a clear improvement in the consistency and quality of delivery from companies that had been long-term members of the business school.

In addition to ensuring continuous improvement in quality and delivery, the Mace Business School also fosters long-term collaborative partnerships with its members. This collaboration builds trust and enables both parties to work closely together to find competitive solutions to the increasing challenges created by the more complex buildings being designed for clients.

Conclusion

The concept of supply chain management took off first in industries where there was natural scope for long-term relationships. For instance, the automotive industry relies on deeply integrated supplier networks. In construction, projects come and go, and there is not the same continuity. But with increased reliance on an external supply chain, the construction industry nonetheless has had to develop its supply chain management skills.

Supply chain partners are selected for construction projects because they contribute with specific, sometimes unique, skills and capabilities. But a complex supply chain with many participants also inevitably involves risk, and risk management is an important part of supply chain management. The best companies find that to maintain consistent quality requires a massive management effort in the supply chain. Getting new partners to perform takes more effort and carries a higher risk; it follows that long-term relationships pay. Mace has through its business school developed the partnership principle in a way that is both innovative and practical. By training its supply chain partners Mace is securing long-term relationships that deliver quality.

Reference

Radosavljevic, M and Bennett, J (2012) *Construction Management Strategies: A theory of construction management*, Wiley-Blackwell, Hoboken, NJ

PART TWO
The impact of BIM and new data management capabilities on supply chain management in construction

Data management for integrated supply chains in construction

06

WES BEAUMONT and JASON UNDERWOOD

Introduction

In a 1962 report Sir Harold Emmerson, referring to the construction industry, commented: 'In no other important industry in the world is the responsibility for design so far removed from the responsibility for production' (Emmerson, 1962). Whilst it is true that this gap has been reduced, there still remains a lack of integration between stakeholders, particularly within the wider supply chain.

The industry is fragmented and adversarial, limiting the potential for integrated teams with open communication and information exchange. However, collaboration is essential in achieving maximum value and, despite advances in technology with the use of web collaboration tools, the level of integration among stakeholders is still low. Additionally, current practices in information are linear and sequential, limiting the ability to add value in the early stages of projects.

A number of countries worldwide have started to mandate the use of building information modelling (BIM). The UK government, in its 2011 construction strategy, in an effort to reduce whole life costs and reduce carbon emissions, mandated the use of BIM 'level two' on all central procurement projects, by 2016. This will, in theory, provide the process and technology that finally closes the gap between construction stakeholders, creating truly collaborative and integrated project teams throughout the entire supply chain, using data-driven procurement and delivery strategies.

However, while the transformation to level two BIM develops the capabilities for the digital procurement of assets, level three (Digital Built Britain Strategy) further serves to facilitate deriving 'value' through big data and the 'smarter' life-cycle management of the built environment. Thereby, the 'smarter' life-cycle management of the built environment is enabled through digital procurement, which is based on a data-driven approach that embraces the capital delivery and operational management of assets along with performance management across assets, sectors and society/ies. In addition, level three BIM will form the basis for level four BIM whereby the focus of deriving value extends to societal outcomes and well-being.

Information management in construction

The success of a construction project is largely determined by the effectiveness of processes, the explicitness of obligations and the capability of stakeholders to communicate a shared understanding. Despite this, current processes encourage silo mentalities in which each stakeholder performs its task in isolation, encouraging local optimization and causing detrimental effects to supply chain performance. Sequential processes create reciprocal workflows (Eastman *et al*, 2011), which are exacerbated when changes or variations occur. As design is an iterative process the industry must make allowances for concurrent working, currently limited by existing procurement strategies. Reciprocal workflow is counterproductive and introduces waste (Womack and Jones, 2003), which reduces value. Ballard and Howell (2003) identified that up to 50 per cent of design time is wasted due to this process. Additionally, in general, procurement strategies inhibit early involvement of the supply chain, reducing the impact they can have on early stages of the product life cycle, where maximum value can be generated.

Project complexity

The construction industry is complex and vast, consisting of 280,000 self-governing but interdependent organizations (BIS, 2013). 'Project complexity' was coined by Baccarini (1996) and defined as, 'consisting of many varied interrelated parts' with large numbers of influencing stakeholders and associated interdependencies increasing ambiguity and uncertainty. This hinders the identification of goals and objectives relating to time, cost and quality, with Baccarini (1996) identifying that, in general, the higher the project complexity the greater the time and cost. Figure 6.1 illustrates the breakdown of project complexity. Virtually all projects are by definition multi-objective, with conflicting goals, and the effects of activities on all goals have to be assessed and trade-offs have to consider the balancing effects of other activities (Williams, 1999).

Data Management for Integrated Supply Chains in Construction 93

FIGURE 6.1 Project complexity

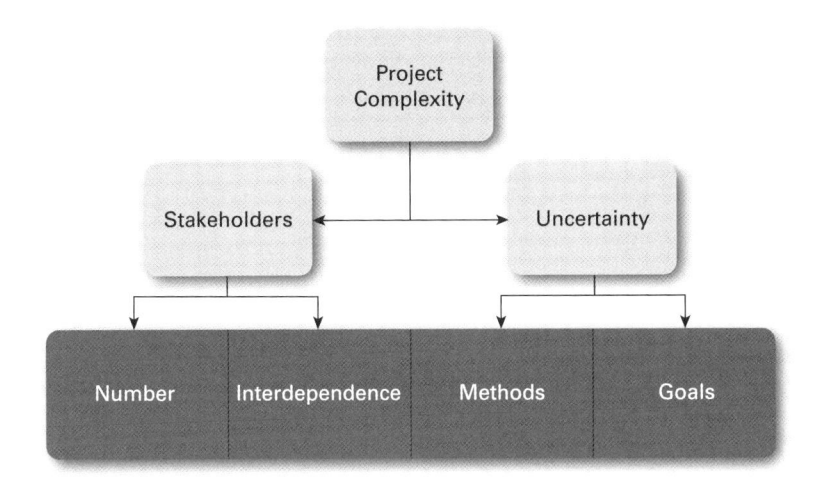

SOURCE: Williams (1999)

Figures 6.2 and 6.3 illustrate a comparison between traditional and modern contractual structures and the evolution of stakeholder relationships. Unbroken lines indicate contractual relationships and broken lines non-contractual relationships. The modern structure represents a chaotic and risky relationship structure in comparison to the much simplified master builder concept.

FIGURE 6.2 Traditional contractual structure

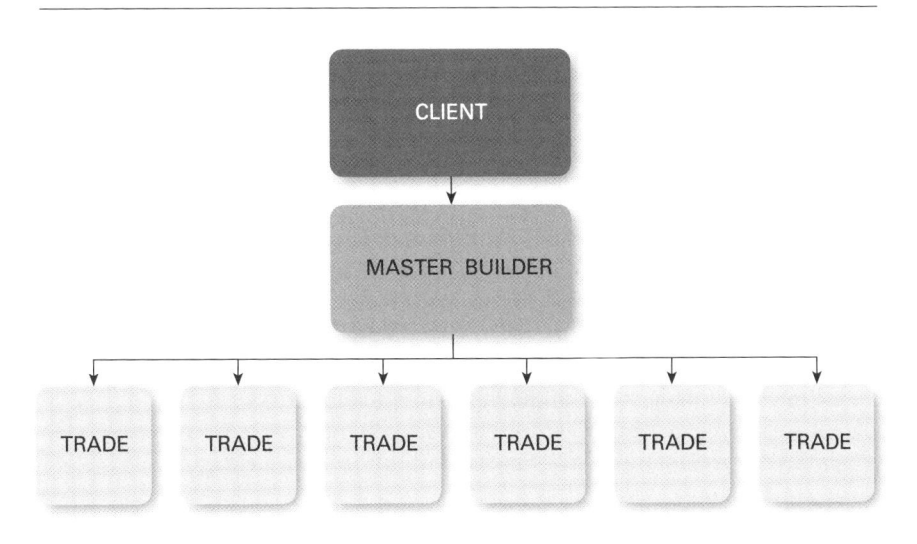

FIGURE 6.3 Modern contractual structure

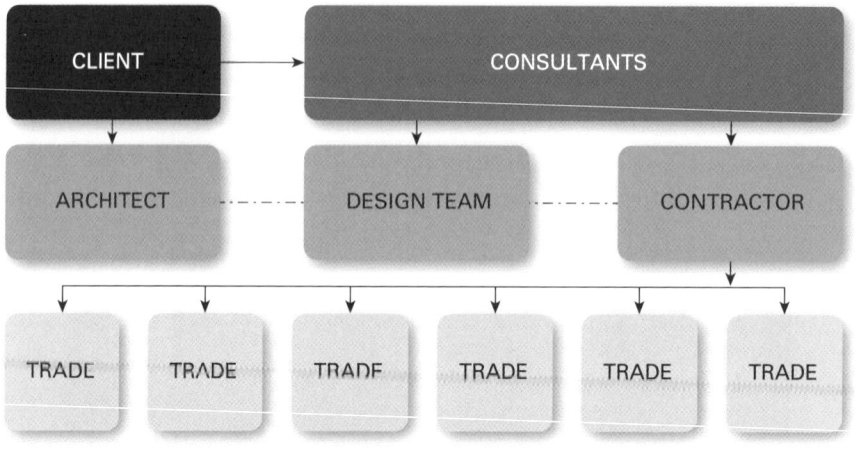

The construction supply chain accounted for £124 billion of intermediate consumption in 2011 (BIS, 2013), representing a huge portion of workload. This illustrates the sheer number of organizations participating in the sector, increasing the number of contractual and non-contractual relationships required. When the wider supply chain is considered in contractual and non-contractual structures the complexity increases significantly.

Winch (1989) observed that the firms forming construction projects are bound together by flows of information and materials. The modern relationship structure hinders this flow and makes information distribution difficult and somewhat risky. To put this into context, research carried out for BIS (BIS, 2013) identified that on a typical medium-size construction project, in the £20 million to £25 million range, the main contractor may be directly managing around 70 subcontracts.

Information distribution

As the industry has progressed, traditional master builders have become rare and principal contractors have evolved into information managers coordinating the activities of the supply chain. The challenge of ensuring that all stakeholders are working to coordinated information can be great, even more so considering that information is re-created or re-entered five to eight times in a project life cycle. Figure 6.4 illustrates the common process of information exchange, representing a chaotic system increasing the potential for errors and discrepancies with information exchange.

FIGURE 6.4 Traditional relationship process

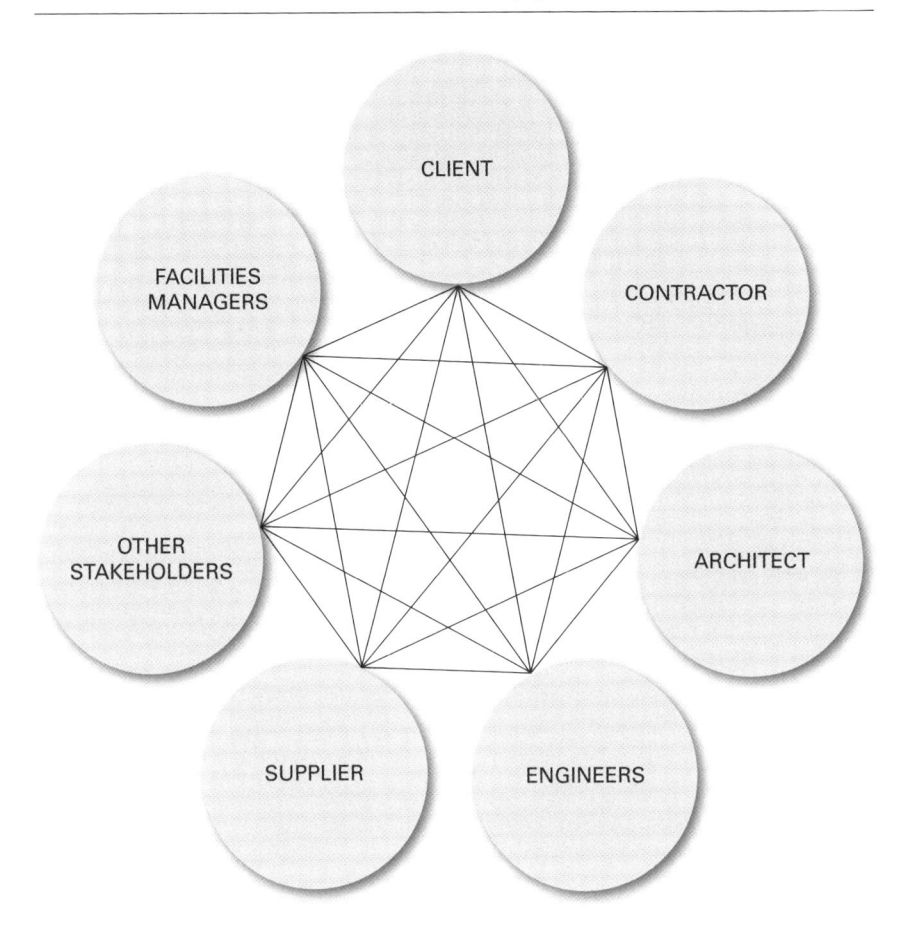

(Diagram: circles labelled CLIENT, CONTRACTOR, ARCHITECT, ENGINEERS, SUPPLIER, OTHER STAKEHOLDERS, FACILITIES MANAGERS, all interconnected with lines.)

Building information modelling (BIM)

BIM is the digital representation of physical and functional characteristics of a facility and acts as a shared knowledge resource for information, forming a reliable basis for decisions during its whole life cycle. A basic premise of BIM is collaboration amongst stakeholders at different phases of the life cycle to insert, extract, update or modify information in the BIM to support and reflect the roles of that stakeholder (Fallon and Palmer, 2007). It enables the reuse of material and ensures that all stakeholders are utilizing the same database of information. BIM requires early collaboration between project stakeholders in order for value to be maximized, with the UK government themselves commenting that: 'BIM not only enables integration, it virtually demands it... it has the potential not just to reduce or eliminate error and unnecessary change, but also to cut out layers of waste' (HM Gov, 2010). By

FIGURE 6.5 Relationships process utilizing BIM and integrated teams

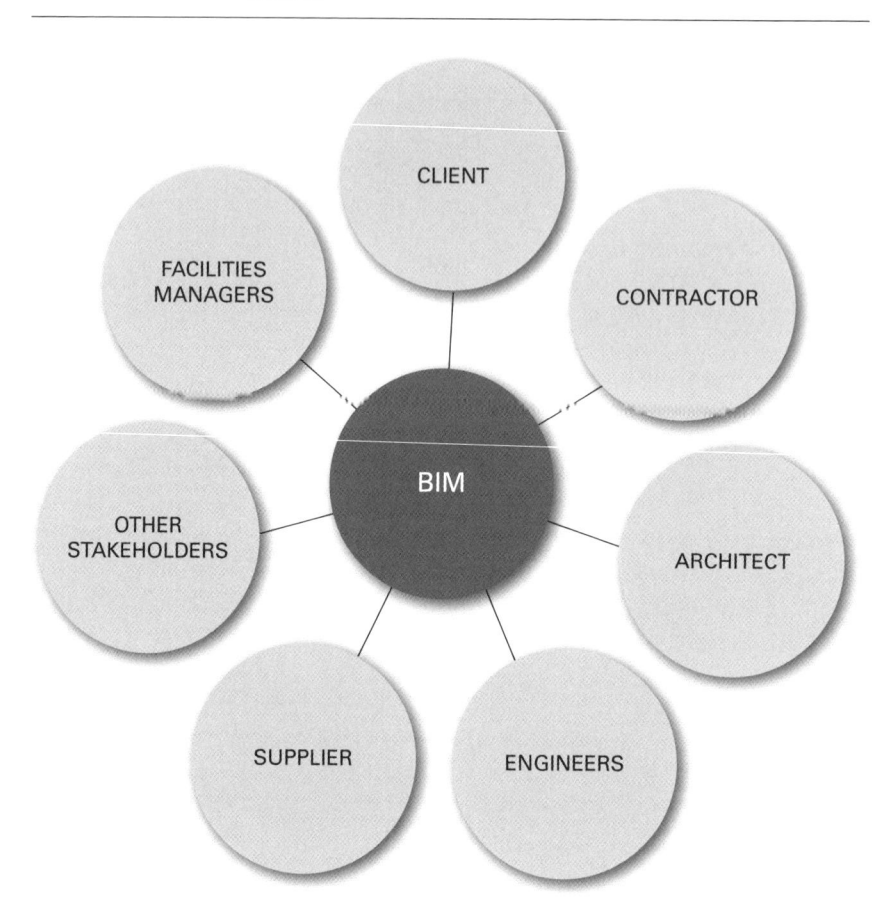

virtue of its nature, the BIM methodology is underpinned by participative and collaborative working, with buy-in required from all stakeholder participants from their earliest involvement.

BIM and the integration it demands can eliminate the gap between design and construction and provide a holistic approach to information exchange, enabling information to be pulled from a shared central location, as demonstrated in Figure 6.5.

The mandate of BIM maturity level two is an attempt to move the industry to a digital, rather than analogue, sector and requires project and asset information, documentation and data to be electronic (HM Gov, 2011). PAS 1192–2: 2013 is the framework for implementing BIM level two and enables information 'to be shared efficiently and accurately between all members of the project team'. This is enabled through a common data environment (CDE), essentially a web collaboration tool utilizing cloud computing. Data created during design and construction can be used during the operation for an asset and for wider socioeconomic benefits and aid the creation of '*smart cities*'. The importance of the information economy has already been discussed in the UK government's recently published information economy strategy. Whilst not defined explicitly, at the time of print, the strategy for level two could be compared to the activity of creating structured data, whilst level three is the strategy for using that structured data for a number of purposes. More is discussed later in this chapter.

Digital technologies, cloud computing and the breakdown of contracts that restrict collaboration will facilitate the adoption of lean processes in the design and construction of projects, reducing inherent waste and eliminating the problems currently associated with design and construction. Training and upskilling of supply chains will allow fully collaborative BIM to become reality, in which all stakeholders input into a BIM and form part of an integrated process, enhancing certainty of delivery. Further advances in technology will not just improve 3D design but bring augmented reality, ubiquitous work spaces and the internet of things to the mainstream, further improving communication lines with the supply chain.

Information, robust processes and people are important in driving value by developing the understanding and capabilities for the life-cycle management of the built environment enabled through collaborative and digital procurement strategies. Furthermore, the need to share information transparently becomes paramount in enabling such strategies, together with an understanding and integration of the associated knowledge domains that are important for the life-cycle management of the built environment and facilitating robust processes for improving decision-making practices. This is underpinned by data-driven strategies in the built environment.

Value proposition of BIM and data-driven management

Whilst 'small data' is still very important, consisting of lists of customers, sales, employees and so forth, the integration of all data in a 'single customer view' enables greater analytical interrogation. Data regarding an asset, created using BIM, can be used during the operation and maintenance of a building, where the majority of whole life costs are borne. In this instance the operational supply chain also benefits. Some of the common pitfalls in supply chain management (Lee and Billington, 1992) and a proposed BIM and data management solution are illustrated in Table 6.1.

The above examples are compounded by the fragmented nature of the industry, with its antiquated procurement processes, which appoint supply chain members at the 'last responsible moment'. A suitable solution to overcome this issue is clearly the use of BIM and data management but also strategies to encourage synchronization and concurrent workflows.

TABLE 6.1 Common supply chain problems and data solutions

Common Pitfall	BIM and Data Management Solution
1. No supply chain metrics If metrics are used then objectives often conflict. If metrics are used and do not conflict then they are not measured often enough to determine patterns etc.	Measure the performance of the supply chain member using data – acquired via key performance indicators and analysed to assess performance and variances. Patterns, discrepancies, variations and anomalies in the data can be identified and root causes established.
2. Inadequate definition of customer service What are we measuring the supply chain on? Low cost? Productivity?	Identify performance measure and compare with peers. For example, productivity on site can be measured and analysed to determine productivity rates against organizations of the same type. This instigates continuous improvement throughout the supply chain and encourages performance improvement.
3. Inaccurate delivery status data Poorly defined completion dates – the granularity of programming information is often too high-level.	Simulations and schedules linked with labour rates to determine accurate and precise delivery (programming) data. Actual delivery should be tracked and stored to determine performance levels and assist in continual improvement measures.
4. Inefficient information systems Systems are not linked and therefore data cannot be merged and analysed effectively. Long planning cycles – updated often incorrectly. In construction the use of multiple systems often means that when changes are made they are not articulated to all stakeholders. Worst-case scenario is that the wrong materials are delivered to the job site.	Linked databases and relational databases, akin to the internet of things. Project information contained within the BIM – supplemented with information added via a database management system. All information is provided to the supply chain to improve transparency and communication.

TABLE 6.1 *continued*

Common Pitfall	BIM and Data Management Solution
5. Ignoring the impact of uncertainties	
Uncertainties – lead times, delivery performance, quality of materials, process time. Often these variables are not tracked.	Lead times, delivery performance, quality and cost should be tracked – outside of conventional BIM with variances identified and explained.
Little is known on transit times.	Transit times measured with the potential for linking with Highways Agency data to precisely identify transit times, for example. Radio-frequency identification (RFID) tags to improve location tracking could be utilized.
6. Simplistic inventory stocking policies	
Uncertainties are dynamic and constantly changing, making it difficult to track changes/errors/discrepancies.	Classification of stocks and visibility of inventory, both current and incoming. This helps to track instances of uncertainty/discrepancy/non-conformance.
7. Discrimination against internal customers	
One output is an input for another. External customers are perceived as being more important than internal customers – links in the supply chain.	Using an ERP (or similar) enables the entire supply chain to track information in real time, across all stakeholders.
	Think of supply chains as internal and external customers. Linking briefing-feasibility-concept-design-procurement-construction-operate-maintain-dispose. All data (construction as information distribution) consistently relayed, with accuracy and precision, across the entire stakeholder group.
8. Poor coordination	
Lack of coordination results in excessive delays, over-inventory and costly mistakes.	Coordinated data, geometry and information stored in a common data environment accessible to the entire supply chain dependent on role, responsibility and information access requirement.

TABLE 6.1 *continued*

Common Pitfall	BIM and Data Management Solution
9. Incomplete shipment methods analysis	
Difficulty in distributing information to the supply chain. In construction this could be due to poor communication networks.	Access via the cloud gives instantaneous access to all stakeholders.
10. Incorrect assessment of inventory costs	
Most common pitfalls here are related to: 1) obsolescence, owing to short product life cycles. In construction design this could be reciprocal workflow; 2) costs of reworking existing inventory to meet changes – again this is reciprocal workflow.	One piece flow, using digital information that is shared regularly amongst the supply chain via a CDE. Digital information enables more efficient change control, which enables easy interrogation for design changes.
11. Organizational barriers	
Organizational barriers inhibit coordination and forge an unwillingness to commit resources to help someone else. This is often exacerbated by long lead times.	Construction activities are interdependent and require tight coordination. Sharing digital information and using lean principles such as 'last planner' encourages commitments to be made. Data captured can be used to identify reasons for missed commitments, capturing root causes, eliminating them in future phases of work.
12. Product–process design without supply chain considerations	
Not considering the supply chain and having inflexible processes incapable of responding to the demand changes in the supply chain. No collaboration with the supply chain creates a risk of delivering incorrect product and building a large inventory incapable of satisfying the customer demands.	Sharing information with the supply chain via the CDE in an intuitive format will enable comments, suggestions and innovative ideas from the supply chain, promoting a collaborative culture. Lean processes such as 'target value design' enable the entire project team to work collaboratively to create a product with the customer in mind.

TABLE 6.1 *continued*

Common Pitfall	BIM and Data Management Solution
13. Separation of supply chain design from operational decision	
Decisions made without considerations of inventory, response times and interdependencies.	BIM is linked with 'soft landings' and facilities/asset management to provide the seamless integration between design, construction and operations.
14. Incomplete supply chain	
Not considering the entire supply chain has negative operational impacts and adds inefficiencies. This can lead to variances, which can lead to delays and poor value creation, adding waste.	Creating vertical (and horizontal supply chains) and ensuring that information is distributed to all, for common understanding. Information sharing creates new knowledge and knowing each other's inventory levels enables the supply chain to respond appropriately – be that with further design information, supplies or labour during construction.

Synchronization and concurrent workflows

As information passes through layers in the supply chain it gets distorted, but the one-step process of acquiring information at its point of origin and storing it in a central database reduces the chance for it to be corrupted (Thomsen *et al*, 2009). Furthermore, using digital technology and CDEs allows concurrent working to take place. Deutsch (2011) identified how information flow can become near instantaneous, and automated workflows ensure that the correct people have access to the correct information at all times and remove opportunities for misinterpretation.

The use of BIM and model components with parametric properties ensures that when changes are made to a component all associated documents are simultaneously changed. This synchronization ensures that all stakeholders are working to the same information, in unison, and eliminates the risk of stakeholders using data that has been superseded. It also significantly reduces redrafting time, which adds no value to the process, increasing lean credentials.

Synchronization and concurrent working is facilitated by the use of data-driven strategies and the use of 'big data'. According to recent research (BARC, 2013) only 14 per cent of European companies already address big data analytics as part of their strategic planning. However, almost half of these companies expect a yearly data growth in their organization of more than 25 per cent, and 60 per cent are planning to invest in big data analytics by 2020 – to improve operational efficiency, customer experiences and present new business models.

Big data and construction

Today, ubiquitous computing such as mobile devices, tablets, smartphones, sensors etc are significantly changing our world and the quantity of data being produced is exploding. The global data volume is increasing at the rate of twice every 18 months to two years, and is predicted to hit 20 exabytes by 2020 (one exabyte represents 1 million gigabytes). Combining data from different sources holds huge potential for the life-cycle management of the built environment, including the management of the integrated supply chain; however, how to find, process and then exploit the vast volume of data in order to derive real value presents the challenge, ie '*big data*'.

What is big data?

We are currently early in the 'Age of Big Data', which is considered the 'new' business and social science frontier. In essence, big data is advancing trends in technology that provide the opportunity for a new business approach to understanding the world and making decisions. The amount of information and knowledge that can be extracted from the digital universe is continuing to expand as users come up with new ways to create and process data. According to Kaisler *et al* (2013) big data traditionally referred to the volume of data that could not be processed efficiently by traditional database methods and tools. While the original definition focused on structured data, most of the world's information resides in massive, unstructured information. Moreover, while the creation and collection of data, information and knowledge continues to increase, this explosion exceeds the capacity of traditional data management technologies, which has not been accompanied by a corresponding new storage medium.

Kaisler *et al* (2013) define big data as: 'the amount of data just beyond technology's capability to store, manage and process efficiently and these limitations are only discovered by a robust analysis of the data itself, explicit processing needs, and the capabilities of the tools (hardware, software, and methods) used to analyse it'.

Similarly, Dumbill (2013) defines big data as: 'being data that exceeds the processing capacity of conventional database systems. The data is too big, moves too fast, or doesn't fit the strictures of your database architectures. To gain value from this data, you must choose an alternative way to process it.'

Therefore, big data is concerned with the notion of smarter and predictive decisions based on data and its analysis rather than on experience and intuition.

Value proposition of big data

For governments, big data is considered as a national challenge and priority along with health care and national security. In particular, the concern for governments is on how big data creates '*value*' – and it is the ability to analyse data in order to develop information that is actionable from which value can be derived (Kaisler *et al*, 2013). Furthermore, Kaisler *et al* (2013) propose five generic ways in which value creation for organizations can be supported through big data:

1 Making big data openly available for business and functional analysis (quality, lower costs, reduce time to market etc) creates transparency.
2 Supporting experimental analysis in individual locations that can test decisions or approaches, such as specific market programmes.
3 Assisting in defining market segmentation at more narrow levels based on customer information.
4 Sophisticated analytics applied to data sets from customers and embedded sensors facilitates real-time analysis and decisions.
5 Facilitating computer-assisted innovation in products based on embedded product sensors indicating customer responses.

A World Economic Forum report, 'Big Data, Big Impact', declared data to be a new class of economic asset, similar to currency or gold. Moreover, big data may well become a new type of corporate asset that provides a key basis for competitive advantage. A study of 330 public US organizations found that they performed better on objective measures of financial and operational results the more they characterized themselves as data-driven. In particular, those organizations in the top one-third of their industry, in adopting 'data-driven decision making', were 5 per cent more productive and 6 per cent more profitable than their competitors (McAfee and Brynjolfsson, 2012).

Combining domain expertise with data science will facilitate organizations in gaining competitive advantage.

What characterizes big data?

While big data may be considered as simply being only about data volume or another way of saying 'analytics' aimed at deriving intelligence from data and translating that into business advantage, there are several key characteristic differences (Figure 6.6) (Kaisler *et al*, 2013; McAfee and Brynjolfsson, 2012; Russom, 2011):

- *Data volume*: measures the amount of data available to an organization, which does not necessarily have to be just the data it owns but also all other data it can access. Therefore organizations are provided with an opportunity to work with many petabyes of data in a single data set.

FIGURE 6.6 Key characteristics of big data

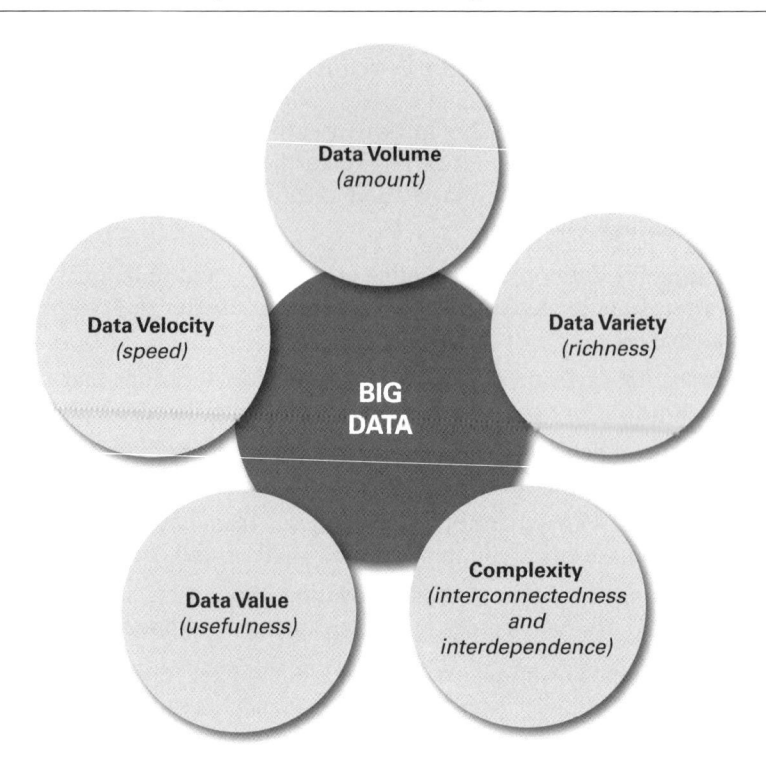

Diagram: Five circles around a central "BIG DATA" hexagon — Data Volume (amount), Data Variety (richness), Complexity (interconnectedness and interdependence), Data Value (usefulness), Data Velocity (speed).

- *Data velocity*: measures the speed of data creation, streaming and aggregation. The speed of data creation can be much more important than the volume for some applications, whereby an organization can increase their agility in relation to their competitors through real-time or close to real-time information. Therefore the management of data velocity goes beyond a bandwidth issue to that of a consumption issue (extract–transform–load).
- *Data variety*: a measure of the richness of the data representation, ie text, images, video, audio etc. The most important sources of big data are relatively new and in many instances ubiquitous, eg social media, smartphones, mobile devices etc. Therefore incompatible data formats, non-aligned data structures and inconsistent data semantics represent significant challenges to effectively using large volumes of data, which can lead to analytic sprawl.
- *Data value*: measures the usefulness of data in making decisions. '*Data science*' is exploratory and useful in getting to know the data, in contrast to '*analytic science*', which encompasses the predictive power of big data. Thus, '*the purpose of computing is insight, not numbers!*'

- *Complexity*: measures the degree of interconnectedness (possibly very large) and interdependence in big data structures such that a small change (or combination of small changes) in one or a few elements can yield a small change or very large changes that ripple across or cascade through the system and substantially affect its behaviour. Or it can yield no change at all.

Challenges of big data

While technology issues such as storage and data transport appear to be solvable in the near term, their long-term challenges require research and new paradigms. Moreover, although the technical challenges of using big data are very real, managerial and cultural issues present even greater challenges, particularly for a traditionally fragmented sector such as construction. Historically, productivity gains were not a result of organizations only adopting new technologies but also, more importantly, the ability to adapt their management practices and change their organizations to maximize the potential. Similarly, a big data transition requires a shift in decision-making culture from organizations relying too much on experience and intuition and more on data. Furthermore, as with any successful transition, organizations need to manage such change process to using big data effectively by considering leadership, talent management, technology, decision making and company culture (McAfee and Brynjolfsson, 2012).

Kaisler *et al* (2013) propose three fundamental issue areas that need to be addressed in dealing with big data:

- *Storage*: while the quantity of data has exploded each time a new storage medium has been invented, there has been no new storage medium for the most recent explosion (eg through unstructured digital channels such as social media, smartphones, mobile devices, sensors etc).
- *Management*: access, metadata, utilization, updating, governance and reference (in publications) are major stumbling blocks. A perfect big data management solution does not currently exist.
- *Processing*: in order to provide timely and actionable information, extensive parallel processing and new analytics algorithms are required for the effective processing of exabytes of data.

In addition, although a data-driven approach proffers significant benefits in relation to value creation, ethical challenges also need to be considered such as tracking employees' movements, continuously measuring their performance against industry benchmarks, ie preserving individual privacy. Conflicting concerns of big data facilitating 'users' being more successful and productive along with having differential impacts across many industries on the one hand, and on the other, a lack of tools and trained personnel to properly work with big data together with creating a new set of privacy incursions and invasive/unwanted marketing, drive competing visions of how to deal with big data (Kaisler *et al*, 2013). Therefore, a major challenge for big data is in achieving an appropriate balance of maximizing the benefits of big data, while minimizing the harms it presents.

Examples of big data

There is anecdotal evidence of creating value from a big data/data-driven approach across a variety of sectors, whereby decisions are increasingly being based on data and analysis rather than on experience and intuition (Brown, Chui and Manyika, 2011; Manyika *et al*, 2011). For example, retailers tailor product selections at particular stores and determine the timing of price discounts by analysing sales, pricing and economic, demographic and weather data. Moreover, by combining monitoring of in-store movements of customers with how they interact with products they are able to reduce the number of items stocked but increase the mix of higher-margin private-label products without losing market share. Shipping companies mine data on truck delivery times and traffic patterns in order to fine-tune routing and logistics. Advanced oil fields optimize production and minimize downtimes by adjusting oil flows from continuously reading and analysing data on well-head conditions, pipelines and mechanical systems. Other examples include online dating services analysing the personal characteristics, reactions, communications etc of members in order to improve their date-matching algorithms; and the police utilizing computerized mapping and analysis of a variety of data in order to predict possible crimes and 'hot spots'. Airline organizations eliminate gaps between estimated and actual arrival times through sophisticated analysis and pattern matching of a significant combination of publicly available data and proprietary company information.

Big data has the predictive power, from a wider societal perspective, to help public health, economic development and economic forecasting (Figure 6.7). Moreover, it has the potential to be 'humanity's dashboard' by providing an intelligent tool that can assist with social issues such as poverty, crime and pollution.

Big data in construction

While big data provides a game changer for almost every sector, the effects can differ for companies and industries, particularly in the early stages of adoption. Being more ready to capitalize on data, or having strong market incentives to do so, enables some organizations/sectors to realize benefits sooner. A study conducted by Brown, Chui and Manyika (2011) examined 20 sectors in the US economy, sized their contributions to GDP, and developed two indices that estimate: 1) each sector's potential for value creation using big data; 2) the ease of capturing that value (Figure 6.7). Financial players were found to get the highest marks for value creation opportunities due to having invested deeply in IT and having large data pools to exploit,

FIGURE 6.7 The ease of capturing big data's value and the magnitude of its potential across various sectors: US economy

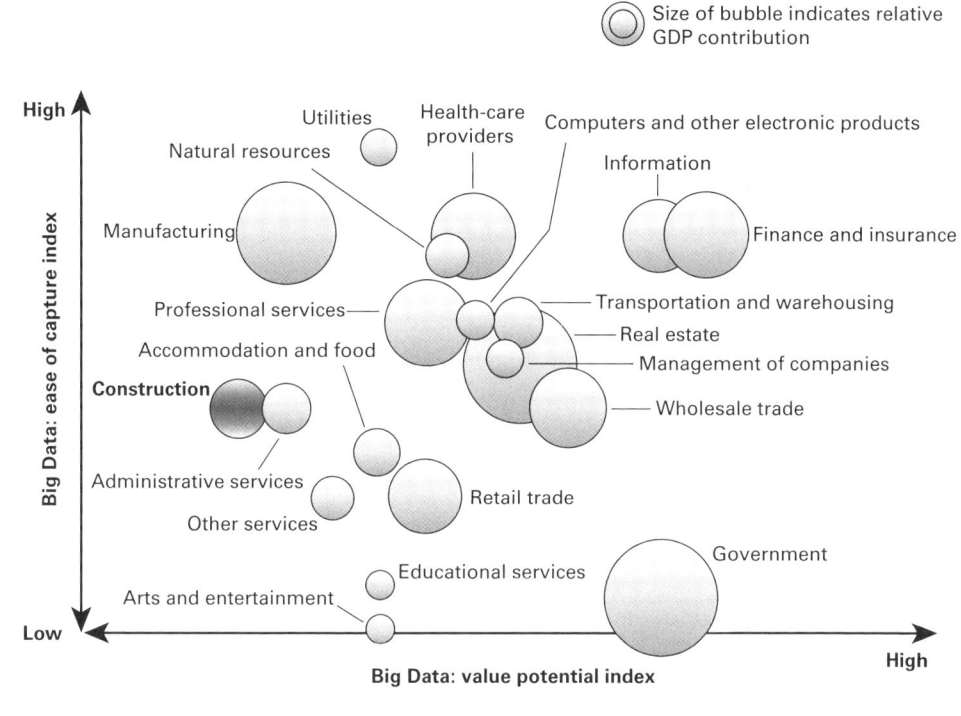

Size of bubble indicates relative GDP contribution

Y-axis: Big Data: ease of capture index (Low to High)
X-axis: Big Data: value potential index (Low to High)

Sectors plotted: Utilities; Health-care providers; Computers and other electronic products; Natural resources; Information; Manufacturing; Finance and insurance; Professional services; Transportation and warehouse; Accommodation and food; Real estate; Management of companies; Construction; Wholesale trade; Administrative services; Other services; Retail trade; Government; Educational services; Arts and entertainment.

SOURCE: adapted from Brown *et al* (2011); Manyika *et al* (2011)

while also being data intensive by nature, thereby using the data innovatively to compete by adopting sophisticated analytic techniques. Furthermore, the public sector was found to be the most fertile terrain for change, but faces steep barriers.

In contrast, fragmented industry structures/supply chains such as those evident in construction complicate the value creation potential of sectors in that the average organization in them is relatively small and therefore can only access limited amounts of data. In construction, 98 per cent of the industry is represented by SMEs whereby the average size of organization is five or fewer people (BIS, 2013; ONS, 2013). On the other hand, the larger players are usually exposed to bigger pools of data and can consequently use this data more readily to create value. However, according to Brown, Chui and Manyika (2011) even low-ranking sectors (in relation to value potential and data capture) such as that of construction could see their fortunes change. This is particularly relevant to the current transformation of the UK construction industry that is being driven through the Government Construction Strategy. The opportunity for increased value creation can occur as the industry supply chains and clients and owner/operators evolve through level two BIM, in developing a greater degree of collaborative and integrated structures, culture, processes etc, along with improved and efficient information management and a shift from a narrowed focus on 'lowest/first-cost' capital delivery procurement to 'value-driven' life-cycle management and digital procurement of assets, to level three and beyond of a data-driven approach, ie big data. Thereby such transformation facilitates the ability to capture value from data; increasing the sector's potential for value creation using big data by developing the sector's capabilities to capitalize on data, together with strong market incentives to do so.

In moving through level two BIM and developing the capabilities for transforming the sector for the digital procurement of assets, level three begins to focus on facilitating deriving 'value' through big data by developing the capability to operate analytic techniques on large data sets from which actionable information can be produced to support more predictive, as opposed to intuitive, decision making. In particular, the life-cycle management of the built environment is enabled through digital procurement based on a data-driven approach that not only embraces the capital delivery and operational management of assets but extends to performance management across assets, sectors, society/ies etc, ie Digital Built Britain (DBB, 2014) (Figure 6.8).

In relation to capital delivery, the greatest challenge in successfully managing a project is finding the right information when it is needed, collecting the right information from different construction sites and managing the distribution of information to other parties. Therefore, leveraging the vast amount of data through smart data systems can be an asset that can greatly benefit capital delivery, with the ability to provide insights for improving project portfolio management, time and budget certainty and performance, risk management, efficiency of site logistics and operations etc (van Rijmenam, 2013).

However, in considering the wider aspect of the life-cycle management of the built environment, a digital data-driven collaborative approach to procuring assets/infrastructure has the potential to deliver greater value that extends beyond simply capital delivery and reducing capex. Understanding and optimizing the operational requirements of assets during the capital delivery of the procurement process, based on insights derived from various sources of data, can achieve improved efficiencies later during the operation of the asset. In addition, improved operational efficiencies can be further enhanced by also considering managing the performance of assets/infrastructure, enabled through big data and smart systems that capture, monitor and measure performance data and combine with other sources to facilitate real-time performance optimization, eg optimized energy performance of smart buildings, not only on single assets/infrastructure but also across large asset/infrastructure stocks for enhanced asset/infrastructure portfolio management. Providing such 'learning' feedback loops to optimize performance or evaluate changes of use enables the planning of new infrastructure more effectively, building it at lower cost and operating and maintaining it more efficiently (DBB, 2014).

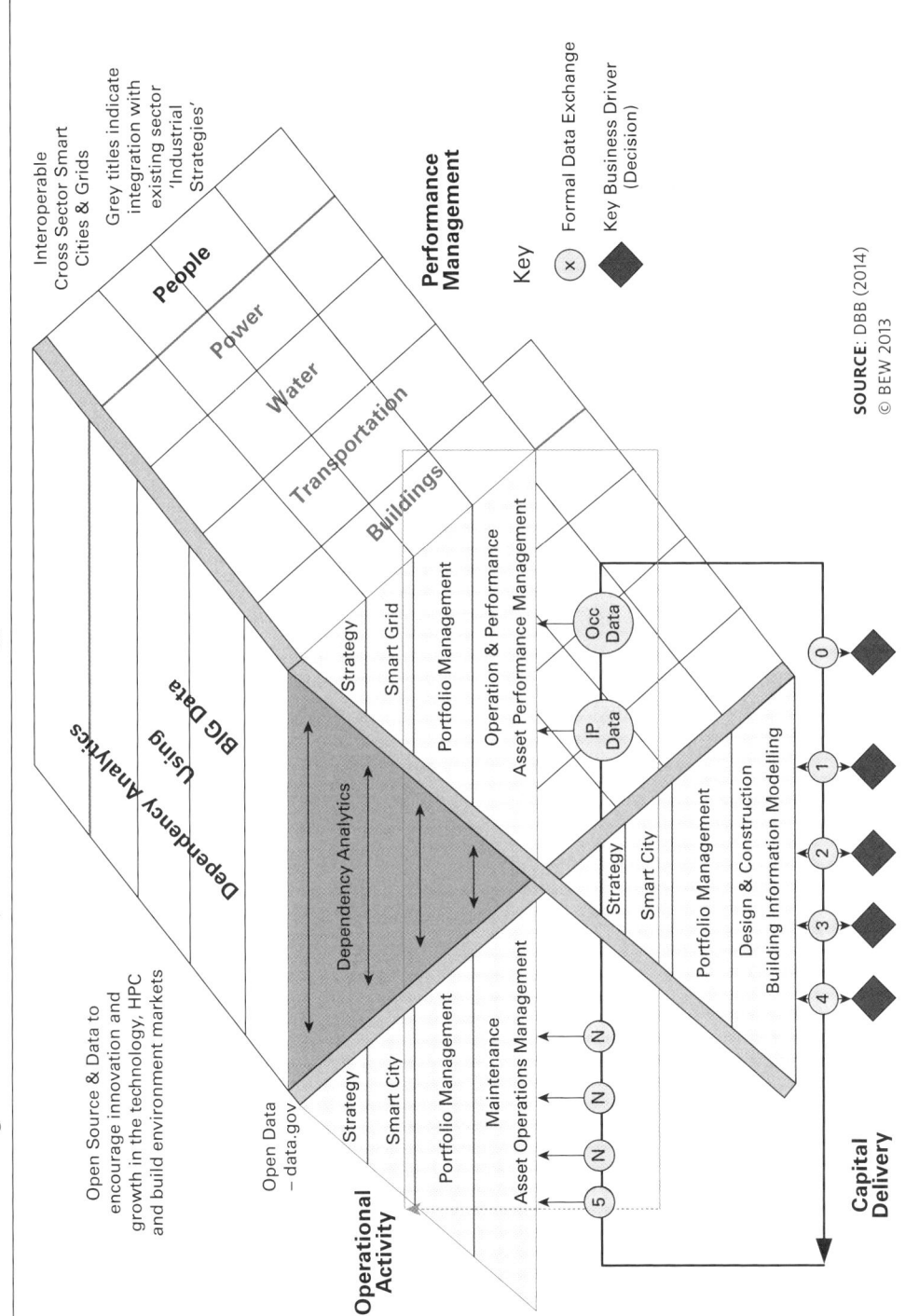

FIGURE 6.8 Digital Built Britain operational model strategy

SOURCE: DBB (2014)
© BEW 2013

Smart citizens, cities and governments

Urbanization has been increasing rapidly since the 18th century from less than 5 per cent of the global population living in a city to more than 50 per cent by 2007 (UNPD, 2007); and this trend is predicted to continue to increase to 80 per cent by the end of the 21st century (Harrison and Donnelly, 2011). While positive benefits accumulate from dense, diverse cities, highly urbanized populations also create many challenges for the planning, development and operation of cities. As discussed previously, the level three BIM/Digital Built Britain strategy is concerned with the life-cycle management of the built environment enabled through digital procurement based on a data-driven approach that not only embraces the capital delivery and operational management of assets/infrastructure but extends to performance management across sectors, society/ies etc, ie smart cities.

The smart city is a recent concept introduced as a strategy to mitigate the challenges generated by the urban population growth by emphasizing the importance of information and communication technologies (ICTs) for enhancing the competitive profile of a city, eg improving economic and political efficiency and enabling social, cultural, urban and sustainable development. According to Caragliu, Del Bo and Nijkamp (2009), a smart city is one where: 'investments in human and social capital and traditional (transport) and modern (ICT) communication infrastructure fuel sustainable economic growth and a high quality of life, with a wise management of natural resources, through participatory governance'.

Significant quantities of data are being produced through ubiquitous computing and big data smart systems can leverage knowledge from this accumulation of information to support the development of smart cities. Moreover, this can be further enhanced through citizens contributing to the smart operation of cities through ubiquitous computing (ie smart citizens), which provides access to real-time information at the level of individual citizens' choices and actions (ie 'making the invisible visible'). In addition, linking communicating sensors to computing intelligence gives rise to the internet of things (the industrial internet) and this growing and largely invisible web of interconnected smart objects and devices promises to transform the way we interact with everyday things (Reed, Gannon and Larus, 2012). Therefore, combining this information with other sources will assist local governments/authorities to manage their built environment much smarter such as improving traffic flow, providing mapping services, supporting relief and aid services in the event of a disaster etc. Moreover, the Digital Built Britain level three BIM strategy will form the basis for level four BIM whereby the focus will extend to social outcomes and well-being (DBB, 2014).

Many cities around the world are already beginning to leverage value by combining and utilizing large data sets to manage their built environment more effectively. For example, Las Vegas manages the risk of utility lines being cut off during construction due to inaccurate historical data through a simulation model of municipal infrastructure network using smart data, which integrates data from various sources and uses specific technologies to generate a 3D real-time model that displays various pipelines and facilities both above and below ground.

Ubiquitous computing, big data, and cloud computing are beginning to change how assets/infrastructure are procured and the built environment is managed. This is not only of concern to the technologies industry but also requires those sectors responsible for the life-cycle management of the built environment to adapt by developing the necessary capabilities.

Data and the integrated supply chain

The effective deployment and use of a big data-driven strategy, including BIM, requires a disciplined and structured approach to data creation, which is openly shareable. BIM level two requires the use and handover of a COBie (construction operations building information exchange) data schema providing a consistent method of data exchange with the ability of capturing data at its point of origin. Creating and storing structured data is a prerequisite for big data processes and enables the entire supply chain to contribute, due to the consistency of processes. One main premise of COBie is the ability to have one input for many outputs.

Whilst COBie is effective at standardizing data structures, there is also a requirement for raw data and information to be distributed around the supply chain. The integrated supply chain requires the management of information flow in three distinct areas: strategic, tactical and operational. At the micro operational level the use of BIM and the CDE provides an integrated supply chain management system.

Integrated supply chain management systems

As technology has improved, the introduction of systems has helped to improve specific functions within the industry. However, the ecosystem of construction includes many legacy and disparate systems that are not interoperable, which contributes to the silo working that is so inherent. Relying on independent systems contributes to requirements loss as information is corrupted or distorted during movement. Up to 50 per cent of initial requirements can be lost (Huovila, Koskela and Lautanala, 1994), contributing to a vast amount of waste and rework.

By adopting an integrated system, with digital information forming the initial input, directly from its point of origin, information can be shared across the entire supply chain. Akin to an ERP system this would involve the information models forming the input and all discipline-specific functions *pulling* information from the central artery. By deploying an integrated system integrated teams can form, with one input facilitating many outputs, which enables the removal of silo working and encourages data-driven management strategies to emerge (Figure 6.9).

FIGURE 6.9 Integrated workflow

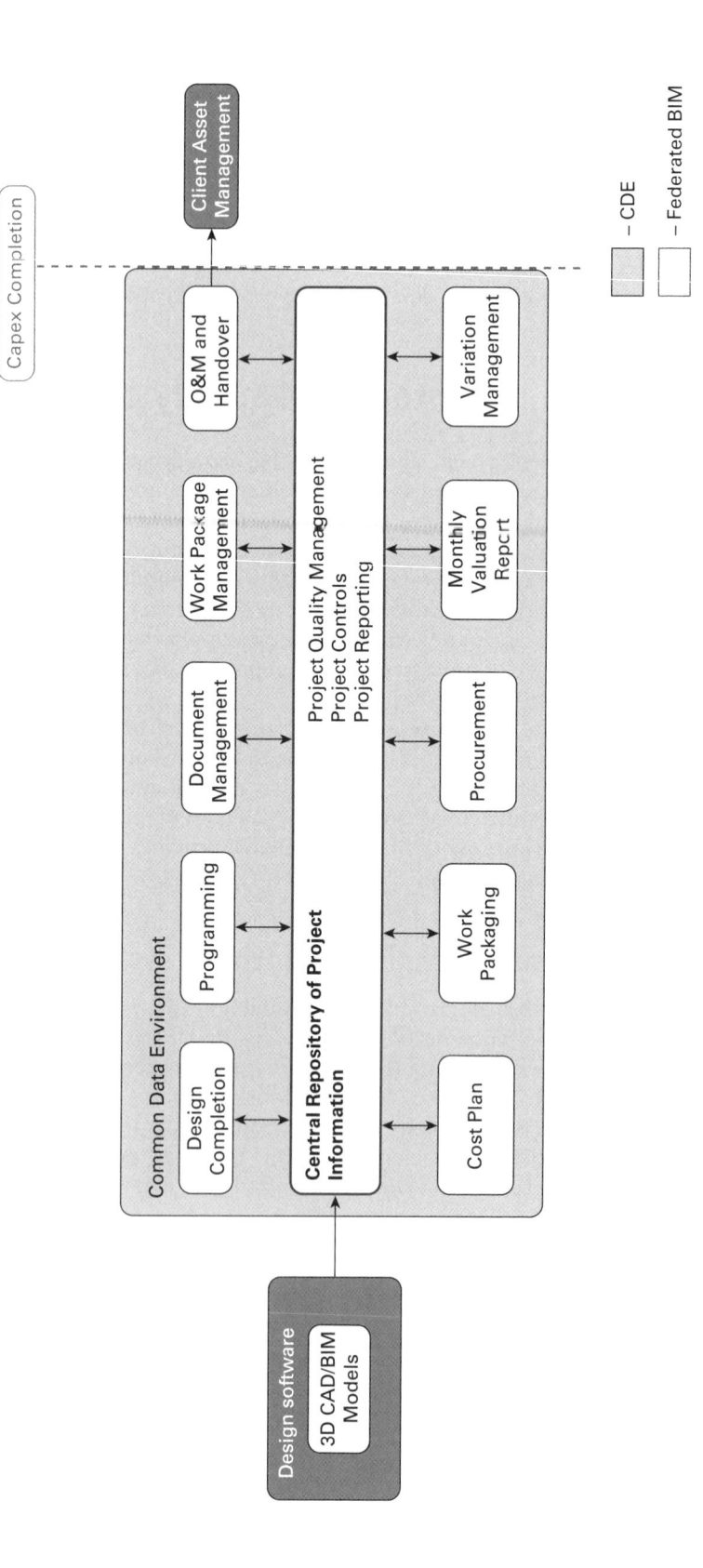

An integrated supply chain management system is akin to an electronic data management system but links organizations via real-time data transfer, project controls and workflows to ensure that the entire supply chain is utilizing the same, up-to-date information. The system provides a transparent system of material and information exchange internally and externally and the use of internal cross-functional management structures.

In 1985 Kurt Salmon Associates in the United States identified that the average delivery time for apparel was 66 weeks, primarily due to inventory or transit procedures, causing major losses due to inflexibility and storage costs. The resulting strategy was based on suppliers sharing information – and the grocery industry in particular adopted a set of standards for electronic data interchange (EDI). Point-of-sale scanning systems relayed information enabling the entire supply chain to forecast more accurately.

Whilst construction differs from manufacturing, the same principles can be applied by accepting that design, procurement and construction is a systematic process of information creation, distribution and use. Using BIM, structured data and the CDE enables quick responses as real-time information can be accessed, interrogated and acted upon nearly instantaneously due to the two-way communication environment it creates. Another premise of BIM is the ability to reuse information created elsewhere, eliminating vast quantities of duplication and rework. Whilst there remains a number of legal issues surrounding this method of working, it facilitates design for manufacture and encourages off-site manufacturing, moving the design and construction process further towards manufacturing.

There are distinct synergies between BIM and lean construction, which is the application of the Toyota Production System (TPS) principles to the construction project delivery process, with the goal of eliminating anything that does not add value to the product. A study by Sacks *et al* (2010) discovered 52 positive interactions between BIM and lean with the following benefits:

- reduced variability;
- reduced cycle times;
- reduced batch sizes;
- increased flexibility;
- increased standardization;
- improved requirements capture;
- improved visual management;
- improved verification and validation processes;
- facilitation of continuous improvement.

There are a number of lean tools that can be delivered in the construction industry more robustly using a BIM and data-driven approach. *Kanban* refers to the process of using signals to indicate when users require additional materials or resources or when tasks are 'made ready'. In the construction context the use of data analytics can go one step further by proactively determining when materials are required to reduce variability. *Pull planning* is a process where members of the supply chain collaborate to make commitments based on currently available information. Having information shared openly is an obvious benefit for facilitating this process. Subsequently *one piece flow* is achieved, a process in which information is made available in smaller segments, as it is created. This reduces waiting time as the supply chain can be made aware of current statuses in near real-time, enabling them to plan more accurately.

By ensuring that information is updated on a very regular basis *andon* (the process of notifying a defect in a manufacturing line) is enabled where the identification of defects – or in the case of the supply chain, errors in the information – are efficiently detected. Moreover, pull planning and the *last planner system of production* (a system of creating predictable and reliable workflow – see Ballard, 2000) enables the identification of the root cause of effects by analysing reasons for commitments being missed. This enables a more scientific process of managing the performance of the supply chain.

Value stream mapping is facilitated as a result of sharing and using common information. The *value chain* identifies end-to-end processes, and activities that do not explicitly add value, such as duplicated effort, are removed. Rather than local optimization, with the integrated supply chain, common real-time information is used to map the process holistically, identifying inherent waste, duplication and non-value-adding activities that exist in the interfaces between organizations in the supply chain. This enables the opportunity to improve joint process efficiency. As a direct result, competitive advantage can be generated in two distinct ways: optimization and coordination.

As iteration waves reduce (the time between data creation and use) the accuracy and precision of information increases, enabling near real-time decisions to be made. This reduces risk as information utilized for decision making is transacted almost to the point of automation, improving objectivity and enabling more proactive and predictive decisions. Removing subjective decision making, in respect of supply chain decisions, eliminates the opportunity for discriminate judgements, wrong interpretations and poor conclusions. This presents a fairer method of analysing the supply chain, potentially reducing inherent risks and opening up newer and more innovative procurement and delivery strategies, including integrated forms of agreement.

As the industry improves its data management skills it will move from analogue to digital decision making, facilitating predictive evaluations and opening up the possibility of nano-second procurement. For example, assets can then either: a) procure themselves based on defined rule sets and accumulated data; b) objectively select the most appropriate partner to procure from; or c) both. This will significantly improve enterprise-level integration.

Enterprise-level integration

Whilst integrating the supply chain at the micro operational level brings efficiency benefits, at the macro strategic level the focus is on what the integrated supply chain does well, its responsiveness to changes and its ability to continuously improve. Data and the internet of things can assist with this enterprise-level supply chain integration.

The benefits of an integrated, enterprise-wide and life-cycle approach to supply chain management will include:

- greater clarity on long-term in-service performance expectations and the consequences of design-stage decisions over life-cycle performance and cost;
- improved predictability using big data and performance data;
- a better understanding of the supply chain market, the availability of resources and improved predictability of future events (based on the availability of commercial data and supplier data);
- location-based demand for services with the opportunity to 'level out the load' in respect of supply chain opportunities, ensuring that variances in demand can be met with better precision;
- reduced project start-up costs due to availability of better information at the beginning of the project;
- portfolio management across multiple projects, programmes or estates;
- organizational 'personality' management with the option of monitoring the performance of different organizations working together to identify positive and negative synergies;
- continuous improvement.

Perhaps more important than any of this is the use of data-driven procurement and management strategies providing a distinct shift from traditional decision making. Using data removes subjectivity and intuitive processes. The use of data, structured and presented with coherence and clarity, forces objective decision making, which can ultimately only be good for the construction supply chain, with clearer and more transparent governance.

Continuous improvement

In the evolving workplace, with greater independencies forming, it is critical to ensure that organizations collaborate for joint success. Moreover, creating an environment where collaboration can flourish and selecting the appropriate stakeholders is fundamentally important. The psychology of the organization should be determined and historical data used to determine the strengths and weaknesses of partnerships. For example, does company A work well with company B under certain conditions? Finding the best match of organizations that can deliver projects collaboratively, be that with interfaces (work packages), interdependencies (with supply and construct) or ability to meet commitments (pull planning), is the basis for ensuring that collaboration brings tangible value.

Using data created during the project life cycle presents a transparent set of information relating to performance. The use of this data removes the subjectivity that could ordinarily be present when measuring the performance of the supply chain.

As referred to earlier, by sharing information and adopting lean principles the root causes of effects can be identified and eradicated. By analysing data and using *optioneering*, which is a key benefit of using digital technologies, cause and effect can be determined. An example from outside the construction industry is the motorsport industry. As single changes are made to a vehicle, the effect of that change can be made and near instantaneous feedback is generated via sensors, engine data and lap times. Using this strategy means that there is little or no subjectivity involved.

Causes for failing to complete planned work should be investigated and those causes removed. This is only feasible when a robust process for providing feedback and learning opportunities for continual improvement are identified. Requirements and data should be captured throughout the entire process and reports submitted in order to fully understand what has happened at each stage. This is better achieved by providing a visual aid to articulate cause and effect.

Data visualization

In order for data to be understood it has to be presented in a format that is intuitive and easily understood by the user. Indeed, the sheer amount of data that is created must not only be structured but presented visually via data visualization, which is concerned with communicating information clearly to aid people in understanding the significance of data by placing it in a visual context. Data visualization can also assist with data mining, which is the extraction of meaningful information from large data sets.

In the construction context it has already been discussed that supply chain management does not generally concern the flow and distribution of goods and materials as much as the management of information. That said, in terms of performance management, the display of data amassed from metrics and key performance indicators in relation to the supply chain can be presented visually. This assists with identifying trends, cause and effect and facilitates more predictive planning, which is useful in areas such as design management, productivity management, quality control, contract administration and invoicing and payment.

The credibility of performance data is of paramount importance; ensuring a single, shared version helps to ensure that people are discussing the same numbers. The risk of formula errors is greatly reduced by hard-coding the calculation logic into the data visualization model, whereas traditional spreadsheets are susceptible to cells not being copied accurately and discrepancies occurring, thus causing errors. Having a shared database of data, presented visually, improves accessibility thus improving objectivity.

The purpose of performance measurement is generally to provide assurance when performance meets expectations and to take corrective action when it does not. Interactive dashboards enable you to manage by exception, ie monitor at a high level and then drill down into areas of concern, finding the root cause and correcting it. Dashboards that are not dynamic in this way tend to present all information at the same level of detail. This results either in not enough detail being available to correct poor performance or time wasted reviewing detailed reports of good performance.

Conclusion

BIM, big data and lean can eliminate the tendency to encourage local optimization of work and reduce variances in productivity in order to enable more accurate forecasting and production rates (Sacks *et al*, 2010). If implemented holistically, the new integrated and lean process will help to depart from the traditional transformation and individualistic view of construction to a more complete view, which gives equal importance to the value and flow concepts along with the transformation concept. However, it should be noted that the use of big data will not replace human intuition but complement existing skills.

The creation of data, of any kind, offers the opportunity to change our decision making from subjective to objective with the use of structured, validated data. Removing human interpretation eliminates the opportunity for opinions, discriminate judgements and poor conclusions. As the data we generate becomes more intelligent we will move to proactive decision making, based on trends, analytics and more objective judgements. The sharing of this data improves transparency, creating a goldfish bowl environment, removing the opportunities for underhand tactics and behaviours synonymous with the adversarial culture that currently exists.

Traditionally procurement has been seen as a mechanism for shifting risk to another party. The visualization of risks enables all stakeholders to understand the landscape they operate in with more clarity. The increase in confidence and trust will open up modern procurement routes, possibly using integrated forms of agreement, sharing risk and rewards. New forms of contract will emerge that reward good behaviour and respond to the return to vertical supply chains.

As we use data more intelligently our needs will become more immediate as decisions are made near instantaneously. The supply chain will need to respond to changing requirements, potentially opening up the sector to start-up companies or *nano-corporates*, as organizations are created to respond to consumers' immediate needs.

By creating an integrated team, composed of the traditional players and supplemented with the nano-corporate, we can see a return to the master builder, albeit in an alternative form. Using data intelligently, and linking that using big data techniques, the industry will likely realize that the journey towards true supply chain integration is based on the realization that we all need each other to survive and we will be better together, integrated, than apart.

References

Baccarini, D (1996) The concept of project complexity: a review, *International Journal of Project Management*, **14** (4), pp 201–04

Ballard, H G (2000) The Last Planner System of Production Control, School of Civil Engineering, Faculty of Engineering, University of Birmingham [Online] http://leanconstruction.org.uk/media/docs/ballard2000-dissertation.pdf [accessed 23 February 2015]

Ballard, HG and Howell, G (2003) Lean project management, *Building Research and Information*, **31** (2), pp 119–33

BARC (2013) Big Data Survey Europe, BARC-Institute, February 2013

BIS (2013) UK Construction: An analysis of the sector department of business innovation and skills

Brown, B, Chui, M and Manyika, J (2011) Are you ready for the era of 'big data'?, *McKinsey Quarterly*, October 2011

Caragliu, A, Del Bo, C and Nijkamp, P (2009) Smart Cities in Europe, 3rd Central European Conference in Regional Science (CERS), 2009

DBB (2014) *Digital Built Britain: Level 3 Building Information Modelling – Strategic Plan*, HMSO, London

Deutsch, R (2011) *BIM and Integrated Design*, John Wiley, Hoboken, NJ

Dumbill, E (2013) Making Sense of Big Data, *Big Data*, **1** (1), March, pp 1–2

Eastman, C et al (2011) *BIM Handbook*, Wiley, Hoboken, NJ

Emmerson, Sir Harold (1962) *Survey of Problems Before the Construction Industries, Prepared for Ministry of Public Buildings and Works*, HMSO, London

Fallon, K and Palmer, M (2007) *General Buildings Information Handover Guide: Principles, methodology and case studies*, industry sector guide of the Information Handover Guide Series Department of Commerce, United States of America

Harrison, C and Donnelly, IA (2011) A Theory of Smart Cities, in Proceedings of the 55th Annual Meeting of the ISSS-2011, September, Hull, UK 55 (1)

HM Gov (2010) *Low Carbon Construction Innovation and Growth Team Final Report*, HMSO, London

HM Gov (2011) Government Construction Strategy [Online] www.gov.uk/government/publications/government-construction-strategy [accessed 23 February 2015]

Huovila, P, Koskela, L and Lautanala, M (1997) Fast or Concurrent: The art of getting construction improved, Proceedings of International Workshop on Lean Construction, Santiago, Chile

Kaisler, S et al (2013) Big Data: Issues and challenges moving forward, 46th Hawaii International Conference on System Sciences

Lee, H and Billington, C (1992) Managing supply chain inventory: pitfalls and opportunities, *Sloan Management Review*, **33** (3), pp 65–73

McAfee, A and Brynjolfsson, E (2012) Big data: the management revolution, *Harvard Business Review*, October, pp 60–68

Manyika, J *et al* (2011) Big Data: The next frontier for innovation, competition, and productivity, June, McKinsey Global Institute

ONS (2013) *Construction Statistics*, No 14, 2013 Edition, Office for National Statistics

Reed, DA, Gannon, DB and Larus, JR (2012) Imagining the future: thoughts on computing, *IEEE Computer*, **45** (1), pp 25–30

Russom, P (2011) Big Data Analytics, TDWI (The Data Warehousing Institute) Report, Fourth Quarter

Sacks, R *et al* (2010) The interaction of lean and building information modelling in construction, *Journal of Construction Engineering and Management*, **136** (9), pp 968–80

Thomsen, C *et al* (2009) Managing Integrated Project Delivery, CMAA

UNPD (United Nations Population Division) (2007) World Urbanization Prospects [Online] www.un.org/esa/population/publications/wup2007/2007WUP_Highlights_web.pdf [accessed 23 February 2015]

van Rijmenam, M (2013) Big Data Can Help Construction Companies Deliver Projects On Time, *Datafloq* [Online] https://datafloq.com/read/big-data-construction-companies-deliver-projects-t/143 [accessed 23 February 2015]

Williams, TM (1999) The need for new paradigms for complex projects, *International Journal of Project Management*, **17** (5), pp 269–73

Winch, GM (1989) The construction firm and the construction project: a transaction cost approach, *Construction Management and Economics*, 7, pp 331–45

Womack, JP and Jones, DT (2003) *Lean Thinking*, Simon & Schuster, London

World Economic Forum (2012) Big Data, Big Impact: New Possibilities for International Development, *World Economic Forum* [Online] www.weforum.org/reports/big-data-big-impact-new-possibilities-international-development [accessed 16 April 2015]

PART THREE
Construction logistics and sustainability

The role of logistics in achieving sustainable construction: a Swedish perspective

07

MONIKA BUBHOLZ, CAMILLA EINARSSON and LARS-GÖRAN SPORRE

Introduction

No business today can afford to ignore environmental concerns; there are demands that logistics should be green and that production must be sustainable. But these are broad concepts, and a company will need a practical approach to translate the idea of sustainability into action and measurable results. This chapter will provide a brief background to the relatively new concept of sustainability and then present a model for analysing sustainability and implementing sustainable solutions.

The sustainability model, developed by Swedish engineering consultants and architects Sweco, was originally used in industrial developments such as manufacturing plants and power generation. The concept, however, was found to be useful and valid across industry sectors and is now applied also in construction projects. From this has been developed a sustainable logistics strategy for construction – or, to put it more correctly, a logistics strategy that allows the overall construction project to be run in as sustainable a way as possible.

The chapter ends by introducing two case studies where this approach has been adopted: one a city-centre mixed development comprising retailing, residential and transport infrastructure and the other a major hospital project. We will hear the views of the logistics manager of one of these projects.

Background

Today sustainability is of central concern for most enterprises. Some examples:

- Both consumers and professional buyers require products that are developed, manufactured and supplied in a sustainable fashion.
- In the media, international organizations are analysed and evaluated from a sustainability perspective.
- Professional buyers produce requirement specifications that will immediately exclude any supplier not pursuing a serious sustainability strategy.
- Shareholders demand that management regularly accounts for the company's sustainability efforts, as set out in, for example, 'Miljö och hållbarhetsinformation i årsredovisningen' (Environmental and sustainability information in the annual report) FAR SRS (a Swedish association for auditors and financial advisors).

It is clear from this that all businesses need to pursue a focused and effective sustainability strategy. This does not, however, involve companies only in long-term commitments, cost and effort; there are also substantial and immediate benefits. This is what we highlight in this chapter.

Sustainability and efficiency are two sides of the same coin. For instance: reducing energy consumption, improving working conditions and reducing the impact on the environment all contribute to the sustainability of the business. But they also enhance efficiency and strengthen the business's competitiveness. The potential efficiency gains are great: for instance, in construction as much as 30 per cent of the total time is wasted by operatives waiting for or looking for materials and/or chasing information and transport, as identified in the report: 'Slöseri i byggprojekt-behov av förändrat synsätt' (Waste in construction projects – a new approach is needed) (Per-Erik Josephsson och Lasse Saukkoriipi, Sveriges Byggindustrier FoU Väst, 2005). Focusing on sustainable logistics can drastically cut this waste.

The concept of sustainability is relatively new. The most commonly used definition is that developed in 1987 by a UN commission led by Gro Harlem Bruntland, former prime minister of Norway, which states: 'A sustainable development satisfies today's needs without jeopardizing the ability of coming generations to satisfy their needs' (Our Common Future: Report of the World Commission on Environment and Development, 1987). Later uses of the sustainability concept often divide it into three main components: ecological, social and financial. For an activity to be regarded as truly sustainable it must be sustainable in all three aspects.

The report 'Klimatpåverkan från byggprocessen' (Impact on the climate from the construction process) (Kungliga Ingenjörsvetenskapsakademien och Sveriges Byggindustrier, 2014) quantifies greenhouse gas emissions from construction. It estimates that the total climate impact of construction activities in Sweden is around 10 million tonnes of CO_2 per year of which

4 million tonnes relate to buildings and 6 million tonnes to other construction – road building, industrial developments etc. In 2012 this corresponded to about 17 per cent of the total emissions of greenhouse gases in Sweden. This is roughly equivalent to the total emissions of all cars in Sweden and more than the combined emissions of all trucks and buses. Obviously, there is room for improved efficiency.

Standards

There are no widely established standards for sustainability. Sustainable buildings are most commonly certified according to LEED (Leadership in Energy and Environmental Design) or BREEAM (Builders Research Establishment, Environmental Assessment Method). They set out requirements concerning the construction process including logistics, material supply and the impact on the environment. LEED stresses the importance of local sourcing; if a sufficient proportion of materials originates from within an 800 kilometre radius from the site, 'credits' are given that count towards certification. Global Reporting Initiative (GRI) is a voluntary standard for sustainability reporting, which includes a special section for buildings including construction, operation and demolition.

The Swedish consultancy Sweco has long been engaged in the development of the built environment where focus on sustainability is a natural part of the work undertaken. Over the years a methodology has been developed that promotes a systematic approach and this has been widely used. Titled 'Sustainable Industry' (Industri i ett större sammanhang) and launched in 2013, a concept was developed that focused on eight dimensions of sustainability, which together provide a comprehensive approach for sustainability in industry (**www.sweco.se**). The eight dimensions, which all have to be considered to fully explore all aspects of sustainability, are:

- the business aspects of the enterprise;
- the people involved in the business;
- the location of the operation;
- the building, including its facility management system;
- the production or construction process;
- the energy use and the energy sources;
- the emissions generated;
- the external stakeholders and the environment.

Each building and each site is unique. However, standard processes and methods for construction can be, and must be, developed in order to gain efficiency and achieve quality and adherence to rules and regulations. Constructing a building is in essence an industrial process and therefore this concept is well suited to developing a sustainable approach to construction logistics.

Sustainable construction logistics

Table 7.1 lists the main factors to be considered under each of the headline dimensions, and then spells out what this typically means in the context of a construction project. The detailed content will always have to be tailored to the requirements and scope of the project being considered.

TABLE 7.1 Sustainable industry concept: dimensions, content and examples relating to logistics

Dimension	Content	Example from a Construction Logistics Perspective
Business enterprise	• Strategic plan • Ethical considerations • Profitability • Risk assessment • Flexibility • Requirements on products from a life-cycle assessment (LCA) perspective	• LCA perspective including the stages construction/facility management/demolition • Long-term strategy encompassing both building design and logistics solutions
People	• Competence • Working environment	• Training and education • Ergonomics • Health and safety • Avoiding the use of, and/or handling correctly and with care any dangerous substances (COSHH) • Less material on site and 'in the way', reducing risk of accidents • Safe lifting
Location	• Resource availability • Stakeholders • Transport	• Priority given to geographical proximity to suppliers • Locating the logistics centre (LC) so as to optimize transport and minimize disturbance • Transport planning • Locating staff facilities (changing rooms, canteen, rest areas etc) conveniently close to the workplace • Convenient and safe access and egress

TABLE 7.1 *continued*

Dimension	Content	Example from a Construction Logistics Perspective
Building (including facility management systems)	• Resource efficient • Flexible • Environment for working/living • Sustainable construction process • Longevity • Cost-efficiency	• Sustainable logistics process • Materials handling • Modular solutions and off-site manufacture (OFM)
Production process (= construction process)	• Resource efficiency (materials, energy, time) • Methods • Sustainable materials • Reuse/recycle waste and surplus materials	• Minimized waste • Effective delivery planning (prepare, organize reception and lay-down areas) minimizes waiting time • Instructions regarding labelling for goods identification • Less material on site resulting in less damage, loss and repeated handling • Optimizing transport • Reusable packaging • Segregation of waste • Return logistics
Energy	• Optimized energy consumption • Sustainable energy sources	• Transport optimization • Planning of material storage requirements reduces the need for heating
Emissions	• Minimize emissions to air and water • Minimize noise and other disruptions	• Minimizing emissions to air and water • Minimizing generation of dust • Minimizing noise • Short and planned transport routes minimize emissions • Segregating waste streams on site
Stakeholders and environment	• Responsibility for impacts on suppliers, customers and other stakeholders • Cooperation for optimized resource utilization	• Supplier selection • Recycling • Using local labour where possible

A sustainable logistics strategy for a construction project

The starting point for construction logistics is to support the construction process, but to do so in a way that is resource efficient, minimizes waste and provides a good environment for both workers on site and residents living in the neighbourhood. Central to the strategy therefore is strict control of deliveries on a just-in-time (JIT) basis to avoid overstocking the site. To minimize transport, loads often need to be consolidated between suppliers, and this is typically achieved using a logistics centre (LC). Figure 7.1 gives a schematic overview.

The material movements start from the respective supplier (right-hand side of Figure 7.1) and reach the construction site (left-hand side of the figure) direct or via the LC. Waste material is sorted directly on site and transferred to the waste station, the LC or back to the supplier as applicable.

Suppliers

Materials from suppliers are delivered when called off against agreed delivery plan.

Materials are sent either as JIT deliveries directly to site or to the LC. Reusable packaging, materials supplied incorrectly, surplus materials and recyclable materials are all sent back on return journeys.

Logistics centre (LC)

The LC can be located on site, depending on the location of the site and space available, or it can be at an external location. Functions at the LC include: goods reception, inspection, storage of materials, picking of materials for sequenced JIT deliveries and consolidated transport of materials to site. The LC also manages handling of materials and packaging to be returned to suppliers.

Site

At the site the materials are delivered as close as possible to each user (trade contractor), ie materials are sorted by floor level and zone. Packaging is collected for reuse or recycling and waste materials are segregated in appropriate waste streams. Non-recyclable materials are sent directly to the waste transfer station. Surplus or damaged materials are returned to the suppliers, either directly or via the LC.

FIGURE 7.1 Logistics strategy for a construction project – a systematic approach

Site Logistics Centre (LC) Suppliers

direct transport materials

JIT delivery from supplier

'Picked' material kits

Material deliveries in sequence from the LC
Consolidated transport

LC

Return logistics packaging and recycling

Return transport to the LC

Return transport to supplier

Waste segregation at source

Waste transfer station

Site

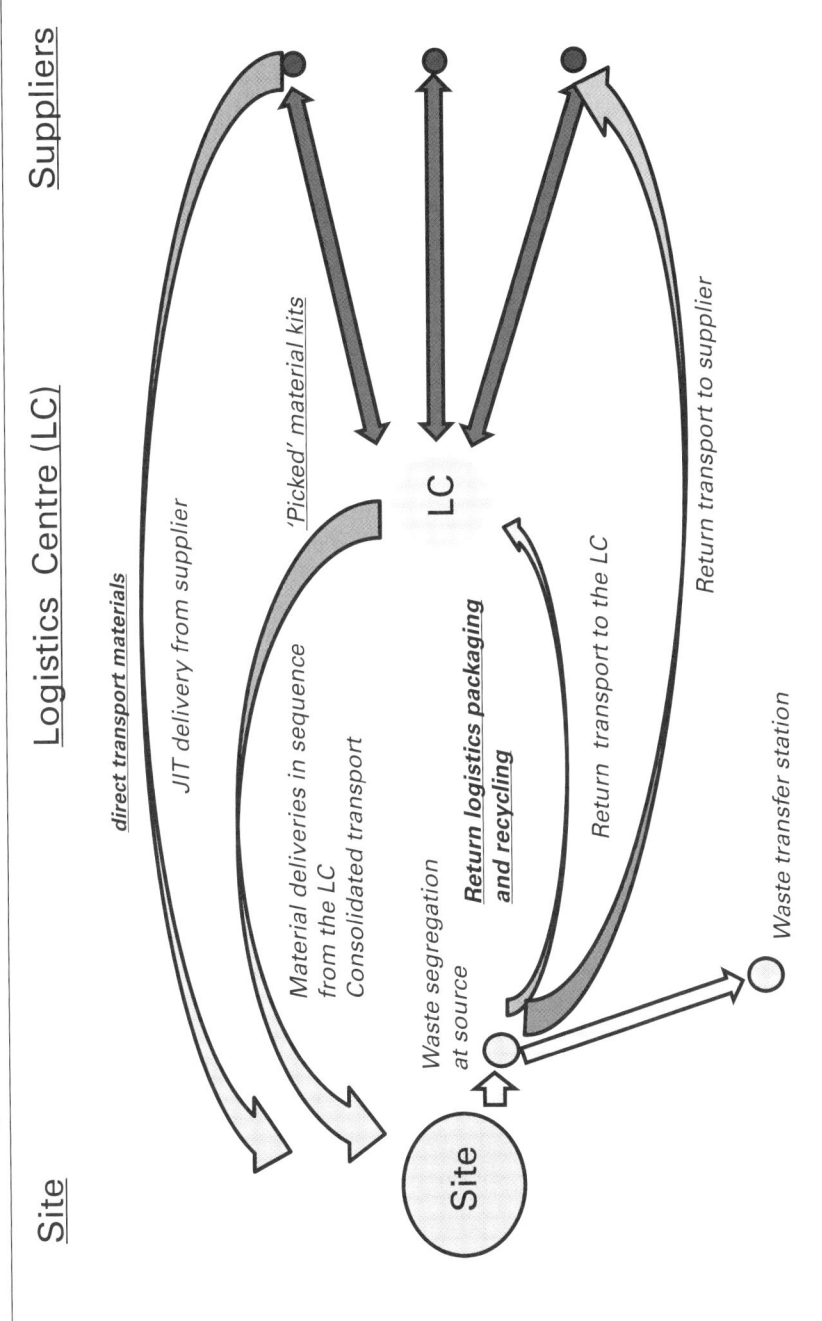

Practical considerations for efficient and sustainable construction logistics

An efficient construction site (and construction process) requires logistics to be well managed and under control; the material flow must run smoothly and waiting time for materials minimized. When deliveries are managed on a JIT basis and material sequences are controlled, the risk of erroneous deliveries is vastly reduced. Furthermore, when material quantities in each delivery are matched to usage, there is much less material lying around in the workplace being in the way, being damaged and being wasted. We summarize this as 'the three Rs' – the right material at the right location at the right time.

Planning

It is in the planning stages of a project that the opportunities to achieve efficient and thereby sustainable logistics solutions are created. During the early construction phase a logistics review takes place where efficient material flow routes are identified and internal transport organized. The review also establishes how materials will be delivered to each floor level and zone. Alternative transport solutions may need to be prepared and could involve delaying construction of certain walls, creating openings in external walls or using lift shafts for delivery. It is necessary to ensure that long materials can be manoeuvred into any required location.

Each project is unique, and the logistics solution must always be tailored to specific requirements and site conditions. As a rule, the need for an externally located LC increases when the site is constrained and/or in an urban or inner-city area. If ample space is available at or in the immediate vicinity of the site then it is useful to place the LC there. Factors to consider:

- If goods receiving areas are limited it will be necessary to schedule deliveries accurately in time or provide suppliers with specific time slots.
- If space is restricted on site, deliveries should be JIT and volumes of materials delivered at any one time should be kept to a minimum. JIT deliveries can come directly from suppliers or from the LC.
- Review the requirements for gate operatives, traffic marshals, goods receiving operatives etc.
- If the time plan is tight and/or space is limited consider evening and/or night deliveries if possible.

The purpose of the logistics process is to support the construction process; therefore the planning must be integrated. Logistics planning needs to be done at different levels:

- A general outline plan should be produced early in the project, based on the material requirements as defined by the construction process.

- A detailed plan should be produced on an ongoing basis, and updated weekly to capture progress and any changes in the programme. This plan is the basis for material call-offs.

The team

When implementing change or developing a new way of doing things, a necessary condition for success is to train those involved. This has to include everyone: own staff and agency staff, subcontractors and suppliers. This is particularly important in environmentally friendly construction and when implementing sustainable logistics, as this is likely to introduce new working methods and procedures to many suppliers and contractors.

Deliveries

Early in the programme, develop clear delivery instructions (sometimes called logistics instructions) and issue them to all contractors and suppliers. Go through the instructions with all concerned and ensure that everyone understands what is expected. It is useful to tie compliance to some kind of commercial reward/penalty.

To avoid unnecessary offloading and reloading activities, materials can be delivered on a JIT basis directly from suppliers; this can be efficient but requires careful coordination. If this can be done it lowers stockholding in the LC and reduces the capital tied up in materials. It can also contribute to reduced waste as less material is lying around waiting to be used, when it is susceptible to damage or loss.

It is useful to organize deliveries according to items required at specific locations. This means that deliveries from the supplier are organized by final location on site. For instance, windows to a building are delivered by the type(s) and quantity needed at each floor level and zone, rather than all windows of a certain type being delivered in one batch. Deliveries are also scheduled in time as construction progresses.

A key function of the LC is to consolidate deliveries. Materials that are needed at the same location on site and within the same time window can be picked to make up a material kit at the LC and then transported to site as part of a consolidated load. This reduces the number of vehicle journeys and handling on site. In this instance the LC performs a value-added service, which reduces waiting time on site.

Vehicles running on renewable fuel sources should, if possible, be used.

Logistics centre

The LC should be established in a geographically suitable location with regard to access and space. This can be immediately adjacent to the site or at an external location. Materials are stored in an organized fashion and transport to and from the site is optimized.

Functions carried out at the LC:

- receiving materials that cannot be delivered directly to site or materials where transport optimization excludes direct delivery to site;
- goods receiving and inspection;
- limited stockholding, ensuring good storage conditions and correct material handling methods;
- picking material kits in sequence to support the construction process;
- consolidating materials for delivery to site;
- receiving materials returned from site to be sent back to suppliers by return transport.

Warehouses, sheds and other storage facilities should be as energy efficient as possible. In the Nordic climate the quality of insulation is important. District heating schemes or heat pump technology should be used where possible.

Lighting is an important safety consideration, but make sure any lights not needed are turned off. Motion sensors are recommended.

Labelling of materials

Labelling is an extremely important element of an efficient logistics process. Labelling systems and detailed design should be agreed with suppliers and specified as part of the purchase contracts. Good labelling is a necessary condition for accurate goods identification, inspection, tracking of materials and payments. Efficient administrative support systems depend on unambiguous labelling.

Packaging design

- Package size and quantities in packages/containers should be adapted to suit the logistics process and materials handling methods used.
- Quality, sturdiness and weatherproofing of packaging should be appropriate with respect to the storage and transport conditions in the project.
- Materials suitable for reuse or recycling should be used, with clear markings advising on waste segregation.
- Packaging volumes should be minimized in order to reduce waste volumes on site. JIT deliveries generally require less packaging.

Deliveries to and from site

- If possible, evenings should be used to bring new materials onto the site; with no trade contractors on site, access is easier – as is availability of hoists and cranes.
- Using third-party logistics companies for site logistics is generally more cost-efficient than depending on trade contractors moving materials around. By presenting materials at the right place at the right time utilization of the various trades on site is improved.
- Waste and surplus materials should be removed in the evening when trade contractors have left.
- By using all available hours, traffic flow around the site can be managed more smoothly.
- Offloading of materials should take place as close as possible to the point of use. Particularly when depending on crane handling, short transport distances save time.

Administrative system support

During the design phase a database is created listing all materials used; this will aid sorting, reuse and recycling of materials during any future demolition. To be effective the database must be maintained and updated with any changes occurring throughout the construction phase.

There are plenty of standard software packages available for use in logistics planning. One example is Log Net (Svensk Bygglogistik AB). Please visit **www.bygglogistik.se/en/services/lognet**

Finance

When operatives are having to wait for materials, cranes and/or lifts, they are not creating any value added; this is a waste of human resources and a waste of project time. By scheduling and booking deliveries, and ensuring they go to the right location, the time usually spent searching for materials is reduced.

Too much material on site frequently leads to substantial levels of damage and waste. One consequence of material damage is the need to reorder – possibly resulting in delays. Limiting the material volumes called off at each delivery reduces waste and waiting time, and the total project cost is lowered.

Less material on site improves housekeeping and makes the site less crowded – reducing the risk of accidents and injury.

Case studies

The following case studies demonstrate logistics solutions at two projects: the first for a hospital in Sweden; the second for a shopping centre in Sweden.

CASE STUDY   'The University Hospital of the future' – University Hospital in Linköping, Sweden

Project summary

'The University Hospital of the future' is a headline linking several construction projects aimed at tackling future hospital care needs. FUS1 is the first stage, and extends over 66,000 square metres in two buildings connected to the existing hospital. One important aspect of the logistics planning was to ensure undisrupted and smooth traffic flow throughout the build programme, as access by ambulances and patients could not be impeded.

A few facts:

- Work on the existing hospital site in Linköping will be taking place over almost a decade.
- Estimated total cost: SEK 3.8 billion (£300m/€390m) for three phases.
- The first phase 'FUS1' will be complete in December 2015.
- 'FUS1' extends over 66,000 square metres.
- The client project manager from Landstinget Östergötland (Östergötland municipality) is Peter Nilsson.
- The overall contract is divided between more than one main contractor.

Logistics at the hospital for the future – FUS1

From the start the project team decided to use third-party logistics in this complex project. Two new buildings had to be constructed, attached to the existing hospital buildings, while the hospital had to remain in use throughout and its operations not disrupted or inconvenienced in any way.

The hospital grounds had no space for material storage or lay-down areas, and roads must not be blocked but kept open for ambulance access. Based on these conditions it was decided early in the project, and specified in the tendering stage, that all deliveries must be controlled and timed (ie no unannounced arrivals). Deliveries should arrive via a checkpoint from where they are released only when signalled by the gate operatives.

The logistics operators (third-party logistics company) deliver materials onto the site during the evenings. The organization on site consists of a logistics manager, a planner and a foreperson who manage and plan the day-to-day operation together with the contractors. Also on the logistics staff are two goods-receiving materials controllers and six gate operatives. Planning and delivery management are carried out using the Log Net system.

The main advantage that the logistics approach at FUS1 has brought has been to secure an efficient flow of materials leading to reduced unproductive time. JIT deliveries in the evenings have contributed to making the site safer, with few accidents or incidents, and with good utilization of all available time.

A disadvantage has been that not all trade contractors are used to planning and are not able to correctly estimate their material needs. This occasionally results in too much material being called off and thus excessive material occupying space in working areas. Some suppliers were also unable to time their deliveries correctly, and this was resolved by introducing a buffer storage area at the checkpoint.

During the most intensive phase of FUS1 550 people were employed on site.

CASE STUDY Triangeln (the Triangle) – Malmö, Sweden

Project summary

In connection with the new award-winning railway station for commuter trains in Malmö, the construction company NCC Construction Sverige AB developed and built a new shopping centre, Triangeln. The project encompassed retail premises, offices and apartments. Construction took place between 2010 and 2014.

Key data:

- a shopping mall of 12,000 square metres;
- space for about 60 shops;
- a two-level, 12,000-square-metre car park below ground;
- 190 apartments over the shopping mall;
- a total cost of around SEK 1.3 billion (£100m/€130m);
- client: NCC Construction Sverige AB;
- main contractor: NCC Property Development AB.

The complexity of the project led to the decision to appoint a third-party logistics company with a dedicated logistics manager with full authority for decisions. The use of third-party logistics was motivated by the efficiency gained by one party taking responsibility for the entire logistics chain.

The site was located in the centre of Malmö, next to an underground railway station and the city tunnel; there was no space available for material storage. The logistics manager was given full authority to coordinate and plan deliveries, to turn away unplanned deliveries and unplanned vehicle arrivals, and to allocate material lay-down areas on the site. The project consisted of three different parts but to ensure optimal performance the logistics manager's role and authority extended across all three parts. The logistics staff included a receiving controller and full-time logistics operatives responsible for distribution of materials.

A further administrator/team leader was available in the final stages of the shop fit-out process when many external contractors were on site and needed coordination. An evening staff consisting of administrator, team leader and logistics operative maintained logistics activities after the main site working hours. The Log Net logistics and delivery planning system was used for all transport planning. Visual planning meetings were conducted once per week, involving the project managers of all contractors working on site.

At any one time, about 400 people were working on site; although over its lifetime more than 1,000 people have worked on the project. The logistics organization consisted, at peak, of five full-time employees during the daytime plus a delivery coordinator and a crew of about 20 people for the evening shift. By using a dedicated logistics team focused on creating a safe site with efficient material flow, the project became more resource efficient with less wasted materials and less waiting time.

Interview with the logistics manager Christos Asimakidis, Svensk Bygglogistik AB

What was your role in the project?
CA: As logistics manager I was responsible for planning all transport requirements, jointly with all site/zone managers representing all contractors on site. I had to create and maintain APD-plans [construction site layout plans], organize the use of the Log Net delivery management system and hold induction meetings with new contractors coming to site to ensure that from the start they learned to 'think logistics'. My role also involved maintaining communication with the client, following up the night-time activities and holding weekly meetings with all contractors, which included both logistics activities and all issues concerning site safety. The role meant total responsibility for all logistics within the project.

Was your role critical for the project?
CA: Before Bygglogistik joined the project there was no computerized system for delivery management. The site was located right in the centre of Malmö, next to an underground railway station and the city tunnel and there was no space available for material storage. Therefore, just-in-time deliveries were necessary. At some critical stages when concrete deliveries and deliveries of off-site manufactured elements coincided in time, detailed logistics planning was absolutely essential. Logistics planning was a new concept to many contractors and therefore a professional external logistics expert was needed to coordinate all contractors on site.

What is your advice to others running large or complex projects?
CA: You should make sure that logistics is part of the project planning right from the start. It is also important to be very strict and to firmly ensure that agreed rules and processes are adhered to; don't allow people to expect to get away with compromises. Make sure that the hierarchy of responsibility for logistics is understood and supported by the management. Try to make sure that all stakeholders and everyone working on site learn to 'think logistics' . Part of this is to invite client, contractors and suppliers to a joint session where a shared understanding of the logistics of the project can be established. Further workshops can be conducted to ensure processes are understood and everyone feels they are part of the operation.

Conclusion

Sustainability is to a large extent the same as minimizing the different resources used. To apply the suggested model for sustainable construction, logistics will certainly improve efficiency and thereby also the level of sustainability. To find relevant quantitative measures to substantiate this is more difficult. Each building project is unique and difficult to compare with others. Also, the building contractors consider their logistics performance indicators to be part of their competitive advantage and are therefore reluctant to publicize them. The advantages gained by the model suggested must therefore be obtained from a more qualitative discussion.

Most models for sustainability today are based on three elements: environmental sustainability, economic sustainability and social sustainability. To be considered as truly sustainable, all three elements must be considered.

Based on interviews with leading personnel from the two projects described earlier, where the suggested logistics structure has been implemented, the following advantages are noted compared with a 'traditional' logistics approach:

- Environmental sustainability:
  - Less construction material needed due to reduced damage during storage and handling.
  - Reduced transport activity (through consolidation) means lower fuel consumption and less noise and disturbance to neighbours.
  - Proper segregation of waste improves opportunities for reuse of material.
- Social sustainability:
  - Fewer accidents on site due to better housekeeping and ensuring that excessive material is kept 'out of the way'.
  - Fewer conflicts arising from missing material and misunderstandings, leading to an improved working climate.
- Economic sustainability:
  - Less damage to building materials.
  - Less waiting time for materials.
  - Improved utilization of equipment such as cranes, elevators and trucks resulting in a lower total need of equipment.
  - Lower total transport costs (note that JIT might increase the number of journeys needed while consolidation will reduce the number of journeys; a balance needs to be found).
  - Time schedules are met to a larger extent, which lowers cost through, for example, improved utilization of working hours.
  - If third-party solutions are used, the logistics cost is made transparent and thereby easier for management to control.
  - The material suppliers get a better overview of expected deliveries and are able to optimize production planning to a larger extent.
  - Risks are made visible and avoidance action can be taken earlier.

Our conclusion is that the suggested model for construction logistics clearly contributes to efficiency and sustainability.

Sweco is a leading international engineering consultant and architect company with its base in Scandinavia. The 9,000 employees are active within the areas of infrastructure, buildings, industry and energy. The mission is to actively contribute to the sustainable development of society.

Reference

World Commission on Environment and Development (1987) Our Common Future: From one earth to one world, *UN Documents* [Online] www.un-documents.net/our-common-future.pdf [accessed 16 April 2015] # Resource efficiency benefits of effective construction logistics

08

MALCOLM WADDELL

Introduction

Resource efficiency in construction and refurbishment projects can reduce costs, reduce risk and help to achieve climate change targets – while reducing the depletion of natural resources.

Sustainable construction involves the whole life cycle of a building or infrastructure project. This involves the overall sustainability of the project from environmental, economic and social impacts. The whole supply chain can work in collaboration to reduce the environmental impact of a construction project. From design to construction, in-use and maintenance through to reuse and demolition at the end of its life, resource-efficient principles help with issues such as biodiversity, costs, durability, resource scarcity, water and energy efficiency, better use of resource, and reduction of overall waste and waste to landfill.

Construction logistics is the control and management of material flow from source to point of use, as well as traditional site services. Taking into consideration resource efficiency and sustainability can have a significant benefit on a whole construction project's sustainability. This chapter will cover the environmental impacts of construction and where effective construction logistics can help to improve the overall sustainability of a construction project.

It will explore the opportunities across the supply chain, such as for manufacturers and suppliers to improve performance by adopting good practice in logistics, or how a principal contractor can improve performance through supply chain logistics planning.

Full supply chain logistics strategies are reviewed with appropriate resources highlighted for further information. Case study evidence will also be demonstrated across a range of project types.

Construction sustainability impact

Across the UK, the construction sector is the largest user of material resources in the UK, consuming around 400 million tonnes of materials per year, accounting for more than half the material consumption in the UK. In 2010, the waste arising across construction, demolition and excavation (CD&E) in England was around 100 million tonnes (GOV.UK, 2012). Within England in 2011, 13.1 million tonnes of construction, demolition and excavation waste were sent to landfill. Managing and disposing of waste costs the industry around 1 per cent of turnover – 30 per cent, or more, of pre-tax profit.

There is significant progress that has been made in the construction industry in the last few years to effectively manage this waste to maximize recovery and recycling and to reduce costs.

The UKCG Environment Group has agreed to work towards the following targets: 1) divert at least 90 per cent of construction and demolition (C&D) waste away from landfill, with the aspiration of achieving zero non-hazardous C&D waste to landfill by 2020; 2) halve construction waste production by 2020 (based on a 2010 baseline of 10.6 tonnes/£100,000). The UK Contractors Group (UKCG) diverted 91 per cent of all construction and demolition waste away from landfill.

Opportunities exist to reduce the amount of materials used at the project conception and design stage and to consider ways to design-out waste. Significant steps have been taken across the construction supply chain to address the waste, including initiatives such as Halving Waste to Landfill, managed by WRAP. This commitment was successful in reducing the amount of construction and demolition waste going to landfill by 65 per cent across the sector. Organizations who signed up and reported had more significant savings of 75 per cent reduction in waste to landfill.

A follow-on commitment is the Built Environment Commitment launched in July 2014 (UKCG, 2014). The commitment is an industry-wide initiative that will aim to deliver a low-carbon, resource-efficient built environment. Many have already begun to change how they work, others are at the start of their journey. The Built Environment Commitment brings all this action together and publicly demonstrates what each organization that signs up is committed to do.

Developed in consultation with industry, the Built Environment Commitment is a strategic priority of Construction 2025 – the industrial strategy for construction (GOV.UK, 2013). The Built Environment Commitment provides an easy and practical framework for action by businesses and sector bodies throughout all areas of the built environment to lower carbon and improve resource efficiency in their everyday activities. The framework gives flexibility to enable individual organizations to make their own journey of improvement. It supports the sector driving collective action, encouraging a consistent approach to measuring and reporting, and promoting sharing of good practice.

Resource Efficiency Benefits of Effective Construction Logistics

The commitment is led by a simple statement of intent to which all signatories sign up and publicly support: 'We commit to take action that contributes to a lower carbon, resource-efficient built environment.'

Signatories then individually establish what they specifically want to achieve in support of the statement of intent, and how they want to get there – they therefore each take an individual journey in lowering carbon and improving resource efficiency. This enables each signatory to reflect, for example: their current performance, corporate priorities, and aspects they can influence and take action on.

The built environment accounts for about half of the UK's carbon impact. An embodied-carbon database was developed by WRAP with the UK Green Building Council to gain an understanding of the carbon impact of different types of construction.

The Green Construction Board has developed a low-carbon route map for the built environment following extensive consultation across government and industry (2012). It serves as a visual tool that enables stakeholders to understand the policies, actions and key decision points required to achieve an 80 per cent reduction in greenhouse gas emissions in the built environment versus 1990 levels by 2050.

Figure 8.1 is taken from the WRAP website and demonstrates different business cases for improving resource efficiency during construction.

FIGURE 8.1 The case for action: resource efficiency in the built environment

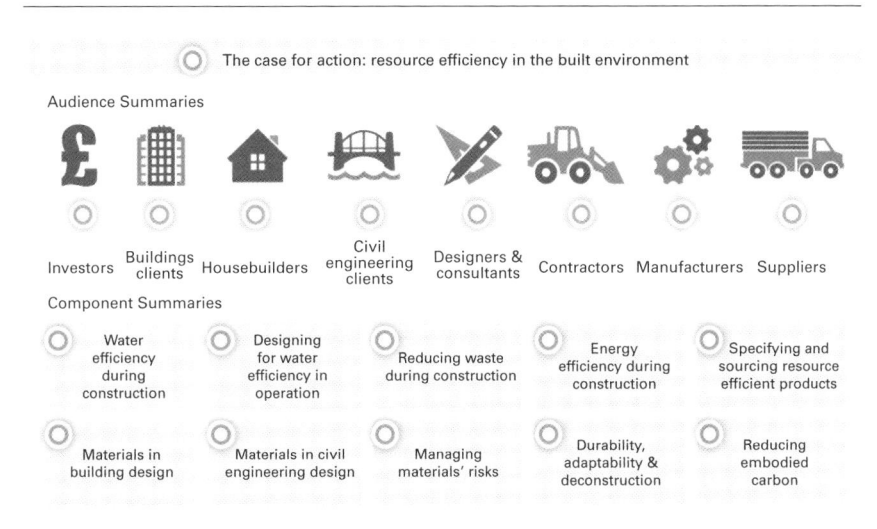

SOURCE: www.wrap.org.uk/construction

There is a range of opportunities to reduce material use, waste, embodied and operational carbon impact and water use such as:

- supply chain procurement;
- specifying and sourcing resource-efficient products that have, for instance, a lower impact in carbon emissions, waste and/or water;
- design for resource efficiency;
- energy efficiency;
- water efficiency;
- effective construction logistics (this will be explored in more detail later in this chapter);
- reuse;
- waste management.

Legislation and standards

The Building Regulations also include reference to sustainability (Planning Portal, 2015). The Code for Sustainable Homes is included within this and is the national standard for the sustainable design and construction of new homes (BREEAM, 2012). The code aims to reduce carbon emissions by creating homes that are more sustainable. It assesses the design of new homes against nine categories of sustainable design:

- energy/CO_2;
- water;
- materials;
- surface water runoff;
- waste;
- pollution;
- health and well-being;
- management;
- ecology.

The code uses a one- to six-star rating system to communicate the overall sustainability performance of a new home. One star is the entry level – above the level of the Building Regulations; six stars is the highest level – reflecting exemplar development in sustainability terms.

Other standards to demonstrate the sustainability of a project, which are used across the UK construction sector, are BREEAM (Building Research Establishment (BRE) Environmental Assessment Methodology), SKA rating (an environmental assessment tool for sustainable fit-outs) and CEEQUAL for civil engineering projects.

Supply chain influence on sustainable construction logistics

Clients

Effective logistics practices should be considered throughout the supply chain. The client can ensure it is included as part of an overarching sustainability policy and it can help an organization to meet its carbon reduction targets.

A client can promote more effective logistics by including it as criteria within the procurement process. This could involve attributing scoring to it in tender evaluation and asking for responses on an organization's approach to logistics. Key performance indicators (KPIs) should be set for organizations to report on how they are performing, such as miles travelled, carbon impact, type of vehicle, driver training and empty miles.

Design

Designers can have the largest influence on resource efficiency in the supply chain. The earlier that such opportunities are identified in the design stage, the greater impact they have. Having resource efficiency on the agenda and using planning support tools and guidance such as Design for Resource Efficiency (WRAP, 2015) can help to identify solutions to improve the resource efficiency of a project. A tool that is being used more and more on construction projects is building information modelling (BIM). This is a digital representation of physical and functional characteristics of a facility. A BIM is a shared knowledge resource for information about a facility, which forms a reliable basis for decisions during its life cycle, from earliest conception to completion.

When using BIM, all materials are specified in detail: dimensions, quantities and other characteristics including environmental data such as embodied carbon. Expected waste volumes can be accurately estimated and efforts can be made to minimize. This helps to avoid over-ordering and identify opportunities for reuse. When using BIM on a succession of similar projects, a continuous improvement cycle can be achieved by involving all parties across the supply chain to improve on report and data integrity. The supply chain is involved in the project at an early phase and the improved relationships and sharing of knowledge will aid in identifying and implementing developing opportunities. When using BIM, it can support resource-efficient logistics through improved product specifications in terms of type and quantity, which improves the development of a material logistics plan and scheduling of material, labour and equipment.

Contractors

A contractor could consider logistics strategies such as employing an on-site logistics specialist, or using a fourth-party logistics operator. Where the location of the site makes it suitable or where economies of scale exist, the use of a construction consolidation centre (CCC) should be considered or options for using an existing CCC or partnering may be appropriate.

Suppliers

Suppliers often operate their own transport or have direct management of the logistics subcontractors, so they have significant opportunities to affect the transport practices. For example, specifying that drivers have undertaken a fuel-efficient training course (or similar) may mean around a 15 per cent saving in fuel cost.

Offering a reverse logistics collection service on the back of deliveries for unused products, reusable packaging or wasted packaging can reduce costs and increase revenue as well as having a reduction in carbon emissions.

A common challenge in construction (and other industries) is where a supplier specifies that their products must be delivered on a vehicle that has a livery that they have contracted to deliver to site or that is bespoke to their brand. This can cause extra costs and 'brand miles' to be travelled where unnecessary transport takes place for no other reason than the requirement to deliver a product on a vehicle carrying a particular brand. For example, a builders' merchant may have been contracted to deliver a product on its own branded vehicles, so a haulier may do extra miles (even passing the final delivery point) to deliver to the merchant who then reloads the product for future delivery. Although there are advantages in terms of brand recognition, by working in partnership with the supply chain, opportunities can be realized for reduced miles, reduced site deliveries, consolidated loads and less handling of products.

Waste management contractors can support contractors by measuring and reporting qualitative and key performance indicators. There is an advisory role in helping the contractor with the accuracy of their data. Improving quality of outputs will therefore increase the viability and likelihood of recovery, recycling and reuse. Guidance and reporting tools can be found on the Construction MRF page of the WRAP website (**www.wrap.org.uk**).

Construction logistics strategies and how they can influence resource efficiency

There is a range of logistics strategies that can be implemented to improve the management of a construction project. Each project has to be studied on its own merits in order to decide what is the most appropriate logistics strategy.

Consideration of how, when and how much material to deliver to site and to which point of the site is a key decision and has an impact on the future use of the materials. Too much material on site can create storage issues, health and safety hazards, decreased productivity and increased waste.

This section gives an introduction to a number of logistics strategies along with case study examples of where they have been implemented effectively. Not all the logistics strategies will work on each type of project and some will be more suitable than others, so consideration is needed on a project for which strategies to consider and implement. An understanding of these is important – not every strategy is right for every project. Engagement with the construction project supply chain should be undertaken at an early stage in exploring these options.

Reverse logistics

This is the process of managing the collection of unused material to be recovered for reuse or resale, or the collection of waste such as wasted products or packaging to be reprocessed. There are a number of benefits to introducing an effective reverse logistics operation such as:

- reduced costs;
- effective waste management;
- reduced carbon – from reduced transport mileage and vehicle use;
- health and safety – vehicles on construction sites are one of the most common causes of accidents, so reducing vehicles on site results in less risk;
- site efficiency – from reduced vehicles to reducing the time that material is on site and identifying opportunities for material recovery.

Where manufacturers can recycle the offcuts of their materials back into new product, take-back schemes are becoming increasingly popular. For example, plasterboard manufacturers in the UK have committed to a voluntary scheme called the Ashdown Agreement. This is in its second phase and at the time of writing, key targets are:

- zero gypsum waste to landfill by 2025;
- zero manufacturing waste to landfill by 2015;
- 50 per cent of new construction waste recycled by 2015.

Reverse logistics can help with the first and third of these targets. The plasterboard manufacturers all use a proportion of recycled plasterboard in their new manufactured product. This can be got from recyclers who provide a collection service. In addition, the manufacturers offer a collection facility for wasted plasterboard from construction sites at a competitive cost via the hauliers they use. This will be taken to a recycling centre near their manufacturing plant for recycle and reuse.

For smaller sites that have deliveries from merchants, they may be able to get a merchant offering a collection service. For example, EJ Berry & Sons Ltd with Recycling Solutions Ltd offer a collection service on the back of their delivery vehicles, which may visit a number of sites on each route. For a £15 million sheltered housing village project managed by construction contractor Leadbitter this solution was offered and made an annual saving of £1,200 in waste management costs for plasterboard, in addition to reduced transport miles of just over 1,000 miles.

Transport

There is a range of ways that transport can be made more efficient and reduce costs and carbon emissions.

4PL

Using fourth-party logistics involves a logistics company that coordinates the logistics providers and can ensure that they operate effectively. This could involve combining loads for collecting from a range of suppliers and arranging deliveries to construction sites whereby routing is more effective, reducing mileage overall and improving vehicle utilization. If, for example, a company has a number of depots that each book their own transport using local hauliers, there is no coordination and return logistics opportunities are missed.

Using a 4PL operator, each depot logs its transport requirements on a central web-based system. All participating hauliers are also on the system and can see available assignments. The system analyses the assignments and the network and proposes optimal transport arrangements, eg multi-leg journeys instead of one-way journeys with empty return legs. This kind of operation can also be extended to cover more than one client – achieving even higher efficiency. The web-based system provides entirely transparent information, allowing costs to be fairly allocated to users.

Aggregate Industries is a leading player in the construction industry, committed to creating a better built environment through sustainable approaches. Using a 4PL operated by Norbert Dentressangle (a major European transport, logistics, and freight-forwarding company), Aggregate Industries increased the return load opportunities by 16 per cent (2013). This led to a 12 per cent mileage reduction and a carbon saving of 4,700 tonnes during its first year of operation (WRAP, 2010).

Transport types

Types of transport used should be considered. On some sites, the mode of transport can provide carbon savings. For example, at Media City in Salford Quays, barge transport was used, which is more fuel efficient than road transport. Rail transport can also be considered where feasible. Where delivery by road is the only option, the type of vehicle should be considered, from van deliveries for small loads to ensuring vehicle optimization for other loads.

Route planning should also be considered as an option for reducing fuel consumption. Often the shortest routes by mileage will offer the lowest fuel use, but if the shortest route would have an adverse impact on the miles per gallon, a route that has a slightly longer distance may be quicker and use less fuel. Computerized vehicle routing systems can be used to highlight typical miles per gallon by road type and total fuel use by route. Truck manufacturers are increasingly offering vehicles with improved fuel efficiency. The up-front cost of investing in these vehicles will be more than outweighed by the future savings from reduced fuel consumption (Fleet Fuel Efficiency, 2012).

By using material logistics planning (discussed later in this chapter) the deliveries can be planned to reduce driver waiting time and inefficient fuel use. An estimated 80 per cent of vehicles delivering to a construction site leave empty. This is an underutilized resource and should be identified for reverse logistics opportunities.

Driver training can also have an impact on costs, reducing fuel use. A variety of training courses are offered from a range of companies. This could be put as a prerequisite in procurement, ensuring drivers have had appropriate fuel awareness and safe driver training. Driver training will clearly have environmental benefits and offers solutions for drivers in different driving scenarios. Fuel-efficient driving teaches various techniques and skills to reduce fuel consumption, thus increasing vehicle efficiency and reducing costs. Examples of how cost savings can be achieved are:

- reduced fuel costs;
- reduced maintenance (such as wear and tear of brakes, engine and tyres);
- improving the resale value of vehicles;
- improved vehicle utilization;
- reduced cost of accidents;
- insurance premium cost reduction.

The style of driving that is coached also reduces stress and fatigue and improves health and safety, reducing the risk of an accident. Examples of some of the solutions are:

- turning off the engine when idle;
- using the vehicle's momentum;
- driving in a higher gear at appropriate speeds;
- smoother driving by anticipating and slowing down where necessary and reducing the use of brakes or high acceleration;
- checking the maintenance of the vehicle regularly as this can impact on its efficiency (such as under-inflated tyres, which in addition to increased risk also increase the fuel consumption);
- load positioning.

Packaging

Packaging is one of the main waste streams in the fit-out stage of a construction project. Wood, plastics, polystyrene and cardboard are generated in large quantities. While these materials can be segregated and recycled often they are stuck together and just thrown in a general skip. Even if they are segregated, this is a labour-intensive process and generates a lot of subsequent handling.

Reusable pallets and packaging can virtually eliminate this waste. Reusing packaging in the construction supply chain can cut cost, waste and carbon emissions compared with single-trip packaging. Construction product suppliers can realize these benefits by working with the supply chain and using various types of reusable packaging.

Pallets can be made very durable and are able to withstand many handling cycles; while the box section on the pallet is collapsible and occupies very little space on the return journey to the supplier.

There is an up-front cost to introducing reusable packaging but this is offset by many advantages:

- often greater product protection, reducing losses from product damage;
- carbon emissions from producing, transporting and disposing of the packaging (even if waste packaging is 100 per cent recycled) are reduced;
- weatherproofing;
- efficient storage, handling and health and safety;
- reduced cost of waste in both total waste (less packaging waste) and handling.

Consideration should be given to the number of break-even trips that are required in order to have a beneficial impact on cost and carbon emissions. Some reusable packaging will only require a few trips to reach a point where it is cost and environmentally beneficial.

Aggregate Industries instigated a trial scheme for the repatriation of pallets to evaluate if reuse is feasible [2011]. Following that trial, Aggregate Industries rolled out the use of reusable pallets to its largest nationwide customer, B&Q. Four new pallets are replacing eight old pallets and they are designed with repatriation in mind. These are relatively low-cost pallets, making it challenging to make a financial case for repatriation. If, however, about 50 per cent of pallets can be reused at least once, then a cost break-even – as compared to one-way pallets – is reached. At this level of reuse considerable reductions in waste can be achieved: wood waste reduction – 996 tonnes per annum; reduction in embodied carbon – 199 tonnes per annum.

If this level of reuse were to be applied across the entire product range, waste savings of up to 3,000 tonnes would be within reach.

Off-site manufacturing

Off-site manufacturing (OSM) has a range of benefits compared to traditional build, including the potential to greatly minimize on-site waste. Through the substitution of a range of OSM methods there is the potential to reduce on-site wastage by up to 90 per cent. Although some waste will be transferred to the factory environment, the amount will be significantly reduced. In this environment there can also be greater opportunities for reuse or recycling. It shortens project lead times, enhances productivity, improves quality and is also an extremely effective waste-reduction strategy.

OSM comes in many shapes and forms, from timber frame construction to whole plots or blocks that can be fitted in place, or bathroom pods or wall sections complete with windows, insulation, wiring etc. Another interesting example of OSM is for mechanical and electrical (M&E) services – pipework, water, waste, power, signal wiring etc; these can be pre-fitted in frame sections 2–3 metres long and then simply lifted into place and connected. This leads to enormous efficiency gains on site and waste is virtually eliminated.

Using OSM changes site practices and means the process becomes a quicker assembly process, thus reducing labour requirements. Other benefits are: reducing the amount of trades and site activities and changing the construction process into one of a rapid assembly of parts. This can provide many environmental, commercial and social benefits, including:

- speed of build;
- programme certainty (less risk of adverse conditions);
- reduced site transport;
- improved health and safety by reduced accidents and risk;
- improved workmanship quality and reduced on-site errors and re-work, which cause considerable on-site waste, delay and disruption.

WRAP produced a range of examples of case studies on off-site manufacture, as discussed below.

Ropemaker is a British Land commercial building on a prominent London city site. The site has 586,000 square feet of net lettable space, with 21 storeys and three basement levels. The high-profile development has impressive green credentials, including a BREEAM 'excellent' rating, and during its construction exploited a number of opportunities for OSM. Products manufactured off site include Podwall washrooms supplied by Swift Horsman, and Technik flooring supplied by Grants Ltd. Both systems were monitored on site using CaliBRE and SMARTWaste tools to evaluate the efficiency of the construction process and measure the waste generated. Other environmental and cost factors were also assessed. More details can be found in the case study. The results demonstrated that:

- The Technik floor product reduces overall waste and costs compared with traditional flooring.
- The Podwall product brings impressive gains in site labour efficiency and waste reduction, leading to a cleaner and more organized site, with the cost of the product being similar to traditional construction.

Jocelyn Park is a housing development owned and managed by South Somerset Homes Housing Association. There are 64 homes on site designed by Calford Seadon, reaching EcoHomes 'very good'. Advanced Panel System (APS) manufactured the timber frame. This case study provides a comprehensive comparison between the APS semi-closed panel timber frame system used in Jocelyn Park and a brick and block system used on the SmartLIFE project, also fully assessed using BRE monitoring tools. Some of the benefits were:

- The APS system has a very similar cost to traditional brick and block.
- Volume of waste reduced by 27.3 per cent during construction using APS semi-closed panel timber frame system.
- 27 per cent less labour required for house construction using APS.
- APS reduces non-added-value time compared to traditional build.

The Royal School of Military Engineering had new accommodation blocks completed in 2013 [WRAP, 2010]. They employed Caledonian Building Systems as the main contractor and the modular approach allowed a considerably shorter project time frame, a high quality of construction, greater certainty of project costs and a significantly reduced number of deliveries entering the construction site. Other benefits were:

- a reduction in vehicle movements of 82 per cent to site as a result of off-site manufacturing;
- labour minimized to around 20–25 per cent of that required for traditional build;
- identified opportunities for minimizing packaging;
- encouraged the use of reusable packaging;
- worked with suppliers to ensure cut-to-size components.

Network Rail's £850 million redevelopment of Reading train station was built in a significantly reduced construction time when compared to traditional construction. This involved a three-storey depot administration building, two ancillary buildings for train maintenance and cleaning staff, a security gatehouse and a train care accommodation building. The steel-framed modules for each building were manufactured off site at the Yorkon production centre. A pre-installed concrete floor option was also installed for enhanced performance. Benefits included:

- improved quality and reduced future maintenance;
- minimized disruption;
- programme times reduced by 50 per cent;
- wasted material reduced by 90 per cent;
- 90 per cent fewer vehicle movements on site.

Just-in-time delivery

One of the core problems in construction is that there is often too much material on site. The results are: congestion, which impedes work and creates safety hazards; damage to materials in handling and storage; double handling when materials have to be moved first to one work-face then another; and reduced productivity.

Just-in-time (JIT) delivery is a service of frequent deliveries in work packs or task loads, 'pulled' just in time for the trade to perform the next task without incurring any delays. Suppliers are not allowed to 'push' materials onto the site until they are required. Staged deliveries and only one or two days' worth of materials on site make for a cleaner and more efficient workplace and lower the wastage rates. To be successfully managed a JIT strategy can benefit from the use of a delivery management system to control the material flows and the use of critical resources.

More frequent deliveries may of course have the adverse effect of increasing transport and associated carbon emissions, which is why it is most successfully employed in combination when the inbound deliveries from different suppliers can be consolidated. The strategy has been very successfully employed in connection with logistics centres, often called construction consolidation centres (CCC).

Demand smoothing

This is a technique that involves analysing the project programme and smoothing the peaks and troughs in demand for either materials or labour. By smoothing out these peaks, 'pinch points' can be reduced as these high areas of activity often result in errors and waste. This would mean that peak periods of activity would be avoided where excess deliveries and work are required, whereby the labour usage can be kept at a more consistent level and periods where labour is being underutilized avoided.

On-site logistics specialist

Employing a logistics team or logistics manager will ensure that the management of deliveries and distribution materials, equipment and plant are dealt with more effectively. This can help planning, for both demand smoothing and JIT deliveries. It will make sure that double and triple handling is eliminated and that materials are stored and delivered to the correct point and handled only at point of construction.

Skilled labour spend around half their time moving material or unloading lorries; having a dedicated team of people for this would mean that trade time would be more effectively used and require fewer hours overall. Unproductive labour time on a construction project is spent waiting for materials, or due to materials being at the wrong place and needing to be moved on one or more occasions.

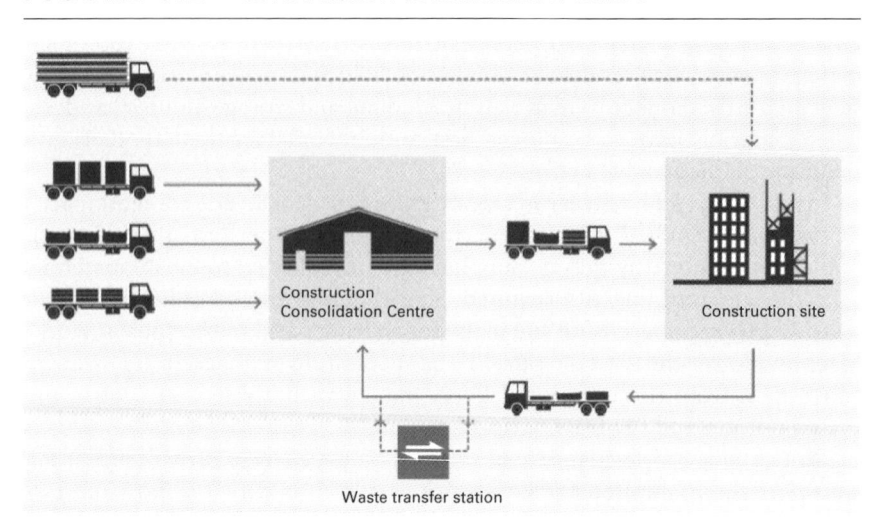

FIGURE 8.2 Construction consolidation centre

Construction consolidation centres

A construction consolidation centre (CCC) is a distribution facility through which material deliveries are channelled to construction sites (Figure 8.2). Specialist material handling, storage and consolidated delivery combine to improve the overall resource efficiency of a construction project.

Some projects will be more suitable for the use of a CCC than others, but if applied to projects of suitable scale and in a suitable location, it has been demonstrated in a range of case studies that using a CCC can:

- reduce overall project costs (though consider sharing these throughout the supply chain);
- make timescales more certain as there is less risk on programme delivery;
- reduce freight traffic to site by up to 70 per cent;
- allow orders to be more bespoke, reducing over-ordering;
- be ideal for reverse logistics such as ease of reuse and recovery of packaging;
- increase productivity of site labour by 30 minutes per day leading to a 6 per cent productivity gain;
- cut waste reduction by 7–15 per cent through less material damage and shrinkage.

CCCs are covered in more detail in Chapter 12.

Waste management and reprocessing logistics opportunities

Waste management contractors have a number of effective logistics methods they can use to improve overall efficiency.

For example, different types and sizes of construction site may have different requirements for waste. Waste management contractors can work with the site and offer the best solutions that will reduce the amount of space needed for waste, offer the best options for segregation and container type for different waste and consider collection schedules [WRAP, 2009].

Collection schedules in other industries are often consistently planned in, but on construction sites a degree of flexibility should be offered that will ensure best container fill thus improving vehicle utilization; this should also vary by material type.

Using equipment for recycling or shredding can reduce skip and transport costs (and the associated carbon emissions). For example, the Green Grinder was used on an 800-flat development project with Higgins Construction in Lambeth, south London in 2014 and reduced the skip requirement for wood waste from 83 skips to 19. The resultant waste could then be used for composting (Figure 8.3).

FIGURE 8.3 Wood waste to be converted to compost

The construction of a hospital in Birmingham was a joint venture between Balfour Beatty and Hayden Young, commonly referred to as the Birmingham New Hospital Joint Venture. It used an on-site waste compactor supplied by the waste contractor Premier Waste UK PLC [WRAP, 2010b], which yielded the following benefits:

- The compactor on site can contain the equivalent of 13 8-yard skips, reducing the movements of compactable waste off site thirteenfold.
- The use of the compactor saved 148 miles per day in waste transport, reducing the wear on the vehicle and equating to approximately 12 gallons of diesel per day.
- The transfer station achieved a diversion rate from landfill of 93–98 per cent of the mixed construction waste collected.

Delivery management systems

Use of a delivery management system can give all relevant contractors and managers on site visibility of planned and actual deliveries. The system will also provide useful follow-up on suppliers' performance with regard to timekeeping and accuracy of deliveries. This is invaluable in ongoing and future negotiations with suppliers. There are a variety of planning benefits including:

- avoiding queuing on site and to the site;
- ensuring the available equipment and labour is planned;
- can be used to record material used and wastage;
- improved productivity on site for labour and material handling;
- delivery vehicles arriving in sequence and on schedule;
- environmental benefits from reduced impact on resources.

One example is Zone Manager, which assists with multi-user planning and real-time operational tools focused on the construction industry (The Logistics Business, 2011). This was used at Media City in Salford. Connolly Construction Facilities Management (CCF) opted to use the full Zone Manager system, including the web-based interface. They decided to allow trade contractors to make their own bookings directly via the web. Whilst this reduces the workload for CCF's logistics team considerably, it must, of course, be tightly controlled. Zone Manager's ability to restrict contractors to specific zones and times, and the ability to prevent 'last-minute' changes, are therefore very important.

Material logistics planning

This helps to effectively manage construction projects to ensure they run smoothly, on schedule and managing the right materials arriving at the right place at the right time.

A material logistics plan (MLP) is a tool used to assist the proactive management of material types and quantities to be used during construction. The MLP covers the management of materials from design to construction (including supply routes, handling, storage, security, use and reuse, recycling and disposal) through to project demobilization and completion.

Using an MLP from the project conception stage can help construction clients and contractors to identify opportunities to introduce logistics strategies, which will help cut costs, improve efficiencies, reduce the environmental impact and increase a company's competitiveness.

By managing deliveries to construction sites more effectively and reducing the number of journeys required, transport efficiency can be improved and help cut costs for both freight operators and their clients. By minimizing the impacts of freight transport we can help to make our country a better place for all.

Efficient logistics planning is good practice for all construction sites, regardless of location, value or complexity. The contractor will benefit from good logistics planning in terms of a well-organized site; effective deliveries and collections; reduced waste resulting from over-ordering or damaged materials; minimized disruption to local residents, businesses and road users. Local authorities frequently require a logistics plan as part of a planning application, and other organizations, such as Transport for London, are instrumental in coordination of activities to keep traffic moving. Transport for London promotes construction logistics plans (CLPs) to provide a framework to better manage all types of freight-vehicle movement to and from construction sites. A developer should draft the CLP as part of the transport assessment. The key stages of MLP are shown in relation to the construction process in Figure 8.1.

Logistics planning should be initiated at the project outset in order to achieve the greatest material savings. Ideally the client should develop and maintain a clear strategy for best practice logistics planning based on their corporate goals and policies. The logistics strategy will define the approach to planning for individual projects. The development of a project-specific logistics plan is generally the responsibility of the main contractor. However, the principles should be identified at project concept and outline design stage in order to minimize wastage through eliminating bespoke designs; for example, reducing the proportion of unique window sizes.

Conclusion

It can be demonstrated that effective logistics practices in construction can benefit the whole supply chain and have tangible sustainability benefits, which go hand in hand with financial and business benefits.

As a summary, the supply chain can benefit in the following ways:

Clients:

- Faster project programmes.
- Improved project certainty such as through using a MLP.
- Promoting logistics planning through a project and demonstrating how it will have lower overall costs.
- Reduced impact on the environment through reduced traffic, a better-organized site and minimization of waste.
- Putting requirements on logistics in the procurement documentation to ensure that carbon impacts and logistics techniques are considered.

Main contractors:

- Improved programme certainty.
- Reduced over-ordering of materials by planning deliveries and allowing for take-back of unused material. Over-ordering at a 15 per cent level is not unusual; allowing take-back should allow contractors to target a 10 per cent reduction in waste.
- Improved site conditions with less material on site and waste, which improves site efficiency and reduces risk of accidents.
- Lower costs and improved competitiveness.
- Reduced waste and carbon emissions, enabling the attainment of environmental objectives.

Manufacturers:

- Offering reverse logistics solutions can improve recycling opportunities and future sales.
- Set up services to recover pallets and packaging.
- Cut-to-size component direct to site will reduce waste on site.
- Review fleet to reduce carbon impact or, if subcontracted transport, impose KPIs and targets on their mileage and carbon emissions.
- Work with industry to develop an action plan for the product to ensure logistics practices are consistent across the sector, such as with resource efficiency action plans.
- Review pack sizes to ensure best vehicle fill.

Suppliers/merchants:

- Offering reverse logistics solutions can improve recycling opportunities and future sales.
- Set up services to recover pallets and packaging.
- Cut-to-size components from suppliers will reduce waste on site.
- Plot-lot ordering will reduce handling and improve efficiency on site.

- Reduce excessive packaging, which reduces the material impact and cost.
- Look for consolidation opportunities and shared transport.
- Discuss and plan scheduling improvements.

Haulier/logistics providers:

- Consideration of vehicle and fuel type will reduce carbon impact and cost and driver training will also have a significant positive impact.
- Faster vehicle turnaround time at sites with planned timeslots, reducing idle time, increasing vehicle utilization. Using a CCC will also reduce vehicle turnaround time.
- Better vehicle fill through shared loads, plot-lot ordering can receive and store materials in a good environment and then deliver smaller lot sizes to site.
- Coordinate and plan deliveries and collections across several suppliers, which will improve vehicle utilization, reduce mileage and reduce overall supply chain costs and carbon emissions.
- Increasing the opportunities of reverse logistics such as collecting unused material or packaging. An estimated 80 per cent of vehicles delivering to a construction site leave empty and this is an underutilized opportunity.
- 3PL companies often have existing depot networks and these can be used to stage deliveries. Economical full vehicle loads are shipped from supplier to depot, and smaller, JIT quantities are then taken to site by suitably sized vehicles.
- On-site logistics management can help by collecting and storing offcuts, reusable materials and surplus materials and managing an on-site marketplace for non-specific materials such as tools, PPE and consumables.

Waste management contractors:

- Offering appropriate receptacles for different materials and packaging.
- Collecting when waste is ready and full may offer reduced costs and transport when compared to scheduled deliveries (on a construction site, this is not as consistent as on other types of projects).
- Alternatively, or in addition, a milk-round collection service of local sites could ensure vehicle utilization and be useful for sites with limited space.
- Using mobile waste processing equipment such as a compactor, shredder or grinder can reduce skip requirements and ongoing transport mileages and carbon impact.

References

BREEAM (2012) Code for Sustainable Homes (CSH) Assessor, *BREEAM* [online] http://www.breeam.org/page.jsp?id=359 [accessed 20 March 2015]

Fleet Fuel Efficiency (2015) Top tips for fuel efficiency, *Fleet Fuel Efficiency* [online] http://fleet-fuel-efficiency.eu/en/fuel-calculator/top-tips-for-fuel-efficiency [accessed 3 April 2015]

GOV.UK (2012) Methodology for Estimating Annual Waste Generation from the Construction, Demolition and Excavation (CD&E) Sectors in England, *GOV.UK* [online] www.gov.uk/government/publications/construction-and-demolition-waste [accessed 5 May 2015]

GOV.UK (2013) Construction 2025: Strategy, *GOV.UK* [online] www.gov.uk/government/publications/construction-2025-strategy [accessed 15 February 2015]

Green Construction Board (2012) Low Carbon Routemap for the Built Environment, *Green Construction Board* [online] www.greenconstructionboard.org/index.php/resources/routemap [accessed 30 April 2015]

Norbert Dentressangle (2013) Aggregate Industries, *Norbert Dentressangle* [online] www.norbert-dentressangle.co.uk/Transport/Optimised-4PL-Solutions-KeyPL/Case-Studies/Aggregate-Industries [accessed 1 February 2015]

Planning Portal (2015) Building Regulations, *Planning Portal* [online] www.planningportal.gov.uk/buildingregulations [accessed 2 May 2015]

The Logistics Business (2011) Zone Manager – Delivery Management Software, *The Logistics Business* [online] www.logistics.co.uk/zone-manager [accessed 12 February 2015]

UKCG (2014) Built Environment Commitment, *WRAP* [online] www.wrap.org.uk/sites/files/wrap/UKCG%20Built%20Environment%20Commitment.pdf [accessed 4 March 2015]

WRAP [2009] www.wrap.org.uk. Please search for 'MRF 107' in the search bar

WRAP [2010] www.wrap.org.uk. Please search for 'RSME Minley' in the search bar

WRAP [2010b] www.wrap.org.uk. Please search for 'Premier Waste UK PLC' in the search bar

WRAP [2011] www.wrap.org.uk. Please search for 'pallets and packaging' in the search bar

WRAP (2010) 4th party logistics (4PL), *WRAP* [online] http://moodle.wrap.org.uk/wrap/modules2008/server_files/module10/page13.html [accessed 5 April 2015]

WRAP (2015) What is Designing for Resource Efficiency?, *WRAP* [online] www.wrap.org.uk/content/designing-resource-efficiency [accessed 4 May 2015]

PART FOUR
Logistics operations

The role of the construction logistics manager

09

ANDY BROWN

Introduction

In this section we look at the role that logistics managers have in the construction industry. This chapter includes a definition of the responsibilities of this recently recognized role, which has been proposed to the industry by the author. It investigates the different strands of the logistics manager's work within the industry and suggests a framework for creating a construction logistics plan (CLP) – the key tool of the construction logistics manager, which should be used to plan how they will deliver each construction project. The chapter ends with a discussion of future developments for construction logistics professionals and a conclusion that discusses the mid-term future of this sector.

The construction logistics manager role is arguably the youngest recognized role within construction operations. Whilst the need has been ever present, it was historically undertaken by a number of personnel within the team, rather than separating into a defined role delivered by one, or a team of individuals.

In the UK the role was born in the 1980s on large, complex sites with difficult interfaces in and around the city of London. As the city has become more developed, and construction has had more regulation applied to it, the need to fully understand these regulations, and be able to overcome the constraints they create, has become more recognized by construction business leaders and innovative businesses.

Technical experience for the role initially came from ex-service personnel, generally trained in logistics by the British Army. This was followed by construction professionals looking to specialize. Only in the last decade has there begun to be some transference from the mainstream construction and logistics sector into the role.

When innovative corporations first envisaged construction logistics as a separate discipline, the construction industry did not use the term logistics. Today, logistics is discussed specifically, in detail, by all of those in the construction process, on sites large and small, whether they have a dedicated logistics manager or not.

Construction is essentially an assembly process. Value is added as components are correctly assembled. In order for the construction process to be successful, resources in the form of materials, operatives, plants, tools, information, services and utilities need to flow efficiently and converge simultaneously at the workface.

Construction logistics is the process of planning, implementing and controlling the efficient and effective flow and management of resources from point of origin to point of consumption for the purpose of supporting the construction process.

These core logistical challenges are faced by almost all large construction projects and programmes in a similar manner, whether a logistics professional is engaged or not. It is for this reason that most industry-leading contractors choose to look for logistics professionals to drive through solutions from inception to completion rather than disseminate elements throughout the delivery team.

The following are generally considered to be the core elements of construction logistics:

- site security;
- temporary infrastructure;
- site team accommodation;
- freight – delivery management, logistics centres, material handling and distribution;
- people – access and egress routes and movement to and within the site;
- temporary services – power, water, drainage, communications and fire safety systems;
- maintenance of temporary infrastructure;
- waste management and recycling (including reverse logistics);
- fire management;
- occupational health and first aid management;
- environmental control and management;
- stakeholder engagement and management;
- monitoring, compliance and reporting.

Clients understand the importance of logistics today. They understand the effect on quality, cost and programme that poor logistics planning can have. They expect it to be done well, and look for confirmation of this in their tender returns.

Within the industry, the number of site logistics managers continues to rise. Senior logistics professionals are now involved in the planning of major projects. The value threshold of engaging a logistics professional early continues to drop as the added value of their involvement continues to be proven.

Logistics professional and service sourcing

There are a number of ways in which the construction industry engages with, and procures, logistics professionals and logistics services. Logistics knowledge is brought into the team via one or a combination of the following:

- in-house dedicated professionals;
- consultancy staff, to be managed by the contractor (or, occasionally, the client on large programmes);
- agency staff, to be managed by the contractor (or, occasionally, the client on large programmes);
- a logistics package contractor (which can be an in-house division or a separate organization);
- third-party logistics (known as 3PL) companies.

In-house professionals

These are the most experienced construction logistics professionals and have generally cut their teeth working for organizations that were the early adopters of the role as a definitive work-stream.

They are generally employed by major UK contractors. (However, it should be noted that not all UK Contractors Group (UKCG) major contractors employ them and the role is still not recognized at some of the household-name contractors at the time of writing.)

Where they do employ them, major contractors will generally engage logistics professionals at tender stage for large, complex or must-win projects.

Consultancy staff

Major construction and project management consultancies may carry logistics professionals whom they market to client organizations and other consultancies alike. These consultants will often provide large construction projects and major programmes with construction logistics advice until such time as a contractor is appointed, and may get involved in evaluating the contractors' offer on behalf of the client.

Multinational logistics organizations often have consultancy arms who are viewing the construction market as an opportunity for them and have begun moving into this market.

Agency staff

As in most other professions, there are plenty of experienced logistics professionals who enjoy the more flexible nature of working through an agency. Often such staff have a number of existing relationships with clients and contractors and they will find their own employment.

These staff should be able to be found right through the construction delivery team, from those representing the client (or their project managers) through to the principal contractor and into the subcontract supply chain.

Logistics package contractors

These were the earliest providers of the logistics professionals in the construction industry. The organization works as a subcontractor to the main or principal contractor and provides a package of works that deliver the logistics elements that support the project, led by a construction logistics manager.

Logistics package contractors will supply staff in a consulting role where they have the capacity to do so or can see a works package or further business development opportunity that could come from early involvement.

Third-party logistics companies

Third-party logistics providers typically specialize in integrated operation, warehousing and transportation services that can be scaled and customized to customers' demands and their delivery service requirements.

These huge organizations are eyeing the equally huge construction market and see opportunity. As such they are offering consultancy and subcontracting services to the construction industry in order to position themselves for what they see as an emerging market opportunity.

There is a split between a logistics professional being positioned in an organization as a consultant and a logistics professional being provided as part of a wider package. The example shown in the box on p 165 illustrates why organizations that can deliver logistics packages as a contractor would be drawn to do so, over and above simply supplying their corporate intellect to manage logistics.

> If a full logistics package is worth a conservative 5 per cent of the works value and the logistics contractor makes (again conservatively) a 10 per cent margin, then a logistics package contractor stands to turn over £5 million and make at the very least £500,000 profit on a £100 million major project. The logistics subcontractor will hope to stretch their scope and increase their margin as much as possible.
>
> However, if they were providing a £100 million project offering their knowledge and expertise in consultancy form, they might provide £400,000 worth of managers over a couple of years and net just £100,000 in profit (with no opportunity to stretch that margin).

We can see from the example why logistics package suppliers tend to wish to supply contracting services rather than consulting services and why many contractors choose to deliver their logistics' element in-house.

The following pages outline roles and responsibilities of the consultant logistics professional and the operational logistics manager. The two roles generally cover how construction logistics professionals consider projects that they are involved in.

Consulting logistics professionals

Always provided in a consultancy position, these individuals can join at any stage in the project's life cycle but are best engaged early when they can join a newly forming programme or project team with their client. To external entities, these individuals should be seen as the client and it is important that the client body empowers them with the correct level of decision-making authority to enable them to be useful within their embedded organization.

There are perhaps four core work streams (over three distinct time frames) when consultant logistics managers might be engaged:

- *Project commencement*: the first is at project feasibility or commencement stage. The logistics professional would be expected to have an input to the development of the client brief and develop options and complete feasibility analyses of these.
- *Project definition stage*: during this next stage logistics professionals would start to create the logistics strategies, programmes, cost plans and business cases required. This will enable procurement strategies to be produced, which will in turn enable the formation of package scopes where applicable.

Scoping logistics and transportation solutions should be based upon robust data, where possible, and the logistics professional will have access to this from previous lessons learned. This will enable the logistics leader to optimally size the element that they are reviewing and bring value to their client.

- *Authority permissions*: parallel to this the consulting manager may well be supporting a planning application or transport and works applications with the client and their design team. By using demand planning to size infrastructure and mitigate construction impacts to local residents and businesses, including the client's own business, the logistics professional brings further value to the project.

  By working closely with transport planners, the construction logistics professional will be able to integrate their assessment of the construction demand in with local demand. The logistics leader will be able to accurately clarify to the authority the modelled effect that their project will have on the local environs – by forecasting the demand profile for material deliveries and personnel movements by the different available transport modes, and identifying and measuring the constraints for material deliveries and personnel movements either as process constraints (eg security passes, duration materials to be held on site, site access timings, environmental considerations etc) or physical constraints (eg site access points, roads, gates, hoists, crane hook time etc).

- *Project delivery stage*: at project delivery stage the client will be expecting project and package management as required by the chosen procurement method. The logistics manager can bring value by creating a set of controls that monitor and manage service quality, as well as report it. Commercially, the logistics budget should be monitored and managed and reported up through the team by those who understand the costs of such items and can challenge them when necessary. Those consultants with suitable experience and an understanding of package contracting will bring best value to their clients at this stage.

At each stage a professional logistics leader will look to approach the subject in a structured and analytical manner as they ensure material, plant, equipment and people flow to the right location at the right time to ensure production targets are met and programme risks are adequately managed.

Table 9.1 highlights areas of focus and techniques that may be employed by the consulting logistics professional when developing a new project plan for a client.

TABLE 9.1 Key construction logistics elements to consider when developing a project plan

Subject	Technique
Site layouts	Creation of time-phased site logistics plans (3D CAD and Building Information Modelling (BIM) systems to show arrangements over time). This enables effective decision making with regard to logistics and transportation solutions.
Space planning	Space planning for plant, equipment and materials (using the same CAD model as used in site layouts; 3D where possible).
Accommodation and welfare	Size and locate all temporary office and welfare accommodation. Create canteen strategy. Create maintenance regime.
Temporary infrastructure	Identify and specify all temporary infrastructure requirements, including roads and footpaths, signage schemes, materials and plant storage areas. Ensure that a maintenance regime has been created.
Temporary services and utilities	Prepare scheme designs and specifications for temporary power, water, drainage and communications networks including base data forecasting. Ensure that these schemes are safeguarded against known and unknown future works (both temporary and permanent) and that a maintenance regime has been created.
Demand flow	Create models that can be integrated to the construction master plan (utilizing BIM technologies where possible) for freight-moving material, plant and personnel. Ensure a level of resilience through multiple transportation routes and modes where possible.
Security	Prepare a scheme design and specifications for providing the security infrastructure. Suitably resource for the sensitivity of the project.
Material strategies	Use specialists in design for manufacture and assembly (DfMA) techniques to establish the optimal materials flows for projects. Review solutions such as off-site prefabrication, modular construction or value engineering of the material supply chain to enable best value for clients and reduce impact on local stakeholders.

TABLE 9.1 *continued*

Subject	Technique
Delivery management systems (DMS)	Specify delivery management, booking and tracking systems that will control the flow of materials to projects, provide a smooth delivery profile, negate queuing vehicles and ensure materials arrive at the right place at the right time. (Use an off-the-shelf system where possible, design if necessary to suit size, complexity and security needs of the project.)
Logistics centres	Adopt a demand fulfilment approach. This is a development of the consolidation centre approach and involves pulling together assembly packs of materials from buffer stocks held in consolidation centres. Combine a DMS with strategically located multi modal logistics centres to smooth demand and promote JIT deliveries.
Workforce management	Design and specify workforce flow systems. Ensure access and egress is controlled and key information is available to enable the safe passage of workers both through the site, and in the local vicinity as they migrate towards transport hubs.
Fire management	Create a fire and emergency management plan for the temporary construction situation (and develop it through all construction phases).
Occupational health and first aid	Assess the needs for occupational health provisions on site and ensure that first aid and emergency protocols are in place.
Waste management and recycling	Promote the recycling of materials generated from construction and using sustainable modes of transport to remove waste responsibly, including utilizing reverse logistics techniques. Establish site-based 'kanban' marketplaces for common supplies and small tool hire, thereby reducing the volume of freight deliveries to site and reducing the need for storage on constrained sites.
Environmental	Create a management plan for environmental monitoring, control and management for the temporary construction condition. Optimize the use of sustainable modes of transport such as water and rail, where available, for freight movement.
Stakeholder engagement	Identify all stakeholders (internal and external) that need to be managed during the construction phase and outline management plans for each.
Planning	Integrate logistics plans that are fully aligned to project master plans. Plans are financially appraised with cost detail and cash flow forecasts.

TABLE 9.1 *continued*

Subject	Technique
Logistics organization and structure	Develop the most suitable organizational structure to deliver the logistics elements of a project, fully integrated into the overall project organization. Plan each resource's commitment and cost.
Commitment to vulnerable road user safety	Adhere to a client policy, a planning constraint, a regional or a national commitment to reducing the risk to vulnerable road users during the movement of freight in and out of the project. These may include Transport for London's Fleet Operator Recognition Scheme (FORS); Transport for London's 'Standard for Construction Logistics: Managing work-related road risks' or the national voluntary commitment to the CLOCS (Construction Logistics and Cycle Safety) Group.
Project communication	Develop standard site preliminaries books to ensure full visibility of Tier 1 contractor preliminary costs and to enable opportunities for the central provision of common site services to be realized.
Metrics	Use experience and tools to calculate key metrics that are fundamental to measuring that the logistics strategy is working. These metrics should enable the safe and efficient delivery of the programme. The metrics should consider using leading indicators rather than lagging indicators, where appropriate.

Construction logistics managers

Below are the operational role and responsibilities that have been developed by the author. These have been agreed with the members of the Chartered Institute of Logistics and Transport's Supply Chain Forum. The agreed roles and responsibilities are becoming adopted by the construction and logistics industries and have been published by *Construction Manager* magazine, *Construction Research and Innovation* magazine and the CILT's *Focus* magazine.

Headline responsibility

The construction logistics manager is responsible for all aspects of the logistics supply chain, stores management, development and optimization of site logistics solutions to meet the needs of the project. The logistics manager will be required to manage the movement of people, goods and equipment at the construction site and control site facilities management. Key interfaces that the logistics manager must ensure early engagement with are the project planner, commercial managers procuring the works and the senior construction manager on the site. The logistics manager should ensure that the construction team are fully aware of logistics activities in support of the build programme:

- *Planning/programming.* Create a construction logistics plan that includes:
  - Planning site set-up to move labour, plant and materials around the site efficiently (eg hoarding, gates, site accommodation, cranes, hoists, security, temporary services, material delivery and waste management strategy, catering).
  - Planning internal and external logistics routes through the project phases focusing on separation of vehicles, machinery and people; lay-down areas and off-loading points.
  - Pre-planning of key asset usage such as hoists to ensure planned assets meet the needs of the programme.
- *Mobilization*:
  - Create a secure site.
  - Assume responsibility for all traffic management internally and externally, weighbridges and road-network cleanliness.
  - Manage installation of site accommodation and manage these facilities.
  - Create operational procedures and method statements.
  - Organize site inductions, ensure induction records are securely stored.
  - Create a schedule of logistics meetings and ensure logistics attendance at site meetings.
- *Supply chain management*:
  - Describe the characteristics of the site: site access/egress; storage capacity and arrangement by programme; labour; hoists, cranes etc.
  - Use the description to produce daily, weekly and long-term movements plans.
  - Understand procurement arrangements.
  - Control materials in and out of site.
  - Undertake planning and integration of key contractors to meet the needs of the planned programme and deconfliction of on-site space and time where appropriate.
  - Assist in the evaluation of potential logistics suppliers and appropriate delivery management booking systems.
  - Be capable of managing subcontractors to deliver their package of goods or services.

- Control variation and communicate foreseeable change early.
- Gain commercial/contract basic understanding.
- Utilize business management system procedures.
- Record keeping and key performance indicator (KPI) production.
- *Programme support*:
  - Embrace the delivery-focused culture.
  - Organize resources to enable contract deadlines to be achieved.
  - Organize resources to work additional hours as required to meet project deadlines (eg extended site hours if required by client).
  - Be responsible for ensuring logistics activities are not a constraining factor on the programme; where deemed unavoidable ensure the issues are communicated in order that deconfliction can occur.
- *Safety*:
  - Ensure the organization's safety policies are followed.
  - Create site-specific safety manual, ensure first aid cover and equipment is present.
  - Be responsible for ensuring that material movements to and from the workface does not cause damage to the works, the workforce or the public.
  - Complete safety inspections to company and client standards.
  - Ensure team has safety training to the company and client's standard programme.
  - Create appropriate logistics awareness training and deliver to site workforce via presentation/toolbox talks (TBTs) as required.
  - Manage and maintain visitor personal protective equipment (PPE) stocks to an agreed number.
  - Produce method statements, risk assessments, and ensure lifting plans are produced.
  - Safeguard vulnerable road users from traffic and transport created by the site.
- *Fire*:
  - Create, maintain and update the site emergency plan (including the site fire plan) reporting to the appointed site fire officer.
  - Maintain fire points and all common life-saving equipment.
- *Site communications*:
  - Create a system to communicate information around the site, eg noticeboards, e-mail distribution lists, monitor displays, web page.
  - Update site safety performance and KPIs to pre-agreed frequency.
  - Ensure local hospital data is regularly updated, communicated and routes are checked.
  - Manage near-miss and project suggestion box. Collate and issue to management team.

- *Signage*:
  - Define and organize all site signage to the agreed corporate standard.
  - Ensure that signage and signage symbols used are internationally recognized.
  - Ensure additional languages are used in signage to ensure messages are understood.
- *Delivery management*:
  - Select delivery management technique, process and system.
  - Provide logistics instruction to all project suppliers.
  - Manage all movements to and from site and keep associated records.
  - Enforce the full use of the organization's delivery management system.
  - Plan to maximize load capacity on all vehicles arriving at site where possible, and ensure suppliers use appropriate vehicles for delivery.
  - Ensure that drivers and vehicles meet the required standards before being accepted to the site.
- *Vehicles, plant, equipment and vertical transport*:
  - Specify and manage plant and equipment.
  - Maintain an asset register of all equipment.
  - Ensure vehicles and plant are operated safely by trained personnel and in a legally compliant manner.
  - Ensure all equipment is inspected, maintained and tested to agreed frequencies.
  - Ensure knowledge of hoists and cranes; create and agree booking system to manage capacity.
- *Security*:
  - Manage guarding resource including rotas and contingency.
  - Ensure adequate training has been provided and certification is valid.
  - Actively police compliance with site rules.
  - Ensure compliance with the Private Security Industry Act (2001).
  - Ensure compliance with the Data Protection Act (1998) and ICO guidelines.
- *Workforce*:
  - Be capable of managing a team of operatives, taking any necessary corrective disciplinary action.
  - Ensure supervisors provide and record TBTs to workforce.
  - Understand the roles of standard logistics operatives: eg labourer, waste operative, carpenter, hoist driver, handyman, traffic marshal, SIA guard.

- Ensure operatives are assured of their roles and responsibilities.
- Ensure competencies of own team are demonstrable.
- Recruit operatives.

- *Environmental*:
  - Complete environmental risk assessment.
  - Create, maintain and regularly update the site waste management plan to ensure the safe and efficient removal of waste from the project.
  - Update environmental reporting on site communications boards and other media.
  - Ensure duty of care certificates from all contractors are kept as required by the project director.
  - Ensure safety, health and environmental monitoring is completed.

- *Corporate social responsibility (CSR)*:
  - Ensure that at least one CSR activity is conducted per month (monthly).
  - Produce project newsletter.

- *Desirable skills and competencies*:
  - A track record of delivery within a construction management or logistics function (over the past three years) that has led to performance improvement, eg cost reduction, process/service enhancements, innovation, winning work etc.
  - A personal commitment to promoting a sustainable approach to logistics procurement and supply chain development.
  - Excellent communication skills that: build empathy and support, engage with individuals at all levels, influence, promote.
  - The intellectual capacity to deal with complex logistics issues – a big-picture view – to implement logistics and supply chain vision, strategy and priorities. A driver of performance improvement.
  - IT skills (Powerpoint, Visio, Word, Excel).
  - An inspirational manager who can get the best out of individuals and teams, can build consensus, work in a matrix structure, deliver performance and outcomes, and can drive professional and personal development of team members.
  - Skilled at managing suppliers: scaffolding, temporary electrics, plumbing, welfare and office accommodation.

- *Desirable qualities*:
  - Professional/lead by example.
  - Passion/can do/constructive challenge.

- A proven track record of integrity and ethical behaviours.
- Open to change/new ideas.
- Sharer of information.
- Supportive.
- Customer focused.
* *Beneficial qualifications*:
  - Construction Skills Certification Scheme (CSCS).
  - Site Management Safety Training Scheme/Site Supervisors Safety Training Scheme (SMSTS/SSSTS).
  - Current full UK driving licence.
  - Recognized safety programme: qualified and up to date.
  - First aid.
  - Lifting supervisor certification.
  - A suitable qualification in traffic management.
  - Institutional membership.

The key document that a construction logistics professional is supposed to produce and use is the construction logistics plan (CLP). This document continues to grow in importance as authorities permitting development take an increasing interest in how capital projects are planned and completed, themselves under pressure from local residents, businesses and other stakeholders.

As such, the author has developed a simple document that guides the reader through all aspects that they should consider within the plan when creating or using one. Created with a blank sheet of paper, this best practice guidance has been formatted to consciously replicate the layout of Transport for London (TfL)'s CLP Guidance documents and it has been reviewed by them.

TfL, the author and the CILT Construction Supply Chain Forum are all keen that the guidance is published and used nationally. All agree that national guidance on CLP will have a positive impact on project efficiency and workplace safety, supporting industry improvements such as the CLOCS campaign.

Creating a construction logistics plan (CLP)

Figure 9.1 sets out a CLP template that the reader is welcome to use, as a guide, or reproduce using the headings, subheadings and guidance notes as prompts. Where an element is not relevant to the project being planned, there is no need to include appropriate headings or subheadings. However, the order should generally be adhered to in order to enable authorities and other logistics specialists to know where to expect to look within any document presented in this format.

FIGURE 9.1 Construction logistics plan (CLP) – best practice format

Introduction	Overview of the site	Include client and key stakeholders
	Key issues or challenges	
	Objectives of this plan	Demonstrate that all construction resources can be delivered (and waste removed); Identify where we can reduce re-time and consolidate (particularly during peak hours); Cut congestion; Reduce project cost and ease environmental pressure; Improve reliability.
Administration Elements	Details of the applicant submitting the CLP	
Site Information	Name of the site	
	Location of the site	
	Size and nature of the development	
	Key personnel	Key personnel R&Rs; Site management organogram; Contact details. Key personnel to include: Logistics team; Security; Crane supervisors; Construction manager(s) and Safety manager(s).
	Planning permission demands	
	Nature of neighbouring residential areas	Who lives there? (Families, age demographic, at home during day etc)
	Hours of site operation	
	Services provision	Any changes to services during the construction phase
Access Management and Travel Planning	Details of Construction Phase Travel Plan document	Include any pertinent references and how to obtain a copy.
	Site access details	Include public transport, cycling and footways.
	Staff, vehicle and pedestrian interfaces	
	Site Parking Policy	
	Details of any parking constraints near the site	
	Arrangements for out of hours working	Security; access changes; street use change.

Logistics Operations

FIGURE 9.1 *continued*

Construction Overview	Details of the scheme	
	Works programme	Showing indicative dates for each stage of construction.
	Overview of the different stages of construction	
	Tower crane and material hoisting layouts	
	Tower crane and material hoisting planned installation and removal arrangements	
	Details of storage for plant and materials	
Traffic Management	Detailed management of traffic at each development phase	
	Delivery scheduling technique proposed	Avoiding peak time deliveries. Include: Notice period for vehicles (eg 48 hours)
	Pedestrian, cyclist, bus and general traffic considerations	
	Local road and site speed limits	
	Construction phase signage required / placed	
Delivery and Materials Management Other Environmental Construction Fleet Transport Needs	Project Waste Strategy	
	Materials Logistics Plan (MLP)	The MLP covers the management of materials from design to construction (including supply routes, handling, storage, security, reduce, reuse, recycle and disposal) through to project demobilization and completion. Implementation of an MLP has a positive impact on the total life cycle of a construction project from conception through design and construction to demobilization and completion. An MLP also complements the actions construction projects are required to take as part of their Site Waste Management Plan (SWMP). http://www.wrap.org.uk/content/construction-logistics

FIGURE 9.1 *continued*

Delivery and Materials Management Other Environmental Construction Fleet Transport Needs	Waste Management	
	Site Waste Management Plan complete and referenced	Apply reduce, reuse, recycle principles:
		Reuse of crushed concrete / aggregate from deconstructing existing structure(s) on site;
		Reuse of excavated material for filling (based on its suitability);
		Potential provision of an on-site soil hospital to remediate soil on site (the current extent of contamination and remediation required is unknown at this point);
		Potential provision of a mortar batching facility on site;
		The use of reusable hoardings;
		The potential for the use of prefabrication techniques and modern methods of construction where practical and viable to do so without compromising quality.
	Environmental rating scheme support	Agreed deliverables required to support BREEAM (or similar rating scheme, eg CEEQUAL) requirements.
	Noise, dust and smoke control	Are there contractual / local authority thresholds, trigger levels etc?
	Minimize vehicle emissions	Vehicle replacement Euro engine standards;
		Driver training;
		Transport CO_2 reporting.
	Monitoring requirements and their targets	
	Number of deliveries	
	Maximum delivery vehicle size	Access, local road network; products (including where they are coming from in world and how much pressure can be applied to the factory to change delivery vehicles if needed).

FIGURE 9.1 *continued*

Delivery and Materials Management Other Environmental Construction Fleet Transport Needs	Access arrangements for vehicles	*Including:* Gate sizes; Site hoarding type; Details of any parking bays to be suspended to allow access for large construction vehicles; Special measures, particularly at access and exit areas, including safety of structures crossed, or that come into close proximity with vehicles accessing site; Overhead power (and shallow underground power); Other hazardous interfaces (eg cranes working, gantries, trains passing though area); Site ground conditions at each phase, and gradients around the site (including access ramps etc); Abnormal loads.
	Proposed vehicle routes	(Show on drawings coming down in scale from point at which vehicles are directed down specific roads) Routes reviewed for restrictions (width allowance; weight allowance; type) (via Video or google earth type technologies).
	Type and number of construction vehicles for each development phase	*Ensure access entry points and work areas are reviewed and analysed where there are concerns.*
	Swept path analysis	
	Parking, loading and unloading arrangements	Crane pick points identified
	Drivers	Welfare (toilets, hand-washing). Communicated driver regulations: Exiting cabs on site (and where they are allowed); vulnerable road users; management expectations.
	Vehicle safety	Contractual requirements for: Driver training; Transport collision reporting; Mirrors; Side guards; Close proximity warning systems; Warning stickers; FORS, WRRR and CLOCS compliance; Collision reporting
Pedestrian Management	Pedestrian access routes (and their physical barrier systems)	For both personnel and the public.
	Safety and directional signage	For both personnel and the public.
	Vertical personnel movement	

FIGURE 9.1 *continued*

Developing and using Policies	Details of policies and procedures to be in place during the construction	*Including:* Site rules; Waste minimization; Use of alternative modes of transport; Vehicle renewal replacement; Consolidation, DHZs, and/or collaboration and off-site fabrication; Winter maintenance.
	Improved vehicle safety	
Stakeholder Engagement	Neighbours	*Including:* Local schools or vulnerable groups using local buildings.
	Coordination with nearby sites	*Coordinating planning meetings with local authority and neighbouring sites. Share daily, weekly, monthly planned schedules.*
	Congestion minimizing techniques	*eg reduced deliveries in peak traffic periods*
	Cleaning of local road networks	
	Protection of the public	Risk assessment. Mitigation placed.
Security Arrangements	Site needs	
	Access management	
	Any local authority	
Operating	Operative training	Security, PVM (Plant and Vehicle Marshaller), Banksman.
	Registering of vehicles entering the site	
	Communication equipment	
	Welfare and office arrangements	*Including drawings where applicable*
	Vertical and horizontal material distribution	
	Hook time analyses, hoisting analyses	
	Temporary service provision	
	Temporary Water Strategy	

FIGURE 9.1 *continued*

Offloading	Offloading space	
	Offloading plant	Type; capability; availability (eg delivery management systems); Safe offloading acceptability (and methodology, if so) outside the site confines for low loaders.
	Safe offloading techniques and systems	(At height, around vehicles eg fall restraint systems). Loading platforms.
	Night time delivery assessment	Safety risk assessment; Local authority acceptance; Neighbour and other stakeholders acceptance; Noise assessment.
Localized Road Works and Temporary Situations	Outline requirement and set out standards for any works that interface with public, or public highway	
Emergency Arrangements	Emergency Preparedness Plan	Document is in place and includes transport and logistics issues.
	Emergency vehicle access	Include signage.
	Fire plan reference	
Monitoring, Compliance, Reporting and Review	Hoarding and site boundary licences	
	Arrangements stated for reviewing this document	Licences and agreements scheduled out into project diaries.
	Details for monitoring the CLP	*Including compliance arrangements, reporting and review*
Consolidation	Load consolidation, logistics zones, etc	

Training required

As a relatively new discipline in the construction process, no formal training has grown up around the logistics management role. As discussed earlier in the chapter, the author's own efforts to define roles and responsibilities for the operational construction logistics manager have been well publicized and are being used by a number of major UK contractors.

Books such as *Managing Construction Logistics* (2010) by Gary Sullivan, Stephen Barthorpe and Stephen Robbins describe best practice for operational logistics management professionals and these should be read by those delivering the role. This should be backed up by development of formal training in the subject if the role is to gain more stature within the construction industry.

There are organizations who feel that they already train and educate their logistics management staff well through practical tuition. However, these organizations should not feel insulated from poor standards across the industry. With only a handful of organizations providing good coaching and training, inevitably they become schooling grounds for the rest of the industry and the organization loses staff through trained staff moving on to companies offering better salaries.

By formalizing and standardizing the training, the author believes that the industry can start to build a sense of belonging and pride into this important role in the construction process. The author, supported by a team from the CILT's Supply Chain Forum, is currently working with the CILT to develop training that will do this, similar to the five-day Site Managers Safety Training Scheme that standardizes this training across the construction industry.

The training is planned to be part online, part project- and part classroom-based, moving up through levels that are QCF/NVQ accredited. As this training is being developed with the CILT it is planned to connect these to grades of membership of the Chartered Institute. The author is working to connect such training to current industry topics such as CLOCS, so that safety improvements made with vehicles are supplemented by a better standard of manager controlling freight movement.

Conclusion

The overriding majority of construction logistics managers working in the UK work either for logistics subcontractors or for main contractors.

In the first instance, where logistics managers are supplied by subcontractors, they are often brought in to deal with problems that the main contractors' construction managers either didn't have the capability to resolve, or felt were beneath them. These managers generally didn't have the choice to say 'no', as job security came down to them pleasing their client, the main contractor. In the second instance, poor-performing construction managers were given the logistics manager role at main contractors. With these two scenarios so prevalent, the role has struggled to attract the best talent, but as of 2014 things are starting to improve.

Educated clients have been investing in engaging logistics professionals early in the process. Large project management consultancies are starting to market logistics planning to their major clients and the logistics professional's standing is starting to improve within the industry. As global 3PL businesses begin to enter the marketplace, they have been offering highly capable individuals to clients, which have in turn improved the quality and understanding of logistics professionals. Pay and career opportunities are starting to move towards parity with construction staff on larger programmes and this has a trickle-down effect to operational logistics managers.

The construction industry is changing fast, advances in IT are enabling projects to be digitally engineered. As the opportunities that digital engineering and BIM are creating become realized, so do opportunities for construction logistics professionals. Ultimately, the construction process should change so that it becomes dominated by the design team, manufacturers and construction logistics experts who move the factory-built elements to assembly. If current trends continue, construction manager numbers on site should be diminished as more intellectual capability moves to factory environments and construction logistics.

Logistics managers who understand the construction process are able to bring the best value to project teams, if they demonstrate how they can reduce risk and create certainty. The logistics professional's standing must be supported by a better standardization of talent through the industry. Standardization will need to be supported by training, as outlined in the earlier section of this chapter.

The author is working with the Chartered Institute of Logistics and Transport and other organizations to do this, including the Chartered Institute of Building (CIOB) and the Institute of Civil Engineers (ICE).

Third-party logistics operators in construction: the role they play and the role they could play

10

PETE FLINDERS

Introduction

Effective supply chain management reduces time requirements and costs in construction supply chains, which traverse diverse markets and a network of channels. Third-party logistics (3PL) operators provide a range of services in the construction supply chain that have reduced waste through collaboration, software and conceptual advances that often adopt best practice from other sectors. Complicated construction site supply chains often delegate material sourcing responsibility by trade on a project-by-project basis, resulting in waste reduction opportunities in the supply chain that 3PLs can drive with the support of stakeholders in the supply chain. More recent agendas to enable construction growth following recession, safety advances and information technology compound to make a compelling greater role for 3PLs in construction.

This chapter introduces a brief history and scope of the 3PL, the impact of the economic downturn triggered in 2008, and presents construction supply chains as complicated and unstructured. Supply chains with a dominant entity such as flagship projects, house building and off-site manufacture offer a greater scope for 3PL engagement. Comparisons to other industries are made with 3PL roles in retail supply chains. The chapter discusses the developments in omni-channel retailing, primary and secondary distribution networks and comparisons to 3PL roles in construction. More specialist international and 'final mile' logistics roles are covered, along with consideration of why the 3PL role is less developed in the construction industry. The evolution of the role from transactional cost savings, through resource provision and network collaboration is discussed, concluding with factors that will trigger momentum in the growth of the 3PL role.

3PL definition

Third-party logistics is the activity of outsourcing activities related to logistics and distribution. Lieb (1992) describes the business process of outsourcing as 'the use of external companies to perform logistics functions, which have traditionally been performed within an organization. The functions performed by the third-party firm can encompass the entire logistics process or selective activities within that process'. Accenture took this further and defined the 3PL as 'a supply chain integrator that assembles and manages the resources, capabilities, and technology of its own organization with those of complementary service providers to deliver a comprehensive supply chain solution' (Cerasis, 2013).

As Cerasis (2013) writes: 'Its beginnings can be traced to the 70s and 80s as companies outsourced more and more logistics services to third parties. Over time these third party logistics service providers (3PLs) expanded their services to cover specific geographies, commodities, modes of transport and integrated their existing warehousing and transportation services, becoming what we now know today as a "3PL".' The use of 3PLs has grown dramatically over recent decades and this looks likely to continue: 'The ability of 3PLs to maintain an increasingly relevant role in today's supply chains will be largely driven by their continued ability to provide value to their customers. This value arises from both accommodating and exceeding customer service expectations in a more cost effective manner than can be achieved by customers performing the activities themselves' (Deepen, 2007).

Fourth-party logistics (4PL) is a relatively new concept that is used 'loosely' and can often be referred to as 'lead logistics providers'. While a 4PL is sometimes described as a non-asset-owning service provider, their role is to provide a broader scope of managing the entire supply chain. A specialist firm (the fourth party) is hired to coordinate the activities of two or more third parties. The 4PL will contract operational logistics to these outsourcing third-party specialists. The extent of outsourcing can be seen as a spectrum with all logistics functions performed in-house at one extreme, through to contracting of haulage, management of distribution operations, to full control of the strategic direction and implementation of a company's supply chain that controls a number of providers at the other extreme (with the latter notion often labelled as a 4PL solution).

Complicated and 'unstructured' supply chain

'Construction has been slower than other industries to realize the benefits that the application of good logistics can provide' (Construction Products Association, 2005). Engagement with 3PLs in the construction supply chain is behind other sectors such as retail, although some channels have greater engagement than others. A simplified view of the construction sector 3PL composition is shown in Figure 10.1.

The current structure of the construction industry provides both opportunities and barriers to improve, as 'the construction industry is not currently optimised for rationalisation of the supply chain' (Department for Business Innovation & Skills, 2013).

Impact of downturn

The fall in construction output since 2008 has generally increased levels of competition and the 'buying' of turnover through the submission of low bids. This is especially relevant in capital-intensive and high-overhead businesses. These price pressures have flowed back up the supply chain, where price reviews have often been worse than the capacity to reduce cost from operations. In fact, there has been inflation exceeding cost increases in areas such as energy, which is a key cost line of some construction products manufacturers. Over the five-year period 2007–12 average industrial electricity prices rose by 35 per cent (19 per cent in real terms), with an increase of 6 per cent (4 per cent in real terms) in 2012. Over the same period average industrial gas prices increased by 56 per cent (38 per cent in real terms) and by 9 per cent (8 per cent in real terms) in 2012. More recent fuel price developments are shown in Table 10.1.

These cost and price pressures through the downturn have had a polarizing effect on the construction logistics market; there has been substantial contraction of specialist haulage fleets including a number of businesses ceasing trading. Yet there has also been a greater consideration to outsource logistics activities to release capital and achieve cost savings.

The construction market structure and price pressure (as opposed to genuine supply chain waste reduction) have restricted the ability of 3PLs to play a greater supply chain collaborative role during the downturn. Cost- and efficiency-reduction decisions have been egocentric at times in attempts for self-preservation of an enterprise in the construction supply chain, sometimes resulting in cost-saving issues being passed back up the supply chain. This has included moves to little-and-often deliveries at shorter lead times. 3PLs have been able to provide collaborative network solutions that share fleet and facilities in order to reduce the cost impact and capacity flexibility to achieve these changing ordering patterns. However, short-term and reactive

FIGURE 10.1 Simplified view of construction supply chain by materials types, highlighting typical characteristics and 3PL roles

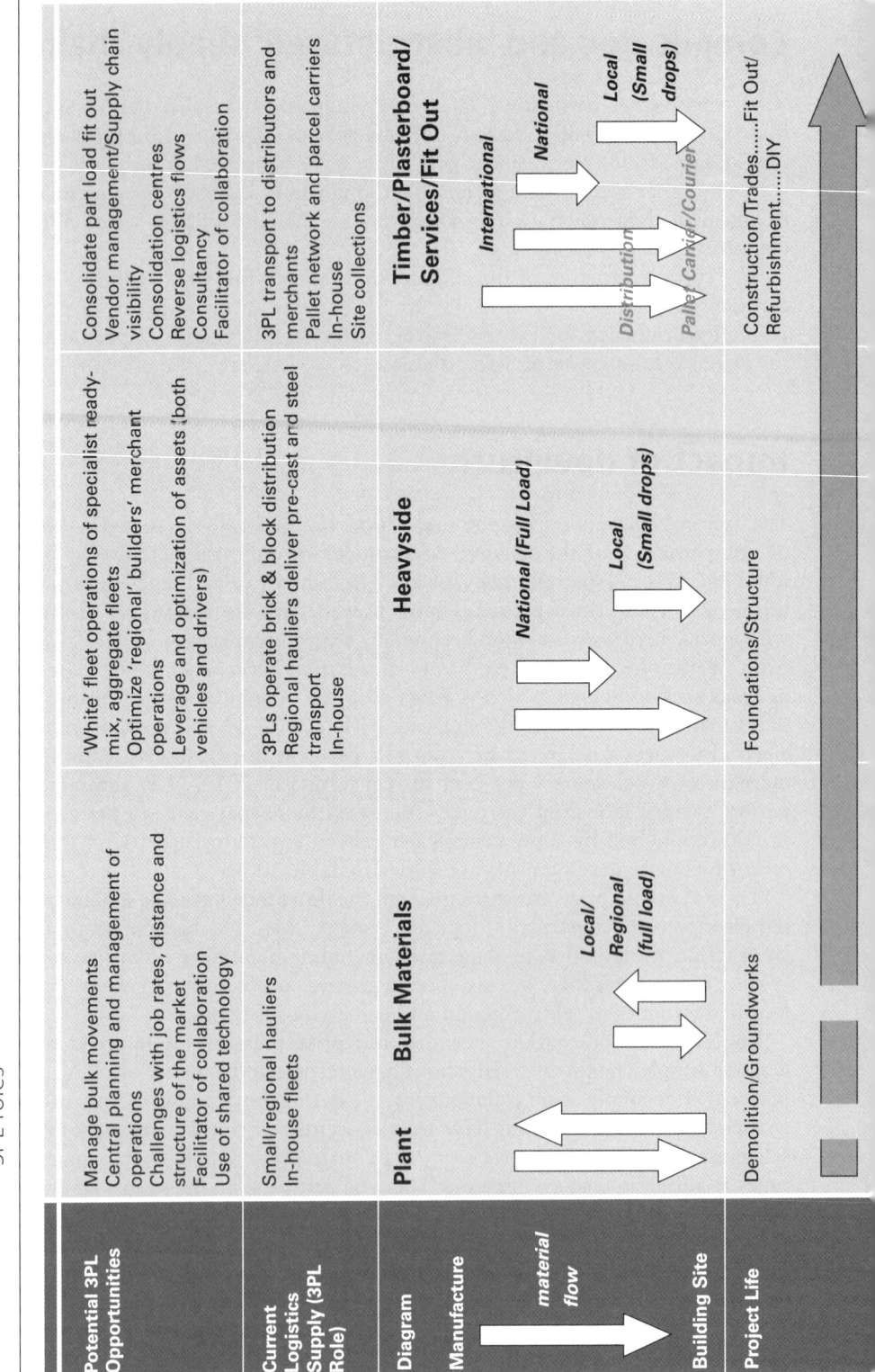

Potential 3PL Opportunities	Manage bulk movements Central planning and management of operations Challenges with job rates, distance and structure of the market Facilitator of collaboration Use of shared technology	'White' fleet operations of specialist ready-mix, aggregate fleets Optimize 'regional' builders' merchant operations Leverage and optimization of assets (both vehicles and drivers)	Consolidate part load fit out Vendor management/Supply chain visibility Consolidation centres Reverse logistics flows Consultancy Facilitator of collaboration
Current Logistics Supply (3PL Role)	Small/regional hauliers In-house fleets	3PLs operate brick & block distribution Regional hauliers deliver pre-cast and steel transport In-house	3PL transport to distributors and merchants Pallet network and parcel carriers In-house Site collections
Diagram	Plant Bulk Materials *Local/Regional (full load)*	Heavyside *National (Full Load)* *Local (Small drops)*	Timber/Plasterboard/Services/Fit Out *International* *National* *Local (Small drops)* *Distribution* *Pallet Carrier/Courier*
Manufacture *material flow*			
Building Site			
Project Life	Demolition/Groundworks	Foundations/Structure	Construction/Trades.....Fit Out/Refurbishment.....DIY

TABLE 10.1 Prices of fuels purchased by manufacturing industry

Compared to Q3 2013, heavy fuel oil consumers in Q3 2014 have seen prices fall by an average of 6.7 per cent in cash terms.
Over the same period, electricity consumers generally saw prices, in cash terms excluding CCL, fall by an average of 0.5 per cent.
Gas consumers generally saw prices, excluding CCL, decrease between Q3 2013 and Q3 2014 by an average of 20 per cent in cash terms.
Consumers of gas oil generally saw prices decrease by 11 per cent in cash terms. Coal consumers generally saw prices, in cash terms excluding CCL, increase by 10 per cent.

Last updated 18 December 2014

competitive pressure in often high fixed-cost enterprises has created barriers for 3PLs to unlock benefits. Some 3PLs have delivered a management, optimization and execution role in enterprises, working as a '4PL' or lead logistics partner. However, these roles have tended to provide value mainly to the contracting entity and not the wider construction supply chain. Conversely, there were a number of high-profile projects during the downturn that demonstrated innovative construction logistics practices supported by 3PLs, including in London the Olympic Park, Crossrail and further developments at Heathrow Airport.

Economic uncertainty has had an impact on 3PLs expanding programmes and launching new initiatives, according to a recent survey of the top European 3PL CEOs (Lieb and Lieb, 2012). This may have slowed the momentum of change in the role of 3PLs in construction in recent years. Therefore, there is a much greater opportunity for 3PLs in construction now, in contrast to the scope and maturity of 3PL roles in some other sectors, such as retail.

The need to coordinate, communicate and collaborate with other companies within the supply chain is a prerequisite for effective supply chain management. Other sectors that comprise large companies have commonly dominated their supply chains, such as in retail, where they impose on suppliers to share information, reduce inventory and invest in new technology. This is also true in the automotive industry, where more advanced supply chain management is recognized, with companies such as Toyota and Nissan. Some high-profile construction projects, such as the Olympic Park and Crossrail, have shown some resemblances with imposed requirements on suppliers. Greater sharing of information, management of inventory and more advanced logistics practices have been evident in some of these projects.

Supply chains that have a dominant entity are able to engage with 3PL expertise on a more structured basis. The drive for cost reduction and efficiencies by the dominant entity provide a clear strategy and trading relationship for 3PLs, who are able to reduce transactional costs through the efficient use of assets, consolidation of overheads, standardization of processes and improvements in coordination.

The concept of large company supply chain dominance enabling 3PL engagement and effective supply chain management provides two questions for construction logistics. First, what is the opportunity and extent of 3PL engagement in dominated construction supply chains? Second, what role do and can 3PLs play in all other construction supply chains?

Supply chains with a dominant entity

The opportunity in dominated supply chains may be limited by the number of large-scale projects, such as Crossrail or the Olympic Park. The role of a 3PL within other sectors often involves the design, implementation and operation of a supply chain network that generally has an existence beyond five years, whereas few construction projects involve a supply chain that operates for this length of time. This is a critical impediment for asset-based 3PLs that require sufficient term length for return on capital for vehicles and distribution centres. Investment in bespoke distribution network assets is unlikely to be approved for projects that expire well before a capital payback period. It is improbable that a bespoke network will fit a second construction project effectively, efficiently and at the exact time the initial project is completed. Less bespoke assets have greater potential to satisfy subsequent projects, but are compromised on their effectiveness and efficiency.

Large-scale 'flagship' projects have engaged with 3PLs, although the scope has often been focused on 'final mile' logistics, not the total supply chain. Solutions that consolidate, security screen and phase deliveries into construction sites have demonstrated innovation and the effectiveness of engaging with 3PLs. Future large-scale projects are limited in number, but offer a greater scope of role for 3PLs to play. However, the structure of contracting on many large projects involves a 3PL as a subcontractor to each bidding construction company and not engaged with the client directly. The 3PL's role in this relationship is to lead the physical delivery of supply chain operations. Effective engagement between the 3PL and the construction company could facilitate an effective and efficient supply chain design that has a greater scope than just the 'final mile' logistics, but this can be limited by early structure imposed by the client or late involvement by the construction company in decision making. Early 3PL involvement can be effective in supply chain design, although the importance of logistics is not always recognized sufficiently to invest in 3PL input prior to physical operations and there can be reluctance by 3PLs to provide a 'free' consultancy service. Conversely, 3PLs are well placed and have a significant USP (unique selling position) over consultancy providers in that they can physically deliver and operate the supply chain.

Large-scale construction programmes are not confined to 'flagship' projects and these can often be overlooked as to their logistical opportunity. House building and other 'repeatable' projects lend themselves to longer-term engagement with 3PLs. These usually comprise a single developer or house builder that has more potential dominance over its supply chain than other one-off construction projects.

The roles that 3PLs could play in future house-building supply chains include the provision of distribution centres, physical transport and systems that provide supply chain visibility and enhanced management. The capability to design a supply chain that aims to get the right material at the right time at the lowest cost (both financial and socioeconomic) is a key offering from 3PLs. There is the further benefit that 3PLs can implement and operate these supply chains, above just a consultancy service. 3PLs can provide IT solutions that provide visibility of material flow through the supply chain and could play roles in supplier management, tracking materials from factory, import or transport, consolidated for efficient delivery when required to building sites. This could reduce delays waiting for materials on site; reduce the need to store materials on site resulting in less waste, damages and overstocks; and reduce the quantity of deliveries to sites. This can unlock procurement arrangements, enabling more bulk-buying framework opportunities and improved management of suppliers, with single information of the delivery of materials to plans.

Potential shifts to off-site manufacture and fabrication of house-building construction not only provide productivity efficiencies in the assembly or construction process, but facilitate further roles for 3PLs to manage materials transport, storage and the delivery of fabricated units to site. This allows house builders to focus on core competences, enjoy transport network and asset synergies and provide a greater control over the effective delivery of materials. Off-site manufacture places greater importance on the supply chain, moves control of transport to the house builder and imposes a significant reliance on the quality of the supply chain. This quality can be assured through the use of a 3PL, providing focused specialists with a network of assets.

Case studies

An example role of a 3PL in a project supply chain, consolidating materials and managing supply for a build, can be seen in the construction of the aircraft carrier, as set out in the following case study.

CASE STUDY Aircraft Carrier Alliance

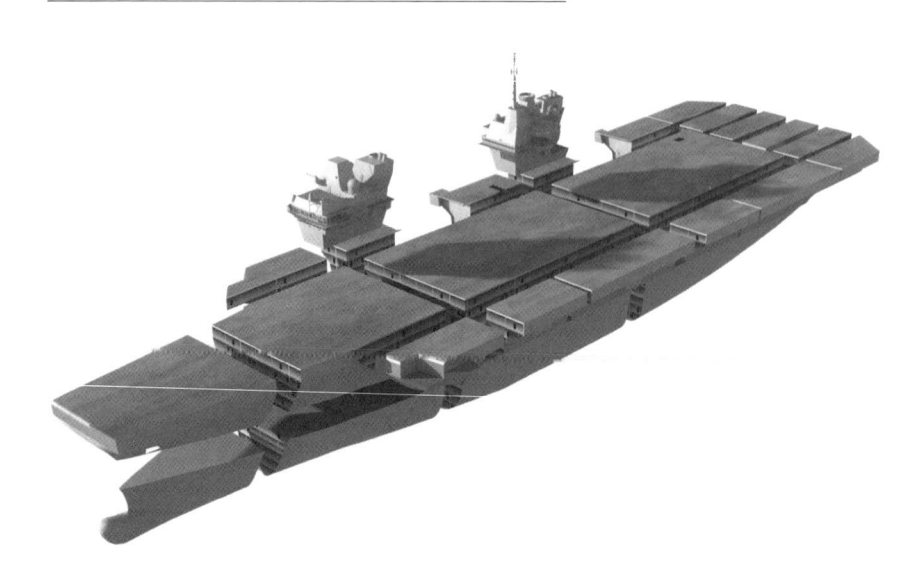

Delivering the nation's flagships

Wincanton is supporting the Aircraft Carrier Alliance (ACA) through the inspection, storage and distribution of parts from over 100 specialist suppliers to manage the build of the Queen Elizabeth class aircraft carriers. ACA is a unique partnering relationship between BAE Systems, Thales, Babcock and the Ministry of Defence: 'In partnership with Wincanton, the ACA now has a new and innovative supply chain solution to successfully manage one of the largest, most complex and highest single value build programmes that the UK defence industry has ever seen' (Dougie McInnes, Supply Chain Director, Aircraft Carrier Alliance).

120-tonne turbine

A 120-tonne £13 million gas turbine assembly (the biggest in the world) is one of the 12.5 million items handled since start-up.

99.7 per cent stock accuracy

Key to achieving in excess of 99.7 per cent stock accuracy is Wincanton's own IT platform, which interfaces directly with ACA's ERP purchasing system providing a single view of inventory.

On time and within budget

Critical to the success of the programme is the need to ensure that the build proceeds to budget and to schedule, particularly in view of the Strategic Defence Review and the public interest in this programme. Any delays to the build create huge impacts on cost and the role that the partnership between ACA and Wincanton plays is key to the successful delivery of the aircraft carriers.

We have used our transport planning expertise, with a control tower approach, to consolidate supplier deliveries, reducing ACA's anticipated transport spend by 60 per cent.

Key to achieving in excess of 99.7 per cent accuracy is Wincanton's own IT platform, which interfaces directly with ACA's ERP purchasing system, providing a single view of inventory. The system also controls weight distribution throughout the racking – critical for items that weigh anything from just a few grams to tens of tonnes.

Over 12.5 million items have been handled since start-up ranging from a single washer to a cut-glass decanter and glasses rumoured to originate from HMS *Victory*, through to a 120-tonne £13 million gas turbine assembly (the biggest in the world).

Construction supply chains comprise diverse materials and industry structures. There is overlap with retail supply chains, with extensive 3PL roles played with DIY retailers. Some of the services provided by a 3PL are demonstrated in the following B&Q case study.

CASE STUDY B&Q

From the beginning we knew we wanted a supply chain partner who could give us a step change in service and value and Wincanton's ability to integrate the container and retail networks has unlocked this potential. We now have the foundations of a control tower that will drive continuous improvement within the B&Q transport network and this will be further established later this year when Wincanton takes on the planning for our two-man multi-channel network.

Rick Jones, Director of Logistics, B&Q

In 2011–12 Wincanton further developed its relationship with leading retail group Kingfisher plc by becoming a strategic supply chain partner to B&Q. As well as continuing to manage and operate the brand's horticulture distribution, Wincanton has become the sole provider of inbound port-to-distribution centre (DC) container movements and will set up B&Q's nationwide transport 'control tower'.

Key benefits delivered include:

- Strategic transport planning to schedule up to 3,000 loads per week for the B&Q network.
- Drawing on Wincanton's wider network to provide additional flexibility at peak operating times through transport collaboration.
- Management of port-to-DC operations, handling around 15,000 containers each year.
- 'Triangular trunks' for containers using tail-lift skeletal trailers to maximize backhauling and direct-to-store deliveries.
- 25 per cent of inbound container traffic transported by rail to strategic railhead.
- Integrated transport approach will reduce CO_2 emissions by an estimated 3,000 tonnes per annum.

During 2011–12, Wincanton also worked closely with B&Q to help shape a multichannel solution around the customer experience, presenting an innovative approach to integrated systems in the supply chain. This type of strategic support underlines Wincanton's market-leading credentials within the retail sector and its growing reputation for providing flexible, agile solutions to meet a range of supply chain requirements.

Omni-channel

There is a movement to 'omni-channel' retailing, which is a more seamless approach to the consumer experience through all shopping channels including internet, stores, direct mail and so forth. Retailers are having to reformulate their supply chain strategies to match the shift in consumer demands. Construction consumers also have a mix of pre-planned distance-purchased goods along with emergency-purchased and often collected goods. Facilitated by advances in mobile technology, there will be increasing demands on construction products retailers and merchants. Consumers will expect to be able to order materials for delivery to sites, check prices, specifications and stock levels online and visit local branches or stores to collect goods at short notice. They will expect the full range to be available and consistent through every shopping channel along with an effective and fast delivery arrangement. A report produced to inform the Industrial Strategy for Construction, 'Supply Chain Analysis into the Construction Industry' (EC Harris, 2013), suggested moves to online transactions could improve performance and reduce transaction costs. It stated: 'the UK construction industry should adapt its structure, in the same way that the Amazon and eBay business model has made a virtue of its highly distributed "tail" of specialist small-scale suppliers'.

These demands create more advanced information technology (IT) requirements that bring together a wider scope of business operations that are often managed independently as well as a much more coordinated physical supply chain. The role that 3PLs will potentially play will include provision of single supply chain IT platforms that provide a single view and management of order processing through to customers, whether ordered online or through physical channels. They could also provide fulfilment 'distribution centres' to pick, pack and deliver through distribution networks to sites.

Primary and secondary distribution networks

The supply chain of DIY retailers has significant similarities with builders' merchants. Large national merchants have implemented 'secondary' distribution networks with centralized storage and transport of materials to depots (the secondary distribution network receives goods from suppliers and disperses these between depots). However, many builders' merchants still operate branches as separate businesses, with transport operations controlled locally. The geographic spread can sometimes result in an overlap between branches, with delivery vehicle planning conducted at branch level. To maximize the effectiveness and efficiency 3PLs are able to provide centralized planning, management and operation of delivery vehicles across branches.

There is potential for 3PLs to operate 'primary' distribution networks for merchants. The primary distribution network combines goods from different supply points for delivery into the merchant's network. Retail supply chains have implemented primary networks since the mid-1990s, with 3PLs providing a key role in combining goods from competing suppliers and distributing these to competing retailers. This provided great efficiency with smaller consignment sizes being delivered more frequently, whilst being consolidated usually in full loads from suppliers to primary distribution centres then again in full loads onto retail distribution centres. This also provided retailers with visibility and influence further up the supply chain.

Greater focus on logistics within large merchant groups should increase the propensity for 3PLs to develop a greater role within a primary distribution network. However, many 3PLs are currently contracted to manufacturers of products supplied to the construction industry and there may be concerns that 3PLs could weaken their existing customers' competitive position, in providing a primary network on behalf of a merchant chain. The role of the 3PL should be to bring these parties together and demonstrate the value to all members of the supply chain in removing waste, although there are further barriers with some elements of the construction supply chain that are fiercely monitored and controlled through the Competition and Markets Authority.

Regional and independent merchants often procure materials through buying groups in order to achieve economies of scale through procurement. Future 3PL roles could involve working with buying groups to provide efficiencies in the physical supply chain to independent merchants.

The role of the 3PL is already more advanced with construction products manufacturers, with many large 3PLs already engaged in this end of the sector. Roe (2007) noted that 'we [DHL] are seeing more businesses in the water, gas and electricity sectors re-engineering their logistics functions, dealing directly with materials suppliers and using supply chain experts as consolidators who can improve co-ordination and efficiency'. The scope of 3PL services with construction products manufacturers has been based around transport and warehousing solutions. However, 'there is a limit to driving value out of tendering transportation and warehousing spending', according to the Sidler (2012): 'the significant savings are in vendor management and reducing cycle times and inventory'. Therefore, the 3PL role in the future should encompass a wider service offering that delivers greater value to the supply chain.

International construction supply chains

Suppliers to construction sites often source materials from outside the UK and usually outsource import arrangements to 3PLs or freight forwarders. These handle the physical transport by road, sea or air and often arrange to complete documentation and clearance arrangements to process materials through the UK border. In a global market roiled by increasing risk, 3PLs are able to focus on speed, flexibility and consistency in technology. The potential for disruption is greater and can have a detrimental impact on the build plan for construction sites. Transport to site is usually contracted by the supplier, not direct to the client or construction company, so supply chain effectiveness can be hampered by distance, culture and language differences. Future 3PL roles will provide greater visibility across the supply chain, to improve the management of these unplanned events, to reduce delays, overstocks and waste. Control of international supply chains by a 3PL appointed directly to the client or construction company could provide further assurance, effectiveness and efficiency in coordinated delivery of materials to sites.

Final mile logistics – construction consolidation centres

Construction consolidation centres (CCCs) are distribution facilities where material deliveries are channelled to construction sites. These show clear resemblance to other goods distribution centres that receive material from a number of suppliers and consolidate them for delivery to a store or business. 3PLs have been operating distribution centres for decades in the UK, so have the experience, systems and facilities to run construction consolidation centres; in particular these can be shared solutions. WRAP (2011) highlights a variety of benefits in shared user CCCs, such as spreading fixed costs, lowering set-up costs per project and optimization of resources.

Despite the published benefits of CCCs there are only a limited number of facilities in the UK, generally focused on London, with presence from some specialist logistics providers. There is a much greater potential role that 3PLs can play in operating CCCs for more projects and in other areas of the UK.

Many deliveries to construction sites are completed with specialist vehicles able to access restricted sites or using mechanical offload equipment (cranes or vehicle-mounted forklifts). 3PLs can help improve specialist vehicle utilization through effective planning, sharing between different projects and material suppliers as well as through more advanced supply chain networks. Wincanton has been able to utilize shipping container haulage routes on return towards ports to transport construction materials from manufacturing locations in the Midlands to strategic locations near to construction sites, where they are transshipped onto specialist crane vehicles for final delivery. This increases the utilization of crane vehicles and fills container vehicles that would have otherwise travelled empty.

Why doesn't the construction industry make better use of 3PL services?

There are many factors that may have influenced the construction industry not to make better use of 3PL services and these include people, process and organization structure cost drivers. These can be interrelated, with a lack of supply chain visibility (poor information process) through the fragmented contracting composition (organizational structure), which is not managed effectively (people's skills). This amalgamation of barriers inhibits the 'push factors' of 3PLs in selling services and the 'pull factors' that invite 3PLs to tender for work. Engagement with transport providers is usually on a transactional level, which is delegated to each trade, who arrange transport, unloading, storage and movement to the installation area on site. It is fairly inconceivable to imagine a town centre convenience retail store being supplied along similar lines to that of a common construction supply chain. Instead of consolidated deliveries with 'shelf ready' packs on flexible wheeled handling units coordinated outside of peak trading periods, the common building site approach to the supply chain could involve store aisles being full of materials that were delivered three weeks early, but missing some key lines, multiple vehicles waiting to unload outside the store with goods being moved by hand and a lot of packaging waste. The retail supply chain rarely accepts these standards, whereas the combination of people, processes and organization structure in the construction supply chain hide many of these wastes. 3PLs have fine-tuned the design, implementation and operation of retail supply chains, so should be well placed to deliver this to the construction industry. A 3PL's success is limited by their ability to engage all suppliers' supply chains into the site, so ultimately require designation by the client or main construction company to achieve this. The cost drivers and root causes classified by people, process or structure are demonstrated in Table 10.2.

These skills, attitudes, common processes and supply chain structure are combined with a diversity of suppliers on each project. EC Harris (2013) found that an average of 50 Tier 2 subcontractors were found on sample projects ranging in size from £20 million to £30 million, with further suppliers involved in the third tier. This spread of responsibility and limited project life impedes longer-term relationships being built with 3PLs. However, project logistics can often have more criticality over less important repeating transactional activities. The skills, expertise and physical networks that 3PLs can provide can offer a more pivotal role in assuring delivery of project logistics. Therefore, despite shorter contract length and a diversity of suppliers, there is a greater opportunity for 3PLs to deliver in construction site logistics. The benefits delivered in a 'project environment' can be seen with, for example, the London 2012 Olympics as outlined in the case study on p 199.

TABLE 10.2 Summary of driving factors as to why the construction industry makes better use of 3PLs

Affecting	Unnecessary Cost Drivers	Root Causes
People	'Someone else's problem'. Lack of duty of care. Lack of motivation. Attitudes/culture. Lack of team working and integration. Lack of trust. Poor management. Skills mix.	Site management gulf between tradesperson and materials costs. Theft and damage. Poor skills regarding cost management. Fear of shortages. Lack of understanding and fitting instructions.
Process	Strategic planning. Balancing of materials supply. Contractual relationships. Tendering, take and sales push. Variance in performance between process steps. Not understanding upstream and downstream processes and interfaces. Volume discounts. Understanding true cost of the process. Programmes that are not kept. Service levels poorly measured. Adversarial contracts and risk pushed down the supply chain.	Over-ordering from other internal processes. Not enough recycling companies. Technical and material properties need over-ordering. Cumulative effect of allowances made in each process step. Sales push. Design processes enhance waste. Materials on-site payment clauses. Variations. Lack of design/dimensional coordination. Poor information and management processes. Poor bills of quantities. Poor handling equipment. Site management processes. Inappropriate specs.
Organizational Structure	Procurement. Recycling advice and it is cheaper to process waste than stop it occurring. Fragmentation. Little understanding of integration. Supply not geared to deliver logistics. Focus is always on site priorities. Forecasting. No optimization of supply chain. Not geared to working on true costs. Communication and information flows. Technology an issue.	Supply chain weakness. Damage by other trades. Bills of quantities. Inappropriate risk. No QA processes. Contractual arrangements.

CASE STUDY   London 2012 Olympics

During London 2012, Wincanton:

- Handled over 15 million items from two London logistics centres with 1 million square feet of space, storing everything from Post-it notes to referees' boats and gymnastic flooring.
- Supplied games equipment for all 35 competition venues and 65 non-competition venues, filling around 60 vehicles per day.
- Installed, moved and recovered in excess of 10,000 lane demarcation and crowd-control barriers during the road cycling, marathon, triathlon and racewalking events.
- Received and receipted 115 trucks full of equipment, including hundreds of beds and artificial turf for the opening ceremony.
- Delivered 500 bulk loads of wholesome water to Greenwich, Lee Valley and Eton.

Teamwork and planning

With over two years of planning, Wincanton played a large part behind the scenes in helping to make the London 2012 Games the outstanding success it was. With three separate contracts, including LOCOG, Wincanton was involved with supplying equipment and support for every single Olympics venue across the UK, handling literally everything from commemorative medals, certificates and souvenir programmes through to furniture for the athletes' village and sand for the equestrian venue. Wincanton is exceptionally proud of the contribution they made.

Involved at a very early stage, they facilitated the supply of equipment for 43 different test events in the run-up to the games, the games themselves and the opening and closing ceremonies. They also advised on health and safety, and provided support staff for the logistics control centre.

Maintaining the supply chain for customers

Away from the official games venues, Wincanton worked hard on ensuring that their customers' supply chains would remain operational during the four-month period of the Olympics. With a dedicated area on their website to keep both customers and colleagues up to date with the latest information on road closures and compliance procedures, they worked closely with Transport for London and LOCOG to ensure that customer deliveries could go ahead smoothly, shelves would remain fully stocked and important documents would reach safe hands.

Evolution of the 3PL role

There are three phases to this: transactional cost savings, access to resources and network collaboration, as discussed below.

Phase one: transactional cost savings

A traditional view as to why companies outsource logistics, as noted by O'Bryne (2012) is that logistics is not a core function/capability and it needs to be handled more professionally:

- in the hope of reducing logistics costs;
- to gain access to specialist IT, equipment and skills;
- to gain flexibility in capacity, and variable cost, due to rising or falling customer demand;
- to move logistics assets off the balance sheet and free up capital.

These have a straightforward application to construction manufacturers, suppliers and builders' merchants. However, it can be difficult to apply to construction site logistics procedures that often contract suppliers to provide delivered goods, or even for trades to arrange delivery and installation, with few logistics assets on balance sheet and a perception that it is the supplier's remit to manage flexibility, equipment and skills. This traditional view demonstrates a basic transaction cost economics (TCE) approach to the supply chain. TCE theory is that companies' decisions are based on minimizing the sum of their transaction and production costs (Williamson, 1985). 3PLs can reduce transactional costs through efficient use of assets and consolidated overheads; with further engagement and visibility, they can deliver standardization and improved coordination. The greater the consolidation of tasks provided by the 3PL, the lower the transaction cost. As demand for 3PLs has increased, the scope of services they offer has grown and as their role has increased, 3PLs have been able to acquire more assets and create synergies. The structure and limited longevity of construction supply chains may position them some years behind retail supply chains in the momentum of TCE decision making, but they do demonstrate a 'power curve' (acceleration factor) of potential opportunity. The supply chains of bulk materials often involve supply chain execution at a local level with transport contracting with a large number of businesses. Many bulk aggregate transport operations are managed by local supply sites and contracted to 'owner–driver' haulage businesses. TCE theory would suggest there are savings opportunities in dealing with fewer suppliers of haulage and centralized management of transport operations. The engagement of 3PLs to manage these supply chains has the potential to reduce transaction costs and could be applied to aggregate, ready-mix and waste transport. An example – a 3PL transport management contract that reduced the number of direct suppliers was implemented in 2006 between Aggregate Industries and Norbert Dentressangle (formerly TDG), where the 3PL procures haulage, minimizes the number of empty running miles through route planning and provides real-time web reporting for planners, hauliers and customers. This can also offer benefits in standardized control of customer service and health and safety practice.

Phase two: access to resources

The competitiveness of companies in the construction supply chain is not limited to just minimizing transaction costs. Competitive advantage can be derived from access to physical assets, such as vehicles and locations as well as knowledge, skills and expertise. The ability to engage with 3PLs can be regarded as an intangible asset and a resource-providing activity (Hobbs, 1996). It is common in the construction supply chain for organizations to rely on outsourcing to gain access to other companies' resources, although uptake in logistics has been limited. There is an opportunity for both subcontract trades and construction companies to elevate their competitive position through long-term and aligned engagement with 3PLs. Transactional engagement can often limit resource opportunities to those of physical service provisions, whereas companies that are more strategically connected and more value dependent provide a far greater range of competitive resources. Strategic partnerships are likely to build from transactional relationships between 3PLs and the construction supply chain, and culminate with a network of relationships across the supply chain.

Phase three: network collaboration

Effective supply chain management views the entire distribution channel as opposed to organizations' logistics in isolation. In other sectors 3PL growth has seen multi-client interactions that span the supply chain. These networks have developed over time through long-term relationships that offer reciprocity, with companies achieving network-wide efficiency whilst 3PLs perform more pivotal roles that orchestrate activities. The greater influence and network provides 3PLs with more opportunity to build assets and capabilities at lower cost, so they generate more value to both 3PLs and supply chain network members.

What will trigger momentum of the 3PL role in construction logistics?

The construction supply chain is diverse and is already significantly engaged with 3PLs in some parts, although it is significantly behind the maturity of other sectors elsewhere. A greater focus on carbon, waste and the cost of these will provide more interest in engaging with 3PLs to achieve fewer emissions and reduce waste – 3PLs can deliver distribution networks, vehicle technologies and systems to manage and report on carbon savings. There are further opportunities for 3PLs to reduce other supply chain wastes, from greater utilization of resources to socioeconomic costs. Greater utilization of resources can be achieved with the integration of vehicle and distribution centre resources with other sectors, improved productivity through off-site kit building and 'line-side supply' of materials when and where they are required, and greater control of inbound long-distance supply chains. Clients may be more prescriptive and demanding of construction companies and their subcontract trades to provide some of these initiatives, as the benefits gain greater recognition.

Waste is not only a fiscal cost, but can have an impact on safety and the social environment. There are increasing expectations on the construction industry to reduce the impact on vulnerable road users, which provides an opportunity for 3PLs to provide the resources and expertise required. Reducing the number of deliveries to sites through consolidation and network design can reduce the social impact on people near to construction sites and is likely to become a more important requirement of clients on construction companies.

The adoption of building information modelling (BIM) processes will provide electronic records of buildings at a much earlier stage. This has the potential to make all the materials in the build visible at an earlier stage and in a single electronic format. Overlayed with planned timings of installation a detailed supply chain can be identified, planned, optimized and managed. The role of a 3PL could be to design each project's supply chain at an early phase using advanced software modelling and execution skills. Part-level data in the automotive supply chain is used to organize and manage the supply chain to achieve vehicle assembly plans whilst following lean principles. In the automotive industry 3PLs are extensively engaged in transporting, storing and managing the flow of materials to line-side assembly operations and are well placed to transfer theses concepts to the construction industry, enabled by the introduction of BIM.

Supply chain capacity and certainty issues in construction products supply may also provide momentum for 3PLs to take a greater role in the construction supply chain. Manufacturing capacity shortages have extended sourcing distance to fill gaps in supply, often increasing international supply of materials. Risks of international supply surety are evident with greater potential consequences of political, economic and environmental events.

Demands of clients and cost control require build schedules to be met, with internationally sourced materials arriving on time; 3PLs can provide software, assets and management of international supply chains that flag events and take advantage of the 3PL's network of resources. This can include a single view of all inbound materials from a range of suppliers.

The ability for 3PLs to bring together all elements of the construction supply chain to a site with overlapping transport solution providers may provide a great opportunity for 4PL-style logistics operators. These would provide advanced IT solutions to provide clear visibility, event management and coordination throughout the supply chain and across multiple suppliers and logistics operators.

Conclusion

The role of the 3PL in other sectors is more mature than within construction, whilst there are significant opportunities for advances to be delivered – 3PLs have the resources, transferable expertise and systems to facilitate progress in the construction supply chain. The sector is diverse and can be complicated and unstructured, which can inhibit effective engagement with 3PLs. There are clear opportunities for 3PLs to deliver similar benefits in 'dominated' supply chains, as can be seen in the retail and automotive sectors. Moves to off-site manufacture and BIM-led information will create a momentum to engage with 3PLs, as the supply chain will require more coordinated logistics expertise, rather than simple transactional transport execution. Large-scale, high-profile projects have demonstrated some effective logistics practices, but there is a greater scope of opportunity with other building programmes, such as with house building. Challenges in changing current people, process and structure norms alongside longevity of 3PL contract lives will still be evident, although the evolution of the 3PL's role will start to diminish these barriers. Overall, there is a great opportunity for the construction supply chain to advance, providing scope to 3PLs, which are well placed to deliver significant benefit to the sector.

References

Cerasis (2013) History, Origins, and Various Definitions of 3PL (Third Party Logistics) [Online] http://cerasis.com/2013/09/16/3pl/ [accessed 17 February 2015]

Construction Products Association (2005) Improving Construction Logistics, Report of the Strategic Forum for Construction Logistics Group [Online] http://www.strategicforum.org.uk/pdf/Logistics%20Report%20August%202005.pdf [accessed 23 February 2015]

Deepen, J (2007) *Logistics Outsourcing Relationships*, Physica-Verlag, Heidelberg

EC Harris (2013) Construction Industry: Supply chain analysis, *GOV.UK* [Online] www.gov.uk/government/publications/construction-industry-supply-chain-analysis [accessed 16 April 2015]

Hobbs (1996) A transaction cost to supply chain management, *Supply Chain Management*, **1** (2), pp 15–27

Lieb, K and Lieb, RC (2012) The European third party logistics industry in 2011: the provider CEO perspective, *Supply Chain Forum*, **13** (1)

Lieb, RC (1992) The use of third-party logistics services by large American manufacturers, *Journal of Business Logistics*, **13** (2), pp 29–42

O'Bryne, R (2012) Logistics Outsourcing Tips: A practical guide – part 1, MHD Supply Chain Solutions

Roe, P (2007) Merchants face supply chain challenge, *Builders' Merchant Journal*, November, p 28

Sidler, B, from Bierderman, D (2012) Ceva looks to a new century, *The Journal of Commerce*, 2–9 April

Williamson (1985) *The Economic Institutions of Capitalism*, Free Press, New York

WRAP (2011) Using Construction Consolidation Centres to Reduce Construction Waste and Carbon Emissions, *WRAP* [Online] www.wrap.org.uk/sites/files/wrap/CCC%20combined.pdf [accessed 28 April 2015]

Managing construction logistics for confined sites in urban areas

RUVINDE KOORAGAMAGE

Introduction

Historical trends and recent research have depicted that there has been an increase in the movement and growth of population densities worldwide. Research undertaken from the United Nations in 2008 highlighted that urban and rural populations were equal. According to the source, the trend with urban growth will surpass rural expansion. Over the past decade there has been significant growth in urban centres, whereby urban population is exceeding rural growth (Biddy, 2009) and this trend is expected to continue.

With continuous urban growth there is a need to further develop and restore existing urban centres to accommodate the increasing population. Such redevelopments and the maintenance of these assets require significant construction work and rework (Roberts and Skyes, 2000). From an economic perspective there is a significant attraction for urban regeneration because of increased revenue and return on investment (Thornton *et al*, 2007). This chapter discusses the relevance of managing construction logistics, particularly forward and reverse logistics in busy congested cities.

Identifying current challenges in managing construction logistics

Achieving high levels of productivity and quality in construction is one of the greatest challenges facing urban centres in the 21st century. As such, research in the field of logistics management has demonstrated that productivity gains can be achieved, particularly if the construction processes are planned from a logistics perspective (Agapiou *et al*, 1998). Deficiencies in the supply and flow of construction material can result in major causes of productivity and financial losses.

Construction materials generally consume approximately 40–60 per cent of total project budgets (Agapiou *et al*, 1998; Ahuja, Dozzi and AbouRizk, 1994; Wong and Norman, 1997) and as a result suitable systems must be put in place to properly manage and control construction materials effectively.

The research work presented in this chapter differentiates itself from existing research by examining the flow of materials to the final workspace area for *confined* construction sites for projects located in *congested cities*. Construction projects in congested cities or confined land space possess numerous additional problems when compared to greenfield rural construction projects. Spillane *et al* (2011) highlight the fact that the critical challenge involving such projects is the difficulty in the management of materials required in such spatially restricted surroundings.

Qualitative research undertaken by Spillane *et al* (2011a) indicated 18 factors that were deemed critical in managing materials and material flow in a confined construction site. A causal loop diagram shown in Figure 11.1 seeks to highlight the various core issues related to confined urban construction sites.

The reader will note that in Figure 11.1 the interrelated variables are indicated with positive polarity (+) and negative polarity (–). For example, in the case of materials getting damaged and reducing productivity it can be deduced that with this relationship both variables move in the same direction, ie more materials getting damaged will lead to greater loss in productivity. (The reader should note that Figure 11.1 has been adapted from Spillane *et al* (2011) and the author has made further modifications to incorporate the movement of materials to the construction site and not just within the site.)

Generally, material management can be differentiated into five distinct groups:

- the measurement and specification;
- the procurement and purchasing process where the order is transmitted to the supplier;
- the administrative and financial process of payment;
- using the materials in production on the job site;
- delivery to site and logistics of checking the order, offloading and storing on site.

FIGURE 11.1 Causal loop diagram: issues with material management on confined construction sites

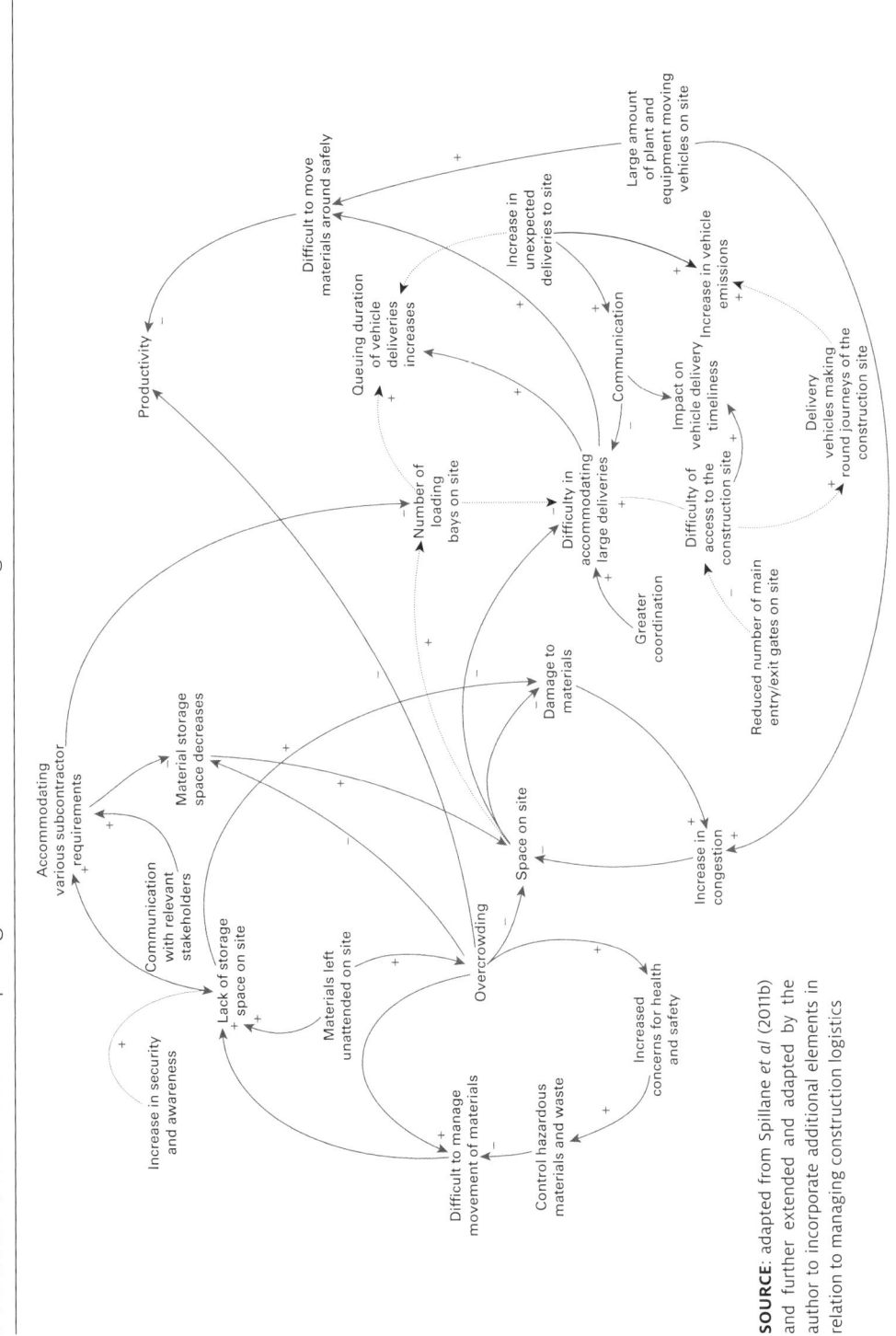

SOURCE: adapted from Spillane et al (2011b) and further extended and adapted by the author to incorporate additional elements in relation to managing construction logistics

The focus of this section is to investigate the last two points above. The ability to achieve efficient material management is important and a site layout design that reduces material travel time is crucial in construction. Donyavi and Flanagan (2009) and Voigtmann and Bargstädt (2010) point out that poor planning leads to inefficiency, a high amount of non-productive actions and consequently disturbed workflow on construction sites, excessive waste, and health and safety-related problems. Voigtmann and Bargstädt (2010) add that disorganized material storage causes additional time for material searches or rearranging storage areas. Site layout management overlaps with material management, which determines the location of offloading, location of the storage materials, protection of the materials and movement of materials to the final workplace (Pheng and Hui, 1999).

Supply chain management is one of the most important solutions for enhancing productivity and efficiency and preventing wasted time and cost (Donyavi and Flanagan, 2009). Additionally in this chapter, the uses of construction consolidation centres (CCCs) are highlighted and signify their relevance in levelling the flow of materials to the construction site and workspace. CCCs are particularly important for projects during the fit-out stage and adopt principles of lean construction in relation to forward and reverse logistics.

Construction logistics processes have a significant impact on the planning and execution of inner-city construction projects. The challenges related to managing and coordinating construction logistics is further amplified in confined construction sites (Lambeck and Eschemuller, 2008; Spillane *et al*, 2012; Loosemore and Uher, 2003). Construction logistics can be related, but not limited, to the following:

- planning;
- coordination;
- material flow to and within the construction site.

Definition of a confined construction site

Identifying a suitable definition for a confined construction site

Spillane *et al* (2012) identify 'confined spaces' as working areas whose characteristics are such that safe access or egress is not possible, leaving the area increasingly hazardous to occupy and work within. For the purposes of this chapter the author will adopt this definition.

A confined construction site is defined as a site where permanent works fit the site footprint, leaving spatial restrictions for other operations (eg plant and material movements, materials storage and temporary accommodation etc). As a result a confined construction site requires effective resource co-ordination beyond regular on-site management input.

Spillane *et al* (2012) distinguish a confined space from a confined construction site. A confined space relates to the characteristics associated with a particular environment within a work package on site where spatial restrictions exist. In comparison, a confined construction site can be described as follows:

> The construction site as a whole is characterized by amplified spatial restrictions, resulting in increased management interface to ensure effective management of the various resources and assorted work packages, to aid in the successful management of the project in its entirety.

Confined construction sites are by no means a new type of site within the construction industry; in fact, with urbanization this is increasingly becoming common.

Spatial congestion on site

Space is a limited *key resource* on a confined construction site. Various simulation tools have been developed to tackle the issues of optimizing space on site with just-in-time (JIT) delivery techniques. One example of such a simulation tool developed by Osman, Georgy and Ibrahim (2003) does not take into consideration how the site layout should decrease site congestion and enhance the safety of the working environment. Achieving numerous goals can be difficult to gauge and as such the formulation of a comprehensive mathematical model, which incorporates these tasks, is complicated. In confined construction sites in relation to multi-storey developments Thabet and Beliveau (1994) identify three distinct problems with construction space:

1 Space constraints mean that storage of construction materials on site is often restricted. In order to circumvent this problem, materials required for numerous activities are stored in construction work areas on the floor.

2 Some activities require a large workspace during execution. This includes mechanical duct installation where materials are initially spread and partially assembled on the ground prior to final installation.

3 Fragmentation of the construction industry adds to the limited workspace availability issue. For instance, work areas are generally allocated to one tradesperson at a time and therefore other tradespeople cannot occupy this space to accommodate their requirements.

According to Ekholm and Fridqvist (2000) the definition of 'construction space' in the domain of computational syntactic lacks sufficient research. Space conflict in construction sites can be classified under a large umbrella. Azmin, Hanafi and Abdullah (2013) and Wu and Chiu (2010) classify these types of workspaces as conflicts and restrictions on a construction site, as shown in Table 11.1.

Congestion on a construction worksite causes expensive inefficiencies to workflow and labour flow, which negatively impact productivity (Horman and Thomas, 2005). Spatial conflict such as congestion at the operation leads to a reduction in productivity in the range of 10–40 per cent; this figure is expected to increase if resources are poorly planned, causing a reduction

TABLE 11.1 Classifying main types of spatial conflicts with the safety, damage and site applicable to spatial congestion on site

Design Conflict	Currently the nature of complex construction projects involves numerous participants. When different participants design their own separate parts of the building, design conflicts may occur. Generally a design conflict occurs when a building component conflicts with another. It should be made clear that the causes of these conflicts are not construction-related. With the involvement of building information modelling (BIM) such conflicts are now greatly minimized.
Safety Hazard	According to Wu and Chiu (2010) and Soltani and Fernando (2004) some of the most prominent safety hazards in construction include being struck by falling objects, motor vehicle crashes, excavation accidents and electrical hazards.
Damage Conflict	A damage conflict takes place when a labour crew space, equipment space, or hazard space required by an activity conflicts with the protected space required by another activity.
Congestion	A congestion conflict occurs when a labour crew and a piece of equipment or material required by an activity requires the identical space at the same time, resulting in a lack of space or space overlap. General scenarios would be when storage space is too small caused by material stacking and overlap, or where too many workers are working on the same building component thus causing congestion. Another example would be when a large number of construction vehicles are entering or leaving the construction site at the same time, thus causing congestion.

in work efficiency by up to 65 per cent because of congestion conflict and 58 per cent because of obstruction of access way. It has been well documented that inadequate workspace and interference during travel leads to access blockage, congestion and safety hazards (Thabet, 1992; Oglesby, Parker and Howell, 1989). As such, spatial conflicts in construction can occur in many areas of the construction site and in various stages throughout the construction process (Wu and Chiu, 2010).

Guo (2001) has demonstrated that resolution of workspace conflicts during construction – by identifying interference between crew moving paths – can effectively increase productivity, especially during the fit-out period (Watkins *et al*, 2009).

Developing a theoretical framework

This section explores the existing literature to develop a theoretical framework through which to identify problems associated with the management of construction logistics in confined sites.

Material flow and material routing management in confined construction sites

Construction material management is differentiated into a number of subtopics, which include routing and material scheduling. Of these subtopics, material management in scheduling and location has been researched extensively whilst few studies have specifically dealt with material routing in construction sites (Yang and Mahdjoubi, 2001; Sikka, Dawood and Marasini, 2006). This section proposes that the integration of these topics is important to understand the management of material flow in construction sites located in congested cities.

The output of Spillane *et al* (2011a) indicated that out of the 18 factors that emerged from the qualitative analysis on health and safety management on confined construction sites, five issues were deemed critical and were weighted and ranked according to a severity index (SI). They are:

- that the contractor's material spatial requirements exceed the available space;
- that it is difficult to coordinate the storage of materials in line with the programme;
- that the location of the site entrance makes delivery of materials challenging;
- that it is difficult to store materials due to the lack of space;
- that it is difficult to coordinate the storage requirements of the various subcontractors.

Contractor's materials' spatial requirements exceed the available space

On average, construction materials take up 40–50 per cent of the total cost of a project. As such, with the increase in utilization of subcontractors and third-party subcontractors (Holt, Olomolaiye and Harris, 2003) the overall on-site management and coordination would increase dramatically. Compression of construction programmes is not uncommon (Nepal, Park and Son, 2006) in the need for on-site management to successfully accept delivery and accommodate the various material requirements of the subcontractors.

For construction sites where the spatial requirements for materials on site exceed the availability of space on site, proactive measures must be introduced in order to minimize hazards and eliminate accidents (Spillane *et al*, 2011b) and increase productivity where possible.

Challenges involved with material coordination and programme

The unavailability of suitable storage locations can have a significant impact on productivity, and as such ensuring that an adequate stockpile of materials on site is essential in the management of production (Horman and Thomas, 2005). The lack of storage space is a leading factor in spatial congestion and results in a significantly reduced level of productivity on construction projects. Where there is a lack of storage space, inventory can become compromised leading towards negative results in productivity and materials management.

Location of site entrance makes delivery of materials challenging

The nature of the construction site layout impacts the management of materials; where this form of management is implemented, monetary savings are then made.

One of the primary functions of an adequately designed site layout is to provide benefit in the movement of materials into and around the construction site (Elbeltagi, Hegazy and Eldsouky, 2004). The supply of materials is fraught with difficulties, not only onto site, but also in getting materials to site (Agapiou *et al*, 1998). With many urban confined-site environments, the location of the site entrance or the site itself can be an issue. The roles of logistics management and supply chain management are essential in the management of materials and the location of the site entrance, both prior to arriving on site and during the delivery and unloading process.

The ability to design and accommodate adequate logistics management plans, site layout plans and materials management plans are all essential in the management of the transportation of materials both onto and around site. Where such site layout plans are not implemented, the movement of materials on site is significantly restricted, resulting in increased manual handling, double handling, waste, lost productivity, increased health and safety risks and potentially project failure. From a materials management perspective materials become damaged, require double handling and are misplaced, due to inadequate management of the limited available space on site. This is mainly attributable to bottleneck effects, where multiple deliveries can result in increased management intervention to alleviate any issue that may arise.

Difficult-to-store materials on site due to the lack of space

One of the main reasons for a lack of storage space on site is overcrowding or congestion of the workspace, which hinders operational productivity of the entire project. An overcrowded construction site may lead to double handling of materials, thus reducing productivity and increasing damage to materials along with increased health and safety concerns (Huang and Hinze, 2003). Inadequate management of materials through over-allocation has also been identified as affecting progress, workflow and overall productivity, due to overcrowding the restricted work area available, while also highlighting the issue of securely storing materials such as ironmongery.

During the fit-out stage spatial variability is indicated by various site layout requirements. For example, the rescheduling of storage areas, rearrangement of means of transportation and other major changes in layout are deemed uncommon (Voigtmann and Bargstädt, 2010).

According to Winch and North (2006) site-based planning is essential to overcome this issue and management of the critical space, including spatial management and reducing congestion on site, has been noted as being fundamental to site management.

Difficult to coordinate the storage requirements of the various subcontractors

In confined construction sites, the coordination and movement of materials to the construction site and around the site can be 'cumbersome' and 'time consuming'. Thomas, Sanvido and Sanders (1989) classify the coordination of materials on site as:

- organization and storage of materials;
- housekeeping of materials and waste;
- planning of material deliveries;
- material availability on site;
- material handling and distribution on site.

Research undertaken by Koskela (1999) shows that almost 40 per cent of the total cost of materials on site is made up of purchasing and controlling the movement of materials on site. Where this task is made more efficient, savings are possible (Koskela, 1999). In Mulholland and Christian's (1999) research project coordination, including material coordination, was highlighted as one of the key issues in projects failing to meet the predetermined project programme. Through acknowledging the requirement to facilitate effective material coordination with the other various tasks and resources on site, such programme slippages could be mitigated or eliminated as the project progresses.

The coordination of materials and other resources has been documented by numerous authors (Thomas, Riley and Messner, 2005; Nepal, Park and Son, 2006; Lu et al, 2007), illustrating that effective coordination of the various resources is essential to avoid waste or non-value-adding activities on site (Formoso et al, 2002). Research has indicated that coordination of materials is an essential facet in the management of materials on site, but where spatial limitations occur, this point is significantly more evident (Thomas, Sanvido and Sanders, 1989).

The effect of spatial time collision on health and safety and productivity

Overcrowding in construction sites is becoming a key managerial issue, particularly in confined construction sites (Spillane *et al*, 2011a). According to the Health and Safety Executive in England, on average seven workers die every year, as a result of being struck by moving plant in addition to more than 90 workers seriously injured (HSE, 2011). Research conducted by Abdelhamid and Everett (2000) indicates vehicular accidents on site as one of the root causes of incidents in the construction industry. Sawacha, Naoum and Fong (1999) add that accidents due to vehicular traffic on site are one of the main elements affecting the safety performance of construction sites and the success of projects.

In confined construction sites this level of health and safety is significantly elevated due to the close proximity of personnel to operating plant and machinery on site (Harris, McCaffer and Edmun-Fotwe, 2006). Research carried out by Uher and Loosemore (2004) demonstrates that 'the use of dangerous machinery within a congested working environment' has a negative impact on the overall health and safety. Overcrowding on site will lead to negative effects both in terms of productivity and safety. Harris and colleagues, and Dawood *et al* (2000) add that the lack of space on a construction site can inevitably lead to 'space conflicts, long journey paths, unavailability of access to rooms, time lost and therefore performance of workers'. Furthermore, Mallasi and Dawood (2002) emphasize that construction project planning is facing a new type of a lack in space, which has reduced the safe movement of workers and vehicles, resulting in accidents. These constraints are coupled with the requirements of shorter deadlines.

In order to minimize or mitigate the possibility of such accidents taking place the HSE (2011) have implemented numerous core strategies to include: minimizing vehicle movements, turning vehicles, visibility and people on site.

The recommendations set out by the HSE (2011) are limited to:

- provide car and van parking for the workforce and visitors away from the work area;
- control entry to the work area;
- plan storage areas so that delivery vehicles do not have to cross the site.

Managing material flow routing to construction sites in congested cities

Transportation costs has been a relatively common area of research (Fang and Ng, 2011) such as routing of transportation (Eilon, Watson-Gandy and

Christofides, 1971), minimization of transportation costs (Bodin *et al*, 1983). However, transportation costs in construction itself have been described as a 'hidden cost' (Shakantu, Tookey and Bowen, 2003). According to the BRE report (2003) this cost can amount to 10–20 per cent of the overall construction cost.

With processes such as prefabrication, pre-assembly, standardization and modularization becoming familiar and common amongst contractors (Sikka, Dawood and Marasini, 2006) this ultimately increases vehicular movements, typically flatbed trailers, HGVs and rigid trucks entering congested cities.

Figures published by the Confederation of British Industry estimates that the annual cost of road congestion to the economy is £20 billion (Sikka, Dawood and Marasini, 2006). Construction vehicles account for a significant proportion of this congestion, as a result construction sites suffer inefficiencies of unreliable deliveries.

In construction, for the majority of the materials purchased, the planning of deliveries is undertaken on an ad hoc basis (Clausen, 1995). This creates a certain level of difficulty often leading to a 'deadlock' in terms of managing and coordinating deliveries for the contractor leading to two different problems. Ordering materials in bulk prior to task execution on site can often lead to financial costs associated with inventories (Georgy and Basily, 2008) if these do not comply with production needs on site (Agapiou *et al*, 1998). Hendrickson (2000) adds that materials may be stolen unless special security is provided, or they may deteriorate during storage. Storage areas on site for building materials often require a large storage capacity, which is rarely available. Furthermore, storage facilities on site are either temporary structures or compounds, and the condition in which the materials are kept leads to damage from ingress of weather and movement of people, plant and equipment (Agapiou *et al*, 1998).

According to Josephson, Larsson and Li (2002) late delivery of materials is the fourth most important cause of rework resulting in delays and cost overruns in projects. Enshassi (1996) emphasizes the potential waste of resources during stocking, handling and transporting, which consequently hinders the value chain. Fang and Ng (2011) argue that cost minimization of construction materials should not purely focus on reducing wastage and rework but also cut down on costs relating to the logistics of the materials, especially those that are bulky and projects requiring extensive fit-outs. An empirical study undertaken in Finland (Wegelius-Lehtonen, 2001) estimated that the logistics costs for supply of plasterboard may account for up to 27 per cent of its purchase price.

Contrary to this argument, ordering materials late can result in late deliveries, which can lead to material shortages, work interruption and consequently delays. Research undertaken by Assaf and Al-Hejji (2006) indicated that late or unreliable deliveries were ranked by contractors as the fourth most important source of delay in construction projects.

In theory, material availability influences activity execution; as such the greatest price that a construction project can pay for uncertainty and randomness is not having the required resources when required (Hamzeh *et al*, 2007).

Material routing and path planning in a confined construction site

This section extends the link made between safety workspace and path workspace and probes into existing research undertaken by various authors. Although past research has targeted the space-scheduling problem, much less literature is concerned with workspaces relating to dynamic working objects on construction sites to include labour and equipment (Wu and Chiu, 2010). The research conducted by Wu and Chiu (2010) and Soltani and Fernando (2004) considered the spatial availability of construction sites relative to scheduling, productivity loss due to path interference and space constraints.

It is not unusual in construction for the site layout and the site plan to change frequently as the project progresses (Soltani and Fernando, 2004). The site layout must not only reflect the logistical problems but should also take into account sustaining high productivity levels for repetitive tasks. This should be coupled with the provision of safe paths, which can be used to control collisions on site.

Yang and Mahdjoubi (2001) highlight the importance of routing materials, which can affect the cost and time during construction projects; as such this can provide 'major productive gains' in terms of reducing waste and working by planning the site from a logistics perspective. Excessive travel routes and distances on site between the processes of unloading and transporting to the exact workplace can be detrimental to the overall productivity of a construction project in terms of labour cost and time (Soltani and Fernando, 2004). This statement is supported by Harris, McCaffer and Edmun-Fotwe (2006), who indicate that the movement of materials, plants and operatives from one place to another almost accounts for 30 per cent delay on construction work.

A theoretical approach to address material flow

Based on the above literature, this section identifies key elements associated with the challenges of material flow in congested cities for confined sites (Figure 11.2). The discussion in the body of this chapter has so far attempted to draw a relationship between the construction site and the external environment as an interface. Existing research predominantly fails to address this link and to investigate the variables that affect this 'interface'.

Material flow in construction projects located in cities is dependent on both the logistics within the construction site and logistics outside the construction site. The section initially began discussing issues relating to confined construction sites then identified how productivity and safety are

FIGURE 11.2 A high-level theoretical framework to address the concepts related to material flow within the context of confined construction sites in congested cities

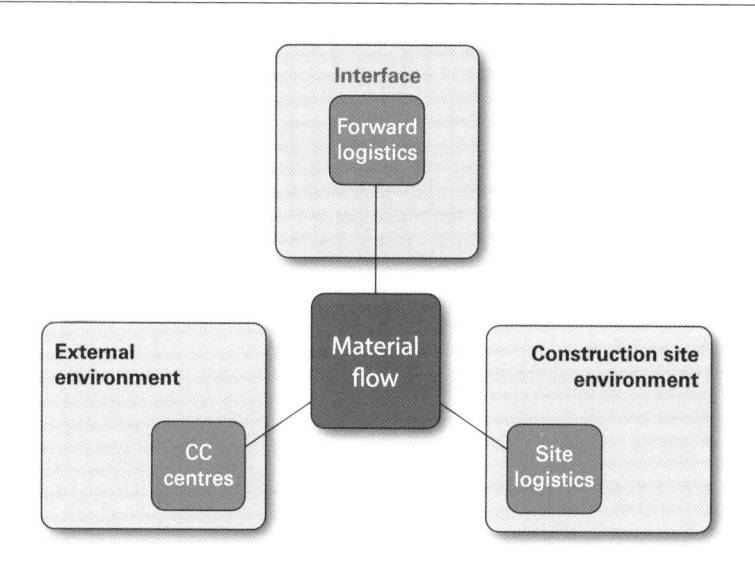

affected by the confined area of the construction site and how this is related to the flow of materials and material management.

Optimizing both productivity and safety in confined construction sites involves an efficient management of materials flowing to the site. The theoretical framework presented in Figure 11.2 closely involves the features shown in Table 11.2, which reflect the parameters of productivity and safety in the overall theme of managing construction logistics. Voigtmann and Bargstädt (2010) emphasize the importance of not only optimizing partial aspects that can be counterproductive. For example, the inclusion of an

TABLE 11.2 Investigating various parameters using the proposed framework

Forward Logistics	Flow of goods and materials directly from supplier to the construction site to minimize queuing time of deliveries.
Construction Consolidation Centre	Temporary material 'holding' area off site to vary and smooth the flow of materials entering the construction site.
Site Logistics	Varying the number of loading bays and material unloading equipment on site to reduce spatial time collisions.

additional loading bay may lead to a reduction in waiting time for delivery vehicles; however, such space must be used efficiently. In confined construction sites, alternative methods of temporary storage should be considered such as loading gantries, and scaffold loading bays that minimize the use of ground space on site.

Conclusion

This chapter commenced by highlighting the root cause problems of construction logistics on site in congested cities. A literature review was carried out to investigate the key elements affecting the flow of materials to site. The output of this literature review was to develop a theoretical framework, as shown in Figure 11.3, which shows to a certain extent the relationship between the various elements associated in the management of construction logistics.

FIGURE 11.3 Theoretical model utilized to develop a logistics model

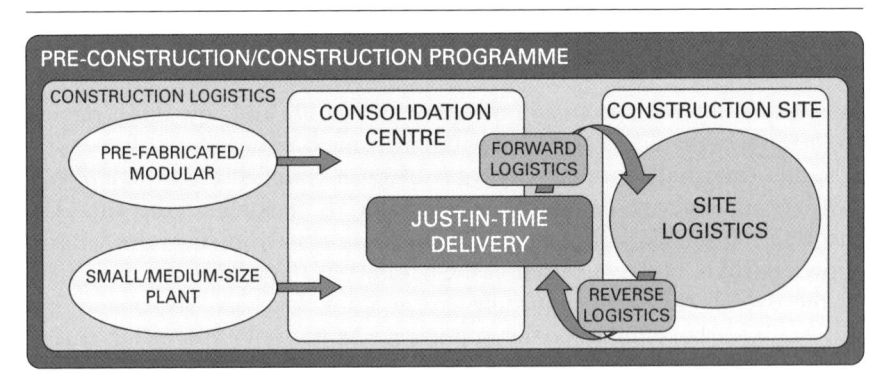

On a macro scale the framework chiefly relates to the supply chain and the flow of materials to the end user. However, with construction projects in congested cities the principle of lean construction, a fundamental theory, is applied to the framework. With the case of forward logistics, materials or plant resources are dispatched to site only when required. This is particularly useful with materials such as plasterboard, which is prone to damage, or ironmongery, which are high-value materials.

The data shown in Figure 11.4, gathered by Wilson James CCC in 2013 and supplied to the author as part of a research project, indicates that the flow of materials to the construction site may not be deemed necessarily as materials consumed or beneficial to the end user, but may also include contractor's/subcontractor's preliminaries.

Figure 11.4 depicts the range of materials that were stored in the consolidation centre. The data also indicated that less than 3 per cent of the

FIGURE 11.4 Variation of materials stored in the construction consolidation centre

Drywall, 17
Other, 102
Scaffolds, 4
Metal, 5
Site services, 11
Internal fixings, 6
Materials returned from site, 31
Internal fittings including M&E, 162
Electrical components, 112
Empty cable drums, 4
Tiles, 9
Ceiling lights, 2
Water heater, 1

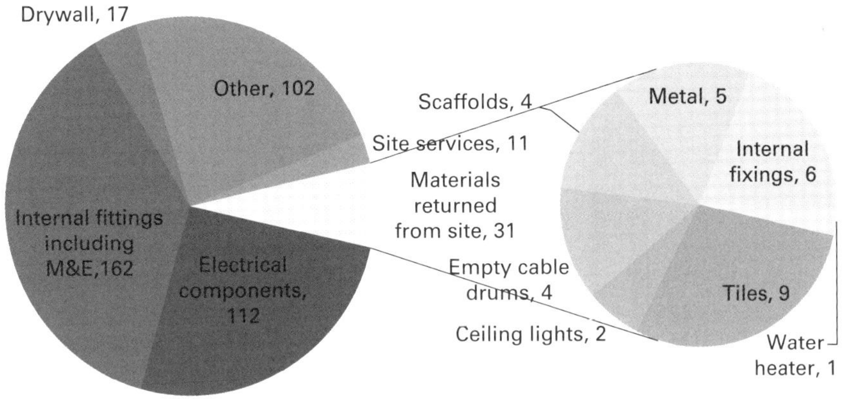

SOURCE: Wilson James Construction Consolidation Centre (2013)

centre was used for storing ancillary plant and materials, such as pedestals and ladder racks. This signifies that the consolidation centre can optimize site space in confined sites by holding and delivering trade contractors' plant or tools to enable their work tasks at the right place/right time.

It is also worth noting that during the five-month operation of the data presented in Figure 11.4, approximately 7 per cent of the materials were returned to the consolidation centre during this fit-out stage. It is difficult to argue the quality of the figure representing the proportion of materials returned, as further data from similar-sized projects are required in order to investigate this further.

The potential benefits of a CCC for this project are highlighted in Figure 11.5 when during this 18-month period the CCC absorbed 74 per cent of the deliveries that would have been made to the construction site. This has a significant impact for a confined construction site in terms of managing material flow. Furthermore, the benefits of adopting such a logistics system attract stakeholders such as local authorities, and can also increase road safety due to the reduction in vehicle movements to the city.

The fundamental purpose of this chapter was to provide a holistic framework engaging the key elements of construction logistics to a certain extent. The management of each of these elements can be complex and should be driven through a simulation model comprising the key elements from the conceptual framework.

The author has put forward that lean construction can be achieved to a certain extent by means of a CCC. The primary theory from a forward logistics perspective is to 'smooth' the flow of materials or plant entering or leaving the construction site. From a site logistics perspective this can be argued as having the materials on site at the right place, right time each time.

FIGURE 11.5 Graph comparing number of deliveries made to site with a CCC versus traditional deliveries to site

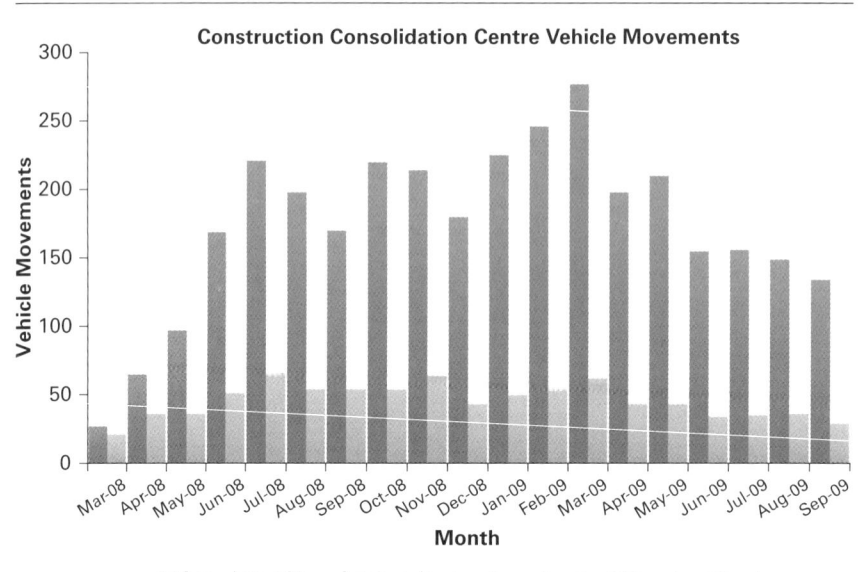

Construction Consolidation Centre Vehicle Movements

■ Calculated No. of deliveries to site using traditional methods.
■ Actual No. of LCCC deliveries to site.

However, this will need to be reflected in the availability of plant resources on site, especially with the vertical movement of material flow in a building project. Lack of site plant such as goods/beam hoist or tower crane may potentially negate the benefits of a CCC.

One key element that has not been thoroughly looked at within the domain of this research is the relevance of the pre-construction/construction programme. Construction projects are programme-driven and resource allocations may alter or in some cases a programme will be re-sequenced. Alterations to the programme will affect the flow of materials to the construction site; therefore the logic on the programme will dictate the flow of materials and resources to site. The project programme should drive the flow of materials to the construction site and delays on the programme will inadvertently impact resources/plant and related activities on the project. The construction consolidation centre not only acts as a short-term buffer but also allows better control of material flow to confined construction sites. This predominantly applies to prefabricated/modular elements.

The benefits of this system can be analysed in numerous directions to include health and safety (on site and off site), benefit in kind for the environment and site logistics. Although not presented in this chapter the author has argued the need to develop a logistics-based simulation model to indicate the financial impact that a CCC may have on the project programme and project value.

References

Abdelhamid, TS and Everett, JG (2000) Identifying root causes of construction accidents, *Journal of Construction Engineering and Management*, **126** (1), pp 52–60

Agapiou, A *et al* (1998) The role of logistics in the materials flow control process, *Construction Management and Economics*, **16**, pp 131–37

Ahuja, HN, Dozzi, SP and AbouRizk, SM (1994) *Project Management: Techniques in planning and controlling construction projects*, 2nd edn, Wiley, New York

Assaf, SA and Al-Hejji, S (2006) Causes of delay in large construction projects, *International Journal of Project Management*, **24** (4), pp 349–57

Azmin, SM, Hanafi, HM and Abdullah, S (2013) Main factors lack of workspace planning that causes workspace on project environment: industrialised building system in Malaysia, *Australian Journal of Basic and Applied Sciences*, **7** (6), pp 408–19

Biddy, P (2009) Land use in Britain, *Land Use Policy*, **26** (1), pp 2–13

Bodin, L *et al* (1983) Routing and scheduling of vehicles and crews, *The State of the Art, Computer and Operational Research*, **10** (2), pp 62–212

BRE (2003) Construction Site Transport [Online] http://www.bre.co.uk/pdf/constructiontraffic.pdf [accessed 23 February 2015]

Clausen, LE (1995) Building Logistics, Number 256, Danish Building Research Institute, Copenhagen

Dawood, N *et al* (2000) The Virtual Construction Site (VIRCON): A decision support system for construction planning, Proceedings of CONVR 2000 conference on construction applications of virtual reality, Middlesbrough, Teesside University, pp 17–29

Donyavi, S and Flanagan, R (2009) The impact of effective material management of construction site performance for small and medium sized construction enterprises, Proceedings of the 25th Annual ARCOM Conference, pp 11–20

Eilon, S, Watson-Gandy, C and Christofides, N (1971) Expected Distances in Distribution Problems, Distribution Management: Mathematical modelling and practical analysis, Griffin, London, pp 151–79

Ekholm, A and Fridqvist, S (2000) A concept of space for building classification, product modelling and design, *Automation in Construction*, **9** (3), pp 315–28

Elbeltagi, E and Hegazy, T (2003) Optimum site layout planning for irregular construction sites, 5th Construction Speciality Conference of the Canadian Society of Civil Engineering, Moncton, Nouveau, Brunswick, Canada

Elbetagi, E, Hegazy, T and Eldsouky, A (2004) Dynamic layout of construction temporary facilities considering safety, *Journal of Construction Engineering and Management*, **130** (4), 534–41

Enshassi, A (1996) Materials control and waste on building sites, *Building Research and Information*, **24** (1), pp 31–34

Fang, YS and Ng, T (2011) Applying activity-based costing approach for construction logistics cost analysis, *Construction Innovation*, **11** (3), pp 259–81

Formoso, CT *et al* (2002) Material waste in building industry: main causes and prevention, *Journal of Construction Engineering and Management*, **128** (4), pp 316–25

Georgy, M and Basily, SY (2008) Using genetic algorithms in optimising construction material delivery schedules, *Construction Innovation*, **8** (1), pp 23–45

Guo, S (2001) Identification and resolution of workspace conflicts in building construction, *Journal of Construction Engineering and Management*, **128** (4), pp 287–95

Hamzeh, FR *et al* (2007) Logistics centres to support project based production in the construction industry, Proceedings IGLC-15, Michigan, USA

Harris, F, McCaffer, R and Edmun-Fotwe, F (2006) *Modern Construction Management*, Blackwell, Oxford, UK

Hendrickson, C (2000) *Project Management for Construction: Fundamental concepts for owners, engineers, architects, and builders*, 2nd edn, Prentice-Hall, Englewood Cliffs, NJ

Holt, GD, Olomolaiye, PO and Harris, FC (2003) Factors influencing UK construction clients' choice of contractor, *Building and environment*, **29** (2), pp 241–48

Horman, MJ and Thomas, RH (2005) Role of inventory buffers in construction labour performance, *Journal of Construction Engineering and Management*, **131** (7), pp 751–856

HSE (2011) Health and Safety Executive, Traffic management onsite. [Online] http://www.hse.gov.uk [accessed 26 September 2013]

Huang, X and Hinze, J (2003) Analysis of construction worker fall accidents, *Journal of Construction Engineering and Management*, **129** (3), pp 262–71

Josephson, P, Larsson, B and Li, H (2002) Illustrative benchmarking rework and rework costs in Swedish construction industry, *Journal of Management in Engineering*, **18** (2), pp 76–83

Koskela, L (1999) Management of production in construction: a theoretical review, Proceedings of International Conference for Lean Construction, USA

Lambeck, R and Eschemuller, J (2008) *Urban Construction Project Management*, McGraw Hill, Professional, USA

Loosemore, M and Uher, TE (2003) *Essentials of Construction Project Management*, UNSW Press, Australia

Lu, M *et al* (2007) Positioning and tracking construction vehicles in highly dense urban areas and building construction sites, *Automation in Construction*, **16** (5), pp 647–56

Mallasi, Z and Dawood, N (2002) Registering space requirements of construction operations using site-PECASO model, International Council for Research and Innovation in Building and Construction, CIB W78 conference, pp 1–8

Mulholland, B and Christian, J (1999) Risk assessment in construction schedules, *Journal of Construction Engineering and Management*, **125** (1), pp 8–15

Nepal, MP, Park, M and Son, B (2006) Effects of schedule pressure on construction performance, *Journal of Construction Engineering and Management*, **132** (2), pp 182–88

Oglesby, CH, Parker, HW and Howell, GA (1989) *Productivity Improvement in Construction*, McGraw-Hill Inc, NY

Osman, MH, Georgy, EM and Ibrahim, EM (2003) A hybrid CAD-based construction site layout planning system using genetic algorithms, *Automation in Construction*, **12**, pp 749–64

Pheng, L and Hui, M (1999) The application of JIT philosophy to construction: a case study in site layout, *Construction Management and Economics*, **17**, pp 657–68

Roberts, PW and Skyes, H (2000) Urban Regeneration: A handbook, Sage Publications, London

Sawacha, E, Naoum, S and Fong, D (1999) Factors affecting safety performance on construction sites, *International Journal of Project Management*, **17** (5), pp 309–15

Shakantu, WM, Tookey, E and Bowen, PA (2003) The hidden cost of transportation of construction materials: an overview, *Journal of Engineering, Design and Technology*, **1** (1), pp 103–18

Sikka, S, Dawood, N and Marasini, R (2006) An integration of construction site logistics & associated vehicle movements towards a sustainable construction. Joint International Conference on Computing and Decision Making in Civil and Building Engineering, Montreal, Canada

Soltani, AR and Fernando, T (2004) A fuzzy based multi-objective path planning of construction sites, *Automation in Construction*, **13** (6), pp 717–34

Spillane, JP et al (2011) Confined site construction: a qualitative investigation of critical issues affecting management of health and safety, *Journal of Civil Engineering and Construction Technology*, **2** (7), pp 138–46

Spillane, JP et al (2011a) Challenges of the UK/Irish contractors regarding material management and logistics in confined site construction, *International Journal of Construction Supply Chain Management*, **1** (1), pp 25–42

Spillane, JP et al (2012) Critical factors affecting effective management of site personnel and operatives in confined site construction (paper has no journal reference)

Thabet, WY (1992) A space constrained – resource constrained scheduling system for multi-story buildings, PhD dissertation, Civil Engineering Department, Virginia Polytechnic Institute and State University, Blacksburg, VA

Thabet, WY and Beliveau, JY (1994) Modelling workspace to schedule repetitive floors in multi-storey buildings, *Journal of Construction Engineering and Management*, **120** (1), pp 96–116

Thomas, HR, Sanvido, VE and Sanders, SR (1989) Impact of material management on productivity: a case study, *Journal of Construction Engineering and Management*, **115** (3), pp 370–84

Thomas, HR, Riley, DR and Messner, JI (2005) Fundamental principles of site material management, *Journal of Construction Engineering and Management*, ASCE, **131** (7), pp 808–15

Thornton, GM et al (2007) The challenge of sustainability: incentives for brownfield regeneration in Europe, *Environmental Science and Policy*, **10**, pp 116–34

Uher, TE and Loosemore, M (2004) *Essentials of Construction Project Management*, University of New South Wales Press, Sydney, Australia

United Nations (2008) Urban Agglomerations, 2007, United Nations, Department of Economic and Social Affairs, Population Division, New York, NY, USA

United Nations (2010) World Urbanisation Prospects: The 2009 revision – highlights, United Nations, Department of Economics and Social Affairs, Population Division, New York, NY, USA

Voigtmann, J and Bargstädt, JH (2008) Simulation of construction logistics in outfitting processes, in *EWork and EBusiness in Architecture, Engineering and Construction: ECPPM 2008*, ed, A Zarli and R Scherer, pp 195–203, Taylor and Francis, London

Voigtmann, JK and Bargstädt, H-J (2010) Construction Logistic Planning by Simulation, Winter Simulation Conference, Baltimore [Online] http://informs-sim.org/wsc10papers/prog10.html#14%20//%20PROJECT%20MANAGEMENT%20AND%20CONSTRUCTION [accessed 23 February 2015]

Watkins, M *et al* (2009) Using agent-based modelling to study construction labour productivity as an emergent property of individual and crew interactions, *Journal of Construction Engineering and Management*, **135** (7), pp 657–67

Wegelius-Lehtonen (2001) Performance measurement in construction logistics, *International Journal of Production Economics*, **69** (1), pp 107–16

Winch, GM and North, S (2006) Critical space analysis, *Journal of Construction Engineering and Management*, **132** (5), pp 473–81

Wong, ET and Norman, G (1997) Economic evaluation of materials planning systems for construction, *Construction Management and Economics*, **15**, pp 39–47

Wu, IC and Chiu, YC (2010) 4D Workspace conflict detection and analysis system, Proceedings of the 10th International Conference on Construction Application of Virtual Reality

Yang, LJ and Mahdjoubi, L (2001) An intelligent materials routing system on complex construction sites, *Logistics Information Management*, **14** (5/6), pp 337–43

Consolidation centres in construction logistics

12

GREGER LUNDESJÖ

Introduction

There are many different ways to organize consolidation of materials in construction and we discuss a number of approaches below. To understand what is meant by a construction consolidation centre (CCC) and how it changes the flow of materials to (and in some cases from) a construction site it is useful to consider what typically characterizes the delivery of materials to construction sites:

- There is a great number of deliveries.
- Different materials arrive on separate vehicles from individual suppliers.
- There is little or no coordination between deliveries and timekeeping by suppliers is often poor, leading to congestion and waiting time at gates, or vehicles circulating in the local area waiting for a slot.
- Many vehicles arrive much less than fully loaded.
- Often vehicles depart empty or nearly empty yet return logistics opportunities are not exploited.
- Often large quantities are delivered, requiring storage on site over long periods.
- There is a wide range of vehicle types requiring different equipment and often making unloading time-consuming.
- The different trades on site each have their own suppliers and the main contractor has little control over the coordination of deliveries.

All these factors make the gates and receiving areas much busier than warranted by the actual volume of materials. Queuing and waiting frequently cause delay and trade contractors lose productive time waiting for or looking for materials. Construction traffic has a negative impact on the local area causing congestion, noise and pollution.

Using a CCC addresses all these issues. Instead of delivering to site, suppliers deliver to a small warehouse (or distribution centre) where materials are stored in dry and secure conditions. From the CCC consolidated loads, possibly for a number of trades and in some cases even for more than one site, are made up and delivered to site on a just-in-time (JIT) basis. Large items and materials for which a full vehicle load is required at one time bypass the CCC and go directly to site; there is no point in offloading at the CCC just to reload the complete delivery again. Naturally consolidation is less important in the early stages of the construction of a building, but it comes into its own during the fit-out stages. Excessive packaging can be removed at the CCC and return journeys can be used to remove surplus materials, packaging and waste from the site. Site traffic is drastically reduced and deliveries run on time. Site productivity improves and waste is reduced.

Consolidation is not a new concept in construction and there are many case studies and reports analysing the operation and benefits of using a CCC. Many date from the first decade of the 21st century. Based on the generally excellent feedback from these early examples one would have expected widespread use of CCCs to follow. But while they are in regular use they are by no means the norm in the industry, and it is relevant to ask why, in fact, they are not more widely used.

FIGURE 12.1 Illustration of the principles of consolidation

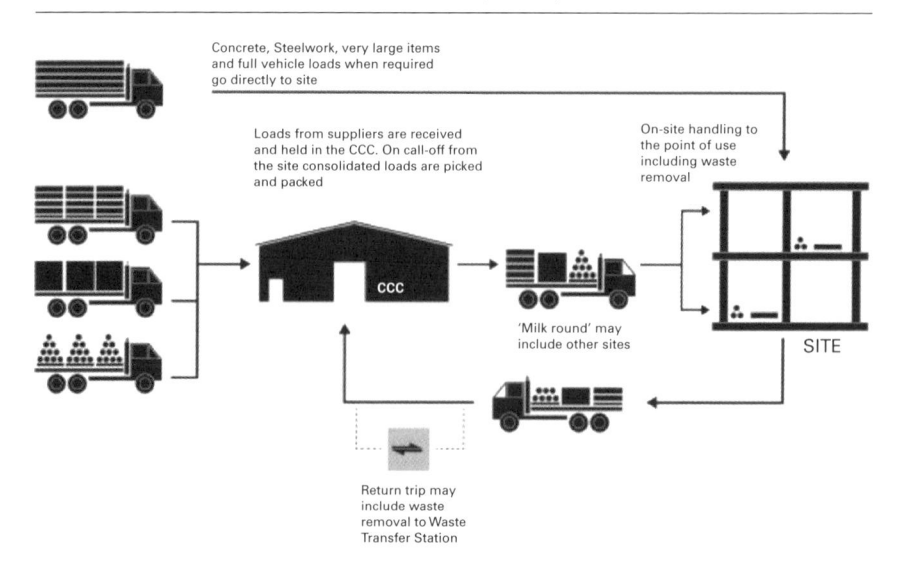

A few well-documented early CCC projects:

- In 2001 the Heathrow Consolidation Centre (HCC) was set up to serve the ongoing construction work at Heathrow Terminals 1–4. The HCC was set up by Mace and was run by construction logistics specialists Wilson James for BAA. The HCC has been thoroughly studied and covered in articles and books, such as *Managing Construction Logistics* (Sullivan, Barthorpe and Robbins, 2010).
- Between 2001 and 2003 a logistics centre supported a large residential project called Hammarby Sjöstad in Stockholm, Sweden. This centre, introduced on the initiative of Stockholm City Authorities, achieved its objectives in reducing traffic and related issues such as noise and emissions. The operation was subject to academic studies, which also found other substantial benefits; in particular significant reductions in waste through better storage, reduced product damage and reduced shrinkage (Ottoson, 2005: 7).
- In London, likewise the authorities encouraged the use of construction consolidation. A partnership between Transport for London, developers Stanhope PLC, the construction firm Bovis Lend Lease and logistics company Wilson James (who also operated the facility) set up the London Construction Consolidation Centre (LCCC), which began operation in Bermondsey, south London in 2005. The LCCC was initially created for a pilot study. After the pilot study Wilson James carried on the activity on a commercial basis; it has relocated to Silvertown just south of City of London Airport. The experiences from this operation have been covered in several articles and books, such as *Managing Construction Logistics* (Sullivan, Barthorpe and Robbins, 2010).

All these early examples of CCCs were studied in some depth, and generally regarded as successful. The benefits of using a CCC based on these experiences and some other more recent examples will be set out in this chapter. Transport for London commissioned further studies indicating that London on an ongoing basis could/should support at least six CCCs strategically located around the city (Anderson, 2007). Following these early, much publicized experiences of CCCs, and both academic and business-case support of the concept, one would have expected strong growth in this approach to construction logistics. This has not happened, and at the end of this chapter some of the reasons for this will be discussed.

The resources, functionality and operation of a CCC

Compared to many modern distribution and warehousing operations the processes of a CCC are very straightforward. In simple terms its purpose is to receive materials in bulk from suppliers, store them securely and, on order from the site, make up loads for daily deliveries. The nature of the typical construction project where different subcontractors have control and ownership of their different materials has an impact on how CCCs are run; and there are different approaches, some of which will be discussed on p 237.

The resources and facilities

When discussing CCCs the process of consolidation is more important than the physical facilities; nothing complicated is required. The resources of an ideal CCC operation include:

- A small or medium-sized warehouse (see p 230). At a minimum an open floor is all that is needed for storage; larger operations will include some pallet racking and shelving areas.
- Preferably a covered area where vehicles can be offloaded/loaded in the dry.
- Outside hard standing for large items and materials not vulnerable to the weather.
- A waste/recycling area for packaging materials and other waste.
- Forklift truck(s) for vehicle loading and handling in the warehouse.
- Vehicle(s) for delivery to site.
- Personnel such as warehouse operative(s), administrator and driver(s).
- Some kind of warehouse management system (see p 231).

In the guidance note for using CCCs to reduce construction waste and carbon emissions (Lundesjö, 2011) examples are given of the differing sizes and types of CCCs that provide useful service depending on the projects served.

For illustration, resources of the largest and smallest are summarized in Table 12.1 which illustrates the rather obvious fact that the resource requirements have to be adapted to the project volume served; they are, however, in warehousing terms neither large nor complex. The focus in consolidation is on the process.

Ordering materials

Trade contractors are usually responsible for ordering and supplying their own materials as part of their subcontract. In a project using a CCC they are asked to request delivery to the CCC rather than to site. The focus of the CCC is to consolidate deliveries to site and not to become a large bulk warehouse. Therefore it is not unusual for CCC operators to require contractors to limit the amount of stock they hold at any one time in the CCC to no more than, say, two weeks' usage. However there is an argument that,

TABLE 12.1 Large and small resources

	Large Multi-Project, Multi-Client CCC	Small Single-Project CCC
Size of warehouse	10,000 m² warehouse space plus large yard area	650 m² warehouse space; the operation housed within a 3PL shared user distribution facility
Throughput in PEU (pallet equivalent unit)	50,000 per year	6,000 per year
Vehicles	1× 26 tonne flatbed with crane 2× 18 tonne flatbed 1× 18 tonne curtain-sided with tail lift 1× LWB Transit 4× forklift trucks The fleet is regularly adjusted to demand	1× rigid flatbed lorry 1× 18 tonne curtain-sided lorry with tail lift 1× large Transit van 1× forklift truck
Operatives	Manager, administrator, warehouse operatives and drivers – in total eight employees	A manager, an administrator, one warehouse operative and two drivers
Construction projects supported	Up to six large inner-city projects simultaneously including a major hospital and large commercial and residential developments	Supporting a single development of luxury apartments

given sufficient space, the guiding principles for supplier deliveries ought to be economic and environmental, ie full vehicle loads, and preferably co-ordinated in time to allow for return logistics opportunities.

It is important to note that this approach will reduce the cost of material supply thanks to faster vehicle turnaround time (see section on p 233 on the benefits of CCCs) and economical order quantities. It is important for the main contractor (who normally pays for the CCC operation) to ensure that these savings are identified and passed on. This might not be as simple as it seems, with delivery costs not always transparent but hidden within fixed price offers, including delivery.

Receiving materials at the CCC

Ideally a CCC should include a covered vehicle offloading area to ensure that materials can always be handled in dry and safe conditions. When vehicles arrive, which should be as per agreed schedule to avoid both conflict with other suppliers and unnecessary waiting time, the CCC operative will offload and inspect the delivery against the delivery note. This inspection is limited to product ID, quantity and damage. The CCC operatives handling goods owned by trade contractors do not have the ability or authority to break open packs for detailed inspections. The warehouse management system is updated so that the materials are shown as in stock in the CCC and available for delivery to site. Often a label is produced identifying the materials, the contractor using the materials and any other information deemed necessary. If not required instantly the materials are put away into storage.

Storage of materials

There are a couple of fundamentally different approaches to the organization of a CCC. The most basic arrangement is to have just an open warehouse floor, with areas painted on the floor allocated to different contractors. All materials for contractor 'A' go in area 'A', for contractor 'B' in area 'B' and so on. While this is the easiest method to administrate, particularly if there is no reasonable warehouse management system in place, it does not utilize space efficiently and will require a large area or will be suitable only when there are relatively few contractors.

A typical construction project has a wide range of materials and the ideal CCC would have floor space for large items and items that can be block stacked, an area with pallet racking for palletized goods handled by forklift truck and some shelving areas for small items. In addition there may be a requirement for a fenced-in lockable area providing extra security for high-value items. This arrangement, where one contractor's items may be in all three areas, requires a warehouse management system (WMS). Compared to the WMS running a modern retail operation this can be a very basic system, sometimes as simple as a large spreadsheet. What is required is basically a database where all materials are registered with details of which contractor they belong to, type of materials, article number, order reference, quantities, dates delivered and location in the warehouse. If, as would often be the case, the CCC is operated by a third-party logistics company (3PL) then the WMS requirement can very easily be fulfilled by standard systems that those companies regularly use. What this means for the CCC is that there is no need to separate zones for all contractors. Instead space can be used efficiently and any individual material can still be retrieved based on the WMS information. The inventory records enable contractors to keep check on their stockholding and plan new orders and deliveries, thus improving forward planning.

Output of materials

The fundamental principle of a CCC-based project is that material supply should be according to a JIT pull system. This means that materials are not pushed onto site to be available 'just in case' but are ordered for when they are needed. This is the responsibility of the trade contractors. Typically this is done on a 24- or 48-hour cycle: eg order today for delivery tomorrow or the day after. The contractor must specify materials required, quantity and (in some cases) delivery location on site. One of the benefits of using a CCC is to drastically reduce the amount of materials on site, therefore the quantities delivered should be just for one or two days' consumption. The methods for ordering can vary from simply phoning in orders to the CCC administrator to using text messaging or e-mail. In some instances connection is provided on site with contractors specifying their orders online. Delivery management systems can also be used for this purpose.

Delivery of materials

The CCC will operate a small fleet of delivery vehicles. Based on the site orders received, the administrator makes up consolidated vehicle loads for the day's requirements.

The delivery operation can benefit from a GPS-based traffic management system. With this, very accurate estimated time of arrival (ETA) can be provided, which is extremely useful to traffic marshals and gate operatives, particularly in restricted inner-city areas. It is a common experience that with a CCC operation deliveries are often within plus or minus 15 minutes of target time, whereas in 'normal' projects it is not unusual for delivery accuracy to be no better than 'morning' or 'afternoon' – if that. The CCC approach means that there will be no queuing at gates and no circulating traffic waiting to get access.

When it comes to the delivery of materials on site there are two main options. Either the CCC operation ends at the offloading area with the individual contractors taking responsibility for their materials once they are offloaded, or there is an on-site logistics team responsible for handling to the point of use or to each individual contractor's material lay-down area. The use of CCCs can lead to substantial productivity gains because there is less time wasted waiting for materials; clearly these productivity gains are maximized with the use of an on-site handling team.

Warehouse management systems

The use of WMS technology brings many advantages to the construction project. It gives a level of control over material usage that isn't there when individual contractors manage their own supply flow directly to site. The inventory control means that low stock levels can be flagged up so that reordering happens in a timely fashion, reducing the number of emergency orders and late deliveries. The system automatically provides a record of suppliers' delivery accuracy in terms of on-time performance, quantity and specification. The system also gives the main contractor improved visibility of trade contractor performance. Poor planning leading to shortages and delays, and emergency orders will show up, as will over-ordering – a common issue in construction.

Value-added processes

The most common approach is for CCCs to consolidate only at full pallet level; ie they receive truck loads of pallets from different suppliers, then make up consolidated vehicle loads comprising a mixture of pallets for delivery to site. It is unusual for pallets to be broken down or for secondary (outer) packaging to be opened and individual packs/items selected. Compare this approach to modern retailing where roll cages are made up with a mixture of products to match the sequence and location of the product in the supermarket aisle, making replenishment as efficient as possible. The full pallet load on the building site might hold more product than is needed in one location, necessitating repeated handling of the materials on a crowded site; while more than one product might be needed in the location leading to several pallets competing for restricted space. Anyone who has visited or worked on a building site will recognize these problems. Following the examples set by other industries, instead of trade contractors having to move materials from location to location, mixed pallet loads can be prepared at the CCC, supplying materials needed at specific on-site locations. An example of where this can work is the making up of a material kit for each ward in a hospital project. The difficulty in achieving this lies in the fact that it could involve more than one trade contractor, so the mixed kit order will only come about through detailed planning and site management, forcing collaboration between different trades and logistics contractors.

Another area where the CCC can provide useful added value is in relation to packaging. In crowded city-centre sites the volume of packaging presents a handling problem on site and leads to additional traffic for waste removal. For some items it is possible to remove secondary (outer) packaging, and in some cases even primary packaging, at the CCC before delivering to site; it is a short journey and materials are handled by logistics professionals. Special handling units (compare the supermarket roll cage) can be used to protect the product on the final leg and on site, and the emptied units are taken back to the CCC on the return leg of the delivery run.

If a work space can be provided at the CCC not only can packaging be removed but in some cases subassemblies or other preparatory work can be undertaken, which otherwise would have to take place on site. An example of this strategy was highlighted in the case study Material Logistics Planning, Central St Giles (Lundesjö, 2009b). The contractor responsible for assembling and lagging the air-conditioning system found that it was far more efficient to carry out this work at the CCC; the work environment was good, and the completed units were loaded on pallets for each location on site. The operator explained that on site, this work would have involved cramped conditions, being up ladders and getting in everybody's way! Furthermore, CCCs are sometimes used to manufacture prototype and demonstration interiors for client approval prior to final completion on site.

These examples show that when a CCC is available, creative thinking by project managers and trade contractors can result in new ways of doing things, thereby easing congestion and making the construction process on site more efficient.

The benefits of using a CCC

There are many well-documented benefits of using a CCC. The most obvious benefits stem from the main reason that CCCs were first introduced: to reduce traffic and congestion around sites in urban and inner-city areas, thus reducing noise and emissions of nitrogen oxides, particulate matter and CO_2. In this primary objective CCCs have been very successful and this is why the use of CCCs has been promoted by, for example, Transport for London and the City of Stockholm.

Studying the impact of using CCCs in some of the early applications of the methodology, several further benefits were discovered and in later applications taken into account as part of the rationale for using CCCs.

The construction industry is a major contributor to the overall volume of waste in society. Product damage from poor site storage conditions and frequent moving of materials as work progresses is a common problem in construction. So-called shrinkage (product being stolen or simple lost) is also not insignificant. As a result, over-ordering, often by 15–25 per cent, takes place with the acceptance that material wastage will be high. The CCC, simply by providing a secure, covered, not overcrowded warehouse facility has a direct beneficial effect on reducing waste. Handling materials on site just once and for more or less immediate use drastically reduces site damage-induced waste.

The use of a CCC facilitates an increase in return logistics. Studies have shown (WRAP, 2012a) that some 80 per cent of vehicles delivering to a construction site depart empty. The planned consolidated delivery pattern that follows from using a CCC makes it easy to use the delivery vehicles for taking unused and packaging materials back to the CCC. Packaging is a major waste stream in construction and attempts to introduce reusable packaging often fail as the return logistics cannot be achieved economically. The CCC is the natural hub for collecting reusable packaging coming back from site. From the CCC, supplier delivery vehicles can collect the reusable packaging; whereas directly on site there normally is not space to marshal return materials, and time pressures for vehicle turnaround prevent methodical return handling.

The use of a CCC has been found to significantly enhance productivity on site. There are a number of ways in which the working practices that follow from using a CCC drive productivity improvements. On traditional sites a significant part of trade contractors' time is occupied in waiting for materials and handling materials rather than completing their primary construction tasks. The problems often start at the gate. Waiting time at gates and offloading areas, queuing for critical resources such as space, forklift trucks, hoists etc steal productive time. The CCC delivers consolidated loads and therefore fewer vehicles on a planned timetable often within plus or minus 15 minutes of schedule, which means that operatives and offloading equipment can be ready and prepared for arrival. This factor alone can have a measurable effect on productivity in an industry where a delivery accuracy no better than within a half-day or day has traditionally not been unusual.

Productivity is also enhanced by the fact that only appropriate quantities of materials are brought to site on a JIT basis. (Note that in construction JIT may refer to, say, daily deliveries; whereas in other industries such as manufacturing it may well be a matter of hours or minutes.) The effect is less material on site. Materials traditionally stored on sites can be in the way, obstruct movement and frequently have to be moved as work progresses into new areas. A working environment clear of clutter promotes productivity. These site-related productivity gains will be enhanced if the use of the CCC is combined with the use of a specialist logistics contractor for the on-site handling to the point of use – utilization of trade contractor time can then be maximized.

The use of a CCC forces the trade contractors to plan ahead at a detailed level. They need to be able to place accurate orders for material delivery on the CCC for their requirements two to four days ahead. The discipline imposed by the main contractor and the CCC operator will not allow them to order excessive quantities 'just to be on the safe side'. Main contractors have expressed the view that this requirement for planning and discipline placed on trade contractors in itself sharpens contractor performance, with fewer conflicts with others on site and a smoother performance.

Using a CCC is also helpful in the promotion of health and safety on site. On-site storage areas are cramped, often out-of-doors and on uneven surfaces ill-suited for storage and handling. Within the CCC materials are handled and stored using appropriate equipment in a safe warehouse environment. Materials are brought to site JIT leaving the site uncluttered; this improvement in the working environment can have a direct impact on site safety. Again the benefit is enhanced if the CCC is combined with the provision of an on-site handling specialist so that handling professionals service the trade contractors to the point of use rather than just to the gate/offloading area.

There are numerous studies that have attempted to quantify these various benefits. Below is a selection of references.

Hammarby Sjöstad, Stockholm

At Hammarby Sjöstad, Stockholm, (Ottoson, 2005) the logistics centre (LC) was introduced specifically to ease the effects of construction – traffic, noise, pollution – for local residents. This was to be achieved mainly by reducing the number of small deliveries, defined as those with fewer than four pallets, through consolidation. Some of the results quoted were:

- number of small deliveries reduced by 80 per cent;
- reduced energy consumption and emissions of CO_2, nitrogen oxides and particulate matter;
- improved living conditions at site for new inhabitants (those moving into properties built in the first phases of the project);
- less traffic congestion at the site;
- improved working environment.

On all these counts the project was deemed a success following evaluation by the City of Stockholm. Subsequent studies by academics also pointed to significant reductions in material waste and shrinkage.

The London CCC

The London Construction Consolidation Centre (LCCC) was set up in 2006 by construction logistics experts Wilson James to serve four projects in central London. The operation was modelled on an original concept established in 2001 at Heathrow Airport (HCC). In *Managing Construction Logistics* (Sullivan, Barthorpe and Robbins, 2010) it is highlighted that many in the industry felt that the CCC concept would be useful only in airport construction projects because of the very particular circumstances that apply:

- the high level of security required;
- the need to deliver the construction project during continuous passenger operations of the airport;
- the stringent commercial needs and absolute requirements to meet handover dates.

In operation, however, the HCC was found to bring further benefits, namely:

- improved productivity on site;
- faster turnaround and better utilization of the suppliers' delivery vehicles, leading to cost reductions;
- reduced damage and waste through better handling methods;
- improved health and safety standards;
- delays due to materials not being available reduced from 6 per cent to 0.4 per cent – a factor of 15, which enhances overall programme certainty and productivity.

These factors contributed to the decision that the consolidation centre concept would be viable also for the central London projects where the main drivers were limited in space on site for offloading and storage, coupled with congested access to sites and the costs of the London congestion charge. Subsequently the LCCC was evaluated in some depth and the following benefits are quoted in the interim and final reports on the LCCC (Transport for London, 2007; Transport for London, 2008):

- a 68 per cent reduction in the number of construction vehicles entering the City of London delivering to the LCCC-served sites;
- an average of two hours reduction in suppliers' journey time by going to the LCCC rather than accessing the central London sites;
- delivery performance of 97 per cent of the right goods delivered correctly first time;
- an approximate reduction in associated CO_2 emissions of 75 per cent (relating to the final stages of the journey);
- significantly reduced product damage and shrinkage leading to an estimated 15 per cent reduction in waste;
- productivity of the LCCC-served site labour force increased by up to 30 minutes per day.

On a site employing 500, this is up to 250 hours per day saved, equating to 30 workers if working an eight-hour shift.

The report Freight Best Practice (Department for Transport, 2007) studied the LCCC from a freight perspective and listed beneficial impact on a number of key performance indicators (KPIs): reduction of freight journeys, reductions in supplier journey times and delivery reliability – with results as stated above. Other KPIs included reduction in vehicle mileage, reduction in number of vehicles used, backloading of pallets and stillages and reduction in waste. The report also looked at the congestion charge savings per annum, as shown in Table 12.2.

The report endorses CCCs as an effective way to reduce both vehicle mileage (and associated fuel consumption and emissions) and traffic congestion in urban areas.

TABLE 12.2 Number of vehicles and cost of congestion charges

	No of Vehicles	Cost of Congestion Charges (at £8 per vehicle per day)
Without LCCC	4,099	£32,792
With LCCC	1,461	£11,688
Minimum saving		£21,104

WRAP

WRAP, the Waste and Resources Action Programme, is a not-for-profit company funded by government and public sector organizations in the UK that promotes the sustainable use of resources in virtually all sectors of society: consumer, retail, construction etc. As the construction industry is a major contributor to overall waste volumes, WRAP has focused on this industry and one of the strategies has been to promote good logistics practice as a way to reduce waste and carbon emissions. (See also Chapter 8 on WRAP's approach to resource efficiency. All WRAP studies are available through the website at **www.wrap.org.uk** under Construction.) Below are a number of relevant studies for using CCCs to reduce construction waste and carbon emissions (Lundesjö, 2011):

- In the study of Unilever House (WRAP, 2007), a central London refurbishment project using the LCCC, the following was reported:
  - In all, some 13,200 pallets (or pallet equivalent) were handled by the LCCC over a two-year period.
  - 90 per cent of all delivered pallets were returned to the LCCC for collection by suppliers.
  - The project also provided an excellent illustration of over-ordering in the industry, and of the waste-reducing effect of using a CCC. At the end of the project 38 full 26-tonne lorry loads of unused materials worth approximately £200,000 remained at the CCC rather than ending up in waste skips.
- WRAP reports on Barts Hospital (Lundesjö, 2009a) and Central St Giles (Lundesjö, 2009b) show a reduction of vehicle journeys into central London of 74 per cent and 75 per cent respectively, with corresponding reductions in energy usage and emissions.

Types of CCC

There are many different types of CCC. In *Managing Construction Logistics* (Sullivan, Barthorpe and Robbins, 2010) three different solutions are suggested:

- concealed consolidation centre;
- communal consolidation centre;
- collaborative consolidation centre.

The concealed consolidation centre is so called because it is not in a separate location but is contained within the boundary of the construction site. This is a useful approach for large, typically multi-building sites, where a warehouse facility can be accommodated and the CCC operation can be carried out, receiving all goods and servicing all the different parts of the site. So while it is not in a separate location the site will enjoy all the CCC functionality and derive the benefits thereof. The Stockholm example of Hammarby Sjöstad referred to earlier can be said to be of this type.

The communal consolidation centre is a facility serving a number of projects for a single contractor/client. This is a good approach for large urban and city areas where there are several projects running concurrently. The facility would typically be run by the main contractor or a specialist logistics company. Dedicated storage zones can be set up for the different projects or the warehouse space can be shared fully depending on how sophisticated are the warehouse managements systems used. The facility is financed by the client via the main contractor, who in turn will try to recoup the costs from the savings made by the various subcontractors: reduced transport, handling, damage etc.

The collaborative consolidation centre would typically be the largest operation of the three alternatives. This is where one CCC is used collaboratively by a number of different clients and main contractors. Operated by a logistics specialist company it is financed by handling charges levied at the clients, depending on volumes handled.

On the construction logistics area of WRAP's website a slightly different categorization of CCC is outlined. Four types of consolidation centres are described:

- *Hidden consolidation.* This is the same approach as with the concealed CCC described above – a consolidation operation within the boundaries of a large site.
- *Single-user consolidation.* This is where a consolidation centre is set up to support a single project. It is typically set up by the main contractor, hiring a logistics company to operate the centre.
- *Shared consolidation centre.* This is a multi-project consolidation centre and encompasses both the communal and collaborative centres described above. This can support several sites for one or several clients/main contractors.
- *Virtual consolidation.* This is the final suggestion described, and it differs from the earlier approaches. This is where a dedicated CCC is not set up. Instead, by collaborating with a 3PL the construction client/main contractor makes use of the 3PL's existing resources in terms of shared user warehouses or depots.

In using CCCs (Lundesjö, 2011), examples are given of three radically different approaches to construction consolidation:

- A shared facility serving multiple clients and multiple sites. The London CCC in Silvertown, London, is operated by construction logistics specialists Wilson James supporting several projects (at the time the report was written six projects used the facility) for different clients/main contractors across central London.
- A single-user single-project CCC. At Nine Elms, London MLogic operated a CCC on a site owned by the large distribution company

DHL, supporting one client, Laing O'Rourke, for a single project: One Hyde Park.
- A single-client, multi-project and multifunctional CCC. This is an operation in Park Royal, London run as a partnership between Sainsbury's and construction logistics specialists Fit Out (UK) Ltd. So while there is a single client (Sainsbury's), there are many sites, with new stores being built and existing stores being refurbished. The CCC is multifunctional in that it not only serves as a CCC but is also a refurbishment centre. During refurbishment projects materials are removed from site and taken back to the CCC, where they are inspected and if possible refurbished for reuse on the current project or stored for future use.

The above list illustrates that there are many ways to approach construction consolidation and while they are very different they can all be successful:

- They reduce traffic to sites and in the urban areas served.
- They facilitate JIT delivery of materials to sites.
- They provide dry, safe and secure storage conditions and professional materials handling methods that result in reduced product damage and shrinkage.
- By providing controlled material flow to site they contribute to programme certainty and financial performance.

There are many arguments in favour of shared and/or multi-project CCCs. Set-up and fixed costs can be shared over a larger volume and there are more opportunities to maximize utilization of resources thereby reducing unit costs. Only large projects tend to justify the initial cost of starting a CCC operation, but once in place smaller projects can successfully benefit from sharing the resource. The arguments in favour of a single-user CCC are often based on the need for security and the ability to tailor the operation entirely around one client/main contractor's operation. With increased engagement by 3PLs in the construction industry, however, one can expect the shared user model to increase, with the 3PL drawing on its existing resource base as in setting up CCCs.

Locating a CCC

To fulfil its function a CCC must be in the right location. This means:

- Good access for inbound supplier deliveries. The CCC should be on a major road close to motorway/trunk road network. There are two reasons for this:
    - to minimize the impact on local roads and communities of incoming deliveries;

- to provide fast turnaround for suppliers' vehicles in order to minimize cost.
- A location reasonably close to the site(s) served. As a rule of thumb this means that the drive time to site should be ideally no more than 30–45 minutes. Allowing for loading and offloading times each vehicle can then do two or three rounds per shift. Fewer than two rounds per shift leads to a high likelihood of poor vehicle and manpower utilization.

In *Using CCCs* (Lundesjö, 2011) these criteria are used to model suitable locations around a number of cities in the UK, illustrating how easily the benefits of a CCC operation could be provided. In reality, however, there are very few examples, and in the UK they are centred on London. The case for CCCs in London was analysed in detail by Peter Brett Associates for TfL (Anderson, 2007) and at that time they forecast that London volumes could support six shared user CCCs on an ongoing basis, for which they modelled suitable locations. However, six shared facilities did not spring up. The LCCC continued in operation and has been joined mainly by single-project CCCs and also some 3PL operations.

Conclusion

Both when studying the literature and when talking to managers in the industry one comes to the conclusion that consolidation centres work; projects using CCCs run well and benefit from them. In spite of this, while CCCs are used, they have not penetrated the industry at anything like the level expected, say, 10 years ago in 2005.

In most cases a CCC is used when the main contractor is forced down that route by specific constraints. Those constraints are normally space restrictions on site (limiting storage and/or access via gates) or restrictions limiting vehicle access such as narrow time windows and on-street queuing disallowed by local councils. While these are good and valid reasons for using a CCC, the advantages identified above – environmental benefits, productivity gains, programme certainty and cost savings that can outweigh the cost of using a CCC – mean that CCCs could be considered much more widely as a construction logistics strategy. So why is it that, if not forced down the CCC route by local regulations or severe constraints, CCCs are so seldom considered? One logistics manager at a major UK main contractor stated that to run a CCC near London of about 3,000 square metres supporting a £400 million project in central London costs about £1 million per year to run. In the extremely competitive bidding environment you just can't win acceptance for that cost, for something that at the end of the project the client doesn't have! The main contractor has to cover the cost, but many of the savings benefit the trade contractors and their subcontractors, such as hauliers. And while case studies point to many savings, few are willing to trust upfront during the bidding situation that those savings will be fulfilled. And even if the savings are fulfilled, the main contractor paying for the CCC might not be able to claw those back from all the subcontractors and suppliers. We have a known cost against hoped-for savings.

Construction, particularly in cities and densely populated urban areas, is an activity circumscribed by planning regulations, traffic regulations and environmental controls. Perhaps this is an area where local authorities should interfere and insist on the use of CCCs, by regulating site access, and perhaps even promoting shared CCC facilities in suitable locations. That way, everyone in the bidding for projects would have to cover the cost and at the end everyone is likely to be the winner.

End note

Shortly before publication of this book Wilson James kindly made available a report (not in the public domain) made by the Department of Engineering and the Built Environment of the Anglia Ruskin University, analysing the effect of logistics and site services on the construction performance of Bart's Hospital Phase 2. While it generally confirms conclusions presented above, it is the most up-to-date study and it is therefore worthwhile sharing some of its conclusions.

For this central London project Wilson James provided a more integrated level of logistics services than has been seen before. Named the Integrated Logistics and Site Services Support Package (ILSSSP), it was tailored to the requirements at Bart's and included the delivery of construction materials from supplier order to point of use, combined with the provision of a range of site services and support. This was managed and delivered as a single discrete work package to main contractor Skanska.

The report identifies the London Construction Consolidation Centre (LCCC) and the on-site team as vital components of a completely integrated supply chain. Specialist logistics management was provided by Wilson James and was itself fully integrated into the Skanska project management team; the effectiveness of the ILSSSP was based upon the central role that logistics played in the planning and management of the project. The report highlights savings and improvements in many areas; here we will mention two. There was an estimated 2–3 per cent saving in materials used by trade contractors and the productivity improvements were estimated to be 6–10 per cent. Further to this the report identifies many environmental benefits in terms of reduced waste, reduced vehicle journeys/mileage, reduced noise and improved safety. The report states that the ILSSSP enabled the project to achieve its programme and cost targets which otherwise would have been significantly increased by the constricted site and restricted access. Improved logistics efficiency through the use of specialist logistics management, specialist equipment and trained, experienced logistics operatives ensured that timely material availability was achieved and waste minimized. It also reduced the management and resource inputs required from Skanska. Furthermore, it ensured that the operation of the hospital was unaffected throughout the duration of the project.

It is clear from the report that this approach not only pays for itself but also offers significant benefits financially, environmentally and socially.

However, some of the difficulties alluded to in this Chapter were also experienced. The report notes scepticism and inertia among trade contractors not keen on adopting new practices. There is an unwillingness among trade contractors to be open about costs – sometimes a lack of awareness of true costs – which means they are unable to appreciate savings; this in turn makes it difficult for the main contractor to fully exploit the potential extra competitiveness in the tendering situation, and later in the project to realise the savings and benefit fully from the strategy. While the integrated approach adopted by Skanska on St Bart's made significant progress in this area, it seems that the report confirms that to move forward the whole industry needs better insight and understanding of all processes and costs in the supply chain, and a more collaborative attitude. But it is clear that for contractors who can master this approach there is strong potential for improved competitiveness on price, construction time and overall performance.

References

Anderson, S (2007) Construction Consolidation Centres: An assessment of the potential for London wide use, Peter Brett Associates for Transport for London

Department for Transport (2007) London Construction Consolidation Centre [Online] http://www.freightbestpractice.org.uk [Accessed August 2010]

Lundesjö, G (2009a) Case Study: Material logistics planning, Barts Hospital, London, Skanska, *The Logistics Business for WRAP* [Online] http://wrap.org.uk/construction [accessed 15 February 2015]

Lundesjö, G (2009b) Case Study: Material logistics planning, Central St Giles Stanhope, Bovis Lend Lease and Wilson James, *The Logistics Business for WRAP* [Online] http://wrap.org.uk/construction [accessed 15 February 2015]

Lundesjö, G (2011) Using Construction Consolidation Centres to Reduce Construction Waste and Carbon Emissions, *The Logistics Business for WRAP* [Online] http://wrap.org.uk/construction [accessed 15 February 2015]

Ottoson, M (2005) Evaluation Report: New concepts for the distribution of goods, trendsetter report no 2005:7, *Civitas* [Online] http://www.trendsetter-europe.org/ [accessed 15 February 2015]

Sullivan, G, Barthorpe, S and Robbins, S (2010) *Managing Construction Logistics*, Wiley-Blackwell, Oxford

Transport for London (2007) London Construction Consolidation Centre Interim Report – May 2007 [Online] http://www.tfl.gov.uk

Transport for London (2008) London Construction Consolidation Centre Final Report – October 2008 [Online] http://www.tfl.gov.uk

WRAP (2007) Material Logistics Plan, Good Practice Guidance: Project code WAS041-001, ISBN 1-84405-370-9 [Online] http://www.wrap.org.uk/sites/files/wrap/MLP%20Guidance%20Document.pdf [accessed 23 February 2015]

WRAP (2012a) Case Study: Reverse logistics on construction sites [Online] http://wrap.org.uk/construction [accessed 15 February 2015]

Delivery management systems

13

RICK BALLARD and NICK HOARE

Introduction

The essence of a construction project is the bringing together of materials, people and equipment in a timely and effective manner in order to create a unique structure. This applies as much to the basic 'production' domestic dwelling as it does to major infrastructure projects; it is just the volumes of materials and numbers of people that differ, and with these come logistical complexity and the need for more management. The scale of some of the world's large infrastructure projects is daunting; the Olympic Stadium in London and London's Crossrail project are just two examples, but there are similar projects throughout the developed world that can never fail to impress. The Crossrail project is a good example of the problems of bringing together materials, people and machinery. It involves the construction of 10 new railway stations across London with 42 kilometres of tunnels (of which half are new), and all this has to be undertaken with the minimum of disruption to traffic and daily life in one of the world's busiest cities. The logistics problems are enormous and the management of delivery transport for both goods and people is essential for the good order of the construction process. It is clear that in projects such as Crossrail the facilities and resources for unloading and storing will be limited and the flow of goods to site and the movement of traffic have to be carefully planned and controlled.

In all but the smallest of construction projects it is just not feasible to deliver all materials to site at the start of the project. Even the smallest jobbing builder knows that the procurement of materials and flow of deliveries has to be managed, not just to control cash flow but to make use of the available space for storage and handling. For larger projects subcontractors are often keen to deliver early so they can be paid early. Materials

FIGURE 13.1 Crossrail construction site

delivered early will occupy lay-down areas unnecessarily and can impede construction, not to mention the risks of loss and damage, so that when the time comes that the materials are actually required there is insufficient available. Modern, lean construction principles demand that materials are delivered as close as possible to actual construction demand, in terms of both time and location.

So managing deliveries is not just about controlling the flow of transport to the construction site. It is also about ordered and controlled storage on site and best use of handling equipment. Managing the supply chain and material flow is as a much a part of the construction process as is digging holes, erecting steelwork or pouring concrete. However good the design, and however skilled and well managed the construction process, failure to control the flow of materials and deliveries to site will increase disruption and reduce productivity, and has the potential to delay the build programme.

In recent years many of the major construction projects in the UK and throughout the world have benefitted from improved systems and processes for delivery management, particularly those in inner-city or other congested areas where traffic is busy and put-down areas are limited. The benefits in those situations are clear but the wider benefits of improved control and better use of resources are there for a much greater range of projects, as this chapter will set out to explain.

What is a delivery management system?

A system can be defined as a set of detailed methods, procedures and routines created to carry out a specific activity, perform a duty, or solve a problem. So in our case the duty to be performed or problem to be solved is the timely, effective delivery of materials and equipment to a construction site, including in many cases the point of use on the site. Whatever system is used, it will involve a set of agreed processes and a means of managing those processes. The key features of a delivery management system are that it:

- provides the basis for managing movement of vehicles coming to and leaving the site;
- can control the movement of vehicles on site;
- gives site managers control over when vehicles and deliveries are expected on site and notification of actual arrivals;
- allows site managers to refuse a delivery if a vehicle is early or late;
- enables contractors working on site to know when their materials are expected and to be notified when they arrive;
- provides control of site lay-down and holding areas for temporary storage of goods;
- provides control of site assets such as scheduling of hoists and trucks to allocate resources for lifting;
- can help to manage delivery to the point of use on site (particularly on large sites) thus reducing double handling and wasted time searching for materials;
- allows for scheduling of waste removal.

There are numerous ways in which these features can be made available to a greater or lesser extent, ranging from a white board in the site office (not uncommon), through the use of spreadsheets (quite common) to fully computerized systems (not so common but increasing). In practice white boards are fine for very small sites where one person can deal with deliveries through phone calls and e-mails and simply add, delete or make changes to entries on the board. But it is easy to make mistakes or even fail to keep up with changes so this really is not a good way to manage deliveries. Spreadsheets are somewhat better than the white board and, depending on the level of sophistication, they can provide significant benefits and go a long way to fulfilling the basic requirements. Their disadvantages are that they are still prone to operator error, they are not truly multi-user and they are not updated in 'real' time, so control and management is limited. Again, they are best used for smaller sites where the site manager can see what is going on and then simply use the spreadsheet system as a decision support tool to help with day-to-day management.

For larger sites or sites with many deliveries then fully computerized systems will certainly bring the greater benefits, albeit at a somewhat higher cost. They can be accessed by many users simultaneously from many different locations, and they operate in 'real' time so that the system is automatically updated for all users as soon as any one user makes a change.

The features of computerized delivery management

A modern delivery management system will help site logistics managers to monitor and control every aspect of the delivery process. An important factor is that as many people as necessary can have access to the system and this is best done with a web-based system that runs on a remote server. If a system runs locally on the construction site then contractors will only have access whilst they are visiting the site. Usually in this situation the organization that hosts the system has a licence to use the software and must maintain all the necessary infrastructure to ensure users can access the system. This might be desirable for high-security projects or where the hosting company's IT department is intent on keeping control, but it does not cater for contractors who do not have a regular presence on site. It may be possible for the project to provide external access to the system but with increasing IT security concerns this is becoming less and less feasible. So usually the best option is to have an externally hosted system that all users can access via the internet. This type of solution, where software is remotely run on a hosted server, is commonly known as 'cloud' computing and there is no doubt that these web-enabled hosted systems bring the greatest flexibility and ease of use. Contractors, suppliers, haulage companies and site management can all access the system from any computer, tablet or mobile phone that has an internet connection.

The core of the system will be the diary management. This is where bookings are made, very much in the same way that appointments are entered in a personal computerized diary. A delivery time slot in the diary is typically a minimum of 15 minutes so appointments can be made on the hour and every quarter hour. For sites with more than one access point the bookings can also be made for a specific gate or control point. The system supervisor (usually appointed by the site logistics manager, or similar) is able to control the number of bookings for each time slot for each delivery point and can also 'blank out' times when no deliveries are to be made.

Key features of a system would be:

- passwords and access control with a range of levels of authorization;
- web interface;
- accessible by suppliers and contractors;
- a bookings diary;
- facilities for authorized personnel to add and manage delivery points and resources such as cranes, tele-handlers and forklift trucks;
- facilities for adding and managing lay-down areas;

- ability to manage multiple entrances to each site;
- ability to manage multiple sites;
- reporting of planned activity and historical activity;
- tracking and control of vehicles on and off site.

The costing structures of these systems will depend on the supplier. Some may provide hardware such as hand-held computers in order to access the system; this may add to the price but overcomes the concerns of giving 'high-tech' devices to logistics personnel on site. Costs may include set-up and customization charges and usually some sort of training will be required. For a hosted system there will be monthly charges and for systems that provide terminals there will be a cost per terminal per week or month. Training and set-up costs might range from £1,000 to £3,000 and monthly costs of a few hundred pounds depending on features and number of users. Terminals might cost from £50–£100 each per week.

The benefits of proper management of deliveries

The benefits of good, computerized delivery management systems are so significant that it begs the question as to why they are not more widely used. For anything other than the smallest construction project the costs are not prohibitive and the benefits from better site control and supplier management are easily realized.

We must also bear in mind that in addition to the benefits for the site there are considerable benefits to the surrounding environment. Ensuring a steady flow of vehicles onto site will address safety concerns in general. Being able effectively to close the site to larger vehicles for critical times of day such as the times of school runs or local rush-hour times offers significant benefits in helping to reduce accidents.

The following are some of the most easily identifiable benefits:

- Supplier management:
  - delivery timekeeping;
  - managing on-time in-full delivery;
  - keeping control of multiple deliveries;
  - giving suppliers confidence that they will be expected and that turnaround delays will be minimized.
- Reducing congestion on the site:
  - improved efficiency;
  - safe working.

- Use of assets:
  - better use of hoists and cranes;
  - improved control of vehicle holding areas;
  - maximize the use of lay-down zones.
- Use of consolidation centres and holding parks:
  - control holding-park areas;
  - improve flow to consolidation centres;
  - minimize congestion;
  - call off deliveries as required and improve traffic flow.
- Labour productivity:
  - deliver close to point of use, reducing time spent finding goods and materials;
  - minimize multiple handling;
  - improve job satisfaction.
- Material management:
  - track deliveries and avoid disputes with contractors;
  - manage waste collections;
  - manage unused returned goods.
- Environmental:
  - minimize congestion in surrounding areas by managing delivery slots;
  - avoid queuing at site access points;
  - manage flow of vehicles onto site;
  - block access at key times of day (rush hour, school opening and closing times etc).
- Site safety:
  - control number of vehicles on site;
  - clear visibility of expected deliveries;
  - better control of use of assets.
- Information for future planning:
  - record patterns of delivery;
  - understand where problems occur and avoid in the future.

It is difficult to quantify the benefits in financial terms as there are so many factors to consider and each site is different. But to put it in perspective let's just speculate on a £5 million project running over two years. The labour cost on such a project could typically be of the order of £2 million, giving an average cost per week of, say, £20,000. The typical cost of a web-enabled computerized management system over two years would be in the region of £10,000 so it is easy to see that the system does not have to do much to improve productivity and reduce delays in order to pay for itself easily in the life of the project.

But it is not just the day-to-day benefits that should be considered. Construction has lagged behind other sectors in recognizing the importance of recording logistics data and using it as a basis for continuous improvement; but this is changing, and management of the logistics process is being seen as part of the effort to maintain competitive advantage, just as it is in the manufacturing and retail sectors. Clearly construction differs in many respects from these other sectors but it still needs to focus on continuous improvement and the best way this can happen is to set targets, measure performance and take action to develop. Delivery management systems have the capability to record enormous amounts of data about site logistics activity and to provide reports on this activity, which can be used to improve operations on current and future projects. Some examples of where measurements can be used to drive improvement are:

- Supplier performance: reports on supplier delivery performance can help identify which suppliers consistently fail to deliver on time or fail to deliver a complete order thus enabling remedial action to be taken with the supplier. This might be trying to understand why the deliveries are a problem for the supplier and working to change operating processes, or in extreme cases it might mean a change of supplier or delivery service provider.
- Use of site assets: careful and detailed monitoring of the history of the use of assets such as hoists, cranes and trucks can provide valuable data on the productivity of those assets and how better use can be made of them. It can also provide support for planning assets on new sites in the future.
- Minimization of congestion: an understanding where and when the site becomes congested with delivery traffic, particularly on large sites with more than one access point, can be used to re-plan deliveries by managing time slots or by changing access points. This can help not only with site congestion but also with traffic build-up on surrounding roads. Again, this can have benefits for both existing sites and the planning of new sites.

Logistics managers need to get into a 'mindset' of collecting operational data and using it to learn and to encourage change for the better. An evidence base is the best way to convince operational staff and senior management of the need to do things differently. Delivery management systems are not the only way to collect this evidence but they should be a key element of the logistics manager's 'toolbox'.

Who is it for?

So who should be using computerized delivery management systems? The current users tend to be larger companies constructing larger sites, often in urban areas where traffic congestion is a problem, but the benefits described earlier are there for both small and large construction companies operating sites of all shapes, sizes and locations. How those benefits are realized depends very much on the logistics managers and the level of importance they place on operating efficiency and data capture for continuous improvement.

A common reason cited by construction companies for not using delivery management systems on small sites is that they believe that the costs will outweigh the benefits. The start-up time and perceived 'learning-curve' may also be an obstacle for shorter projects. A way around both of these issues is to have a multi-site system either bought in or developed internally. The system is then always available and logistics managers moving from one site to the next will be familiar with it. The system then becomes as much a part of managing the business as is an accounting system or attendance management system; it simply becomes the way in which things are done.

There is little doubt that effective delivery management has to be a 'must have' for busy city sites where roads are congested and access is limited. Combined with some form of holding park or consolidation centre they can reap enormous benefits both in real savings and in demonstrating consideration of other road users and local residents. Indeed, an increasing number of local authorities require information on how deliveries will be managed as part of the planning process, and this more often than not means the use of a delivery management system.

There are of course construction sites where delivery management systems are absolutely essential for the control of traffic and the management information they provide. Examples are airports, defence establishments and similar sites where security is paramount. In these high-security sites notification of the time of every delivery is required, control of movements on to the site has to be monitored and time of leaving is carefully checked. Good delivery management systems do all these things and allow as many people as required to have visibility of what is going on.

Another area where the benefits are clearly visible for small projects is where the development is within the boundary of what is already a larger development. Examples are educational establishments such as universities or large hospital campuses where there is already a large flow of people and traffic. Delivery management can help not only to control the movements to and from the construction site but also on and off the larger campus, thus helping to maintain high levels of safety.

The future

As with all software, computerized delivery management systems are improving and developing all the time. They are providing more flexibility to deal with a different range of users, more flexibility to manage multiple sites simultaneously and they offer ever increasing reporting capability and management information.

Some applications already allow users to access all or part of the system from a wide range of personal devices such as smartphones and tablet computers. But options for this are continually improving, giving site supervisory staff, contractors and suppliers greater opportunities for mobile communication and access to up-to-date, real-time delivery information.

Developments include the ability to track deliveries whilst they are on the road. This could cover tracking of a particular vehicle or tracking of a particular load. The latter is especially significant for managing the delivery of highly valuable materials or for deliveries that have a critical time slot in the build schedule. Some of these systems make use of vehicle telematics incorporating positioning systems using the GPS or other satellite systems, whilst others use the capabilities of mobile phones to monitor position. The advantage of the telematics systems is that they are fixed as part of the vehicle and are tamper proof. However, it does mean that tracking will only work if the delivery system is fitted with telematics and that the delivery management system has access to the telematics data. Hence there is limited flexibility in the use of delivery vehicle. Data from mobile phones is perhaps not so robust, in that the phones are not fixed to the vehicle, but they offer far more flexibility because any mobile phone can quickly be set up to provide the data. This means that in principle any delivery can be tracked for minimal cost. There is also the potential to link specific materials with the delivery, and track the delivery at material level. This could include the use of bar coding or RFID (radio frequency identification) tags. The latter are more expensive than bar code labels and require more costly equipment for reading the code but they are able to carry far more information and be read at greater range.

Building information management (BIM) systems are becoming increasingly sophisticated with the ability to show, in 3D graphic detail, the development of the construction in time. These models are usually described as 4D models. The latest incarnations of these, sometimes called 5D models, can include other information such as the costs but also the detailed quantities of materials required at each location. The planning of lay-down areas is also important as these must not interfere with the production plans. This information is a key driver for deliveries to site and so it makes sense to link deliveries with the plan. It is likely that in the future delivery management will become linked to the BIM system with the planned material requirements determining what should be delivered and the delivery management system providing information on what and when materials have been delivered or are planned to be delivered. Developments in BIM are discussed further in Chapter 6.

Case studies

CASE STUDY Royal Adelaide Hospital

The new Royal Adelaide Hospital (new RAH) (Figure 13.2) will be Australia's most advanced hospital and is the single largest infrastructure project in the history of the state of South Australia. It is set on a 9-hectare site among the parklands at the west end of Adelaide's central business district (CBD) and forms part of the broader health and biomedical precinct. It will employ close to 6,000 people and accommodate 85,000 inpatients per year. The facility was delivered as a public–private partnership under the State Government's Partnership SA Model, forming part of the South Australian reformed health system. The main contractors responsible for the design and construction aspect of the project are Hansen Yuncken and Leighton Contractors, operating in a joint venture known as HYLC.

A major construction project such as this in the heart of an important and busy business district is clearly going to create some major logistical challenges. Much as the new hospital is a desirable new asset for Adelaide there has been a limit to the level of disruption that the business district was able to accept. Hence good delivery management has been crucial to the success and timely delivery of the project. There was no doubt that a fully computerized real-time system was needed to control all transport activities in and around the site.

The site logistics planners were keen to learn from the experience of major European infrastructure projects and opted to employ a system developed in the UK but make use of the hosted service. The system they chose was Zone Manager, which had already been used on major UK projects such as Canary Wharf in

FIGURE 13.2 Royal Adelaide Hospital

London and Queen Elizabeth Hospital in Birmingham. The software could, in theory, have resided on a system in the UK but it was decided to use a local server in Australia to ensure that response times were optimum for local users. The installation and support was all undertaken by the Zone Manager developers in the UK, as was the customization of the system to meet the specific requirements of the site. At no time was there ever any need for the UK team to visit Australia – and all helpline support was provided by telephone, by e-mail or by direct log-in to the system.

The fact that South Australia and the UK are just about as far apart as it is possible to be on Earth demonstrates just how powerful and successful 'cloud' computing can be.

Facts and figures

HYLC Joint Venture are the first contractors in Australia to adopt a comprehensive online booking service to manage the construction logistics:

project value:	1.85 billion Australian dollars
tower cranes:	Eight, three of these work two shifts
concrete:	155,000 cubic metres of concrete
man and material hoists:	10 including 6 units PEGA 5032 modified for the project
concrete:	268 slabs, 4,200 columns poured from 155,754 cubic metres delivered via five static pumps, 22,250 truck loads
reinforcing steel:	18,000 tonnes
piles:	2,500
hours worked:	3.5 million man hours and up to 1,700 people on site daily

CASE STUDY Media City UK, Salford

Media City UK in Salford, Greater Manchester was a very significant development in what was a busy but rundown area. It was part of a major redevelopment programme that took place over a number of years. The construction took place on a 200-acre site that was constrained by the Manchester Ship Canal on one side and a major road

FIGURE 13.3 Media City

artery on the other. The canal was used for delivery of some materials and removal of some waste by barge. The development comprised more than 700,000 square metres (almost 8 million square feet) of new and refurbished floor space for business, retail and residential property. It is now home to the BBC in Manchester as well as other major businesses. The construction site was large by most standards, with several access gates from the surrounding road network and the canal. Yet despite its size it had limited space for holding vehicles on site so an off-site area was found to allow delivery vehicles to be marshalled prior to being sent to site.

Connolly Construction Facilities Management (CCF) who were responsible for the site logistics opted for a fully computerized delivery management system on a hosted server with web interface. They decided to allow trade contractors to make their own bookings directly via the web. Whilst this considerably reduced the workload for CCF's logistics team it was essential that it was tightly controlled. By using the features of the delivery management systems CCF were able to monitor and control what contractors were able to do with their deliveries. Booking rules and zone capacities ensured that all bookings would comply with the operational constraints of the site, thus minimizing the need for further intervention by CCF.

The web interface also enabled CCF to operate real-time control of deliveries. By providing the remote holding park and gate operators with laptops equipped with 3G modems, they were able to ensure that vehicles were booked onto the system in real time thus providing an up-to-the minute view of what was on site to anyone with access to the system.

CASE STUDY   M1 motorway widening

MVM was a joint venture made up of Vinci, Sir Robert McAlpine, Morgan Est plc, Gifford and WSP, established specifically to carry out the widening of the M1 in the East Midlands region of England. The £340 million contract to widen the M1 between junctions 25 and 28 was carried out on behalf of the UK Highways Agency, a body with responsibility for management of the UK's motorways and major trunk roads. Approximately 23 kilometres of motorway were widened between Sandiacre at junction 25 and Pinxton at junction 28. MVM was keen to ensure that the site logistics were well managed, partly to ensure the smooth running and timely delivery of the project but also to minimize disruption to traffic on what is one of the UK's busiest stretches of motorway. Deliveries to the construction areas had to be made by travelling along the cordoned-off hard shoulder and any hold-up or blockage could cause a major disruption to the work. Unusually for the construction industry they recruited a logistics manager from outside of the sector and chose someone from the retail industry, which is known for giving logistics a much higher profile in day-to-day management of the business.

FIGURE 13.4 View of the M1

The new logistics manager, knowing that well-planned delivery management was essential in retail, saw the opportunity to use this experience and decided on the use of a computerized delivery management system. Particular requirements for this project were: 1) real-time management and information with remote access for contractors and suppliers; 2) remote access from the entrance gates at the various junctions on what was essentially a linear construction project, not unlike the Crossrail project referred to in the introduction to this chapter.

The system chosen allowed the logistics team to plan and schedule deliveries and the real-time management meant that the team had full visibility of all deliveries and vehicle movements on site. The web-access module also meant that the entrance gates could access the system using laptop computers in the gatehouses. The remote nature of some of the sites did pose problems with mobile data connectivity, which had to be overcome.

Deliveries were entered by MVM's logistics team in the main offices near junction 27. These were immediately visible to the gate operators on site so that they could control access. The system allowed the team to reject unplanned deliveries or to accept them, where space was available, and to maintain records of supplier performance. Rejecting unplanned deliveries helped to keep the limited storage areas uncluttered and prevent unplanned blockages along the delivery route. Unplanned deliveries were sometimes accepted but it is important to know why these had happened. Reports showed which trade contractors were best or worst at following the delivery plan, enabling them to be managed and encouraged accordingly.

CASE STUDY MidKent College

Focus Environmental used the Zone Manager delivery management system to help manage the logistics operations during the construction of the MidKent College of Further and Higher Education in Gillingham (Figure 13.5). This comprised three buildings with teaching accommodation and associated facilities. By some standards this was a small project but its locality in a busy and sensitive residential area demanded good delivery management and careful control of traffic.

FIGURE 13.5 MidKent College

Following the good experience of this project Focus Environmental set up a company-wide multi-site system so that they can now use this in a range of small, medium and large projects across the country. The ability quickly to set up a new site and operate it for just a few months means that they are able to provide web-based delivery management to projects where a dedicated system was previously not viable. The delivery management system has become part of the normal way of running their site logistics.

Conclusion

Logistics management of a construction project has to ensure that goods and materials delivered to site arrive in a planned and coordinated manner. They must arrive when the contractor needs them, which means not too early and not too late, and they must be unloaded as near to the point of use as possible. Good delivery management avoids congestion on and around the site, minimizes site storage and maximizes the use of assets such as cranes, hoists and lay-down areas. Similar considerations apply to the disposal of waste, reclamation of unused materials and removal of equipment for which there is no longer any requirement.

For all but the smallest construction project, a modern computerized delivery management system, accessible via the web, will bring the greatest benefits. The ease of access, multi-user capability and use on a range of devices will ensure that the logistics management team can have a complete view of 'real-time' delivery activities with minimum of effort. Many companies are now using such systems on a wide range of project types and sizes, as routinely as they would use project management or other IT systems – and the benefits can be seen in better project management, improved safety and reduced environmental impact.

Computerized delivery management systems will continue to be developed, providing greater visibility of materials in the supply chain and increasing capability for logistics management to track and control deliveries. Delivery management systems are now considered to be essential for congested inner-city projects and for sites with high security requirements, but as this chapter has shown, they can bring benefits on all significant construction projects, wherever those projects are located.

GLOSSARY

Business literature is notoriously jargon-ridden and the fields of construction and logistics are no exceptions. While far from comprehensive, the glossary below may be helpful for some readers.

aggregate   Extracted granular material used in construction. Discussed in Chapter 3.

aggregating   To bring many parts together to form a whole, a total. In the context of this book the term is used to describe how the many different components needed to build (eg a house) are brought together – aggregated – into kits appropriate for each stage in the build process. See also Chapter 2.

andon   A part of the Toyota Production System (and of lean production) it means 'signboard'. It is a method typically using visual displays for communication, alarm and alerts. It can be used by operators, for example, to alert about defects or shortages.

big data   Large data volumes that cannot practically be managed by conventional tools and databases. Discussed in Chapter 6.

BREEAM   Building Research Establishment Environmental Assessment Method. This is an assessment method and rating system for buildings; it sets best practice standards for sustainable building design, construction and operation. Read more at www.breeam.org.

building information modelling (BIM)   BIM is a way of holding information about a facility in a digital format. This includes architectural, structural, materials and services information etc. One important aspect is that BIM allows the sharing of information between stakeholders, so that everyone in the project is using the same up-to-date data. BIM thereby reduces errors, facilitates integration and cooperation and cuts waste. See Chapter 6.

CD&E   In construction this refers to construction, demolition and excavation.

CEEQUAL   A scheme for sustainability assessment, rating and awards within civil engineering. See www.ceequal.co.uk.

common data environment (CDE)   A shared, common source used for collecting, managing and disseminating data on a project. Typically this would be achieved using a collaborative web tool. It ensures that everyone works to the same information thereby minimizing mistakes and rework, and instead facilitating cooperation. The concept is discussed in Chapter 6.

consolidation centre (CC) / construction consolidation centre (CCC)   A location, often a warehouse, to which suppliers deliver their materials (which are stored for a limited time if necessary) and where loads for onward transport are made up, incorporating a mixture of materials – ie consolidated loads. See also LC.

construction logistics plan (CLP)   A document that covers the logistics information for a construction project. This includes site plans, location and access information, vehicle routes and traffic management, storage and lay-down areas, crane and hoist arrangements, waste and environmental information etc. See Chapter 9 for a detailed description.

construction operations building information exchange (COBie)   A data standard that helps to organize information about facilities, buildings and infrastructure. It can be incorporated in spreadsheets. COBie is used in BIM.

Construction Skills Certification Scheme (CSCS)   A certification to provide proof that an individual has the required training and qualifications. See www.cscs.uk.com.

delivery management system   A computerized system for planning and booking deliveries to construction sites. Apart from booking access to gates it is often also used to plan other resources such as forklifts, hoists and cranes.

demand smoothing   Smoothing the peaks and troughs in a construction project programme in order to avoid periods of understaffing leading to overtime and conversely idle periods with staff underutilization. The term is also used in marketing and production where it can refer to attempts to manage the level of customer demand.

enterprise resource planning (ERP)   Typically a suite of software applications that together will provide an integrated view of a company's business processes including procurement, production, distribution, inventory control, sales, human resources etc.

first/second fix   This represents the different stages in, for example, electrical work and plumbing. In electrical installation, first fix can represent the wiring in the wall and second fix the 'external' sockets and switches.

fourth-party logistics (4PL)   A 4PL is a logistics partner that manages and coordinates the resources of other logistics operators. A business may use one or several 3PLs to run its transport fleet, warehouses etc; a 4PL could then be brought in, without further logistics resources, to optimize the overall performance. Chapters 8 and 10 both touch on this concept.

global reporting initiative (GRI)   An organization, active globally, that promotes sustainability reporting. Learn more at www.globalreporting.org.

holding park / holding area   A location, reasonably close to a construction site, where delivery vehicles pull in and report their arrival. They are held there until called forward to the site by the logistics controller. This avoids queueing and congestion on site – vehicles only turn up when required and when site operatives are ready to receive them.

just-in-time (JIT)   Originally a production philosophy, famously pioneered by Toyota in the 1950s, which aims to minimize inventory by delivering materials to downstream processes only at the right time, to the right place and in the required quantity. Note that while in some manufacturing industries the volumes delivered JIT may represent only a few hours' production or even less, in construction this would typically be one to three days' worth of materials.

kanban   A scheduling system for just-in-time production developed at Toyota.

Glossary

Last Planner According to the Lean Construction Institute The Last Planner® (sometimes referred to as the Last Planner® System) is a production planning system designed to produce predictable work flow and rapid learning in programming, design, construction and commissioning of projects. Last Planner® was developed by Glenn Ballard and Greg Howell.

lay-down area A defined area on a construction site for temporary storage of materials immediately before use. This can be just an indicated area on the floor close to where work is taking place, and as work progresses the area follows.

lean A lean methodology means maximizing value while minimizing waste; or, put differently, to create more with fewer resources. Waste here refers to all kinds of waste, in fact waste is anything that does not add value.

Leadership in Energy and Environmental Design (LEED) A set of rating systems for design, construction, operation and maintenance of green buildings. See www.usgbc.org.

logistics The methods and processes by which products and services are delivered to the right location, in the right quantity and quality, at the right time. There are many definitions – see Chapter 1 for a wider discussion.

logistics centre (LC) In the context of this book a logistics centre is a facility, typically a warehouse, where goods from different suppliers are unloaded, stored if necessary and then delivered in consolidated vehicle loads to the site when required. See also CCC.

logistics planning The detailed planning of all materials and resources, such as manpower and equipment, in space and time, to support an activity. The activity can be a military operation, a retail distribution system, a manufacturing operation or a construction project.

material logistics plan / planning In construction this refers to logistics planning focused on the supply of materials to a process as opposed to the site service-related activities of logistics.

mobilization The preparatory stages of a construction project. This includes detailed logistics planning, procedures and method statements, communication with contractors and other stakeholders etc, as necessary for the construction to commence.

off-site manufacturing (OSM) The manufacture of modules in factory conditions away from site. Complete modules are then delivered to site and assembled. Modules can be, for instance, complete bathrooms in a hotel project, or complete toilet podwalls for commercial buildings. See also Chapter 8.

plant and vehicle marshaller (PVM) This refers to the operative responsible for directing vehicles and cranes on a construction site (the term Banksman is also used).

return logistics / reverse logistics Generally this refers to returning unused materials, resuable packaging and waste from a site to where it can be reused or recycled. An additional objective is to make use of otherwise empty vehicles on their return journeys after deliveries, thereby improving vehicle utilization and reducing total traffic volumes.

sales and operations planning (S&OP) An iterative management process (or rather strategic and tactical planning process) that seeks to optimize production levels with respect to demand while considering all processes from sourcing through manufacturing, distribution and sales.

shrinkage   Material losses in the project and on site. This can include both damage and theft of materials.

site waste management plan (SWMP)   A system of planning and monitoring waste levels at all stages of a construction project, thereby promoting efficient use of material resources.

soft landings   A term used in the BIM context referring to effective and smooth progress through design and construction to operation of a building. Promoted by the UK government in its BIM policy. See www.bimtaskgroup.org.

supply chain management (SCM)   A definition by the Council of Supply Chain Management Professionals: 'Supply chain management encompasses the planning and management of all activities involved in sourcing and procurement, conversion, and all logistics management activities. Importantly, it also includes coordination and collaboration with channel partners, which can be suppliers, intermediaries, third party service providers, and customers. In essence, supply chain management integrates supply and demand management within and across companies.'

sustainability   There are many definitions. The Brundtland Commission of the United Nations defines it as: 'sustainable development is development that meets the needs of the present without compromising the ability of future generations to meet their own needs' (United Nations General Assembly (1987) Report of the World Commission on Environment and Development: Our Common Future).

target value design   Often part of a lean process, a process and a philosophy to deliver customer satisfaction within target costs.

third-party logistics (3PL)   The outsourcing of logistics and distribution activities to a third party – a 3PL company.

Toyota Production System (TPS)   This philosophy is described in 'The Toyota Way' and has been adapted to many industries, among them construction.

UK Contractors Group (UKCG)   An association for contractors and their supply chain partners operating in the UK. Read more at www.ukcg.org.uk.

warehouse management system (WMS)   A computerized system to manage and control material in a warehouse. The system holds information on material type, quantity, location, time received and delivered, supplier data, customer (user) data, order references etc.

Waste & Resources Action Programme (WRAP)   Funded primarily by the UK government WRAP is a not-for-profit organization with the mission: 'to accelerate the move to a sustainable resource-efficient economy through re-inventing how we design, produce and sell products, re-thinking how we use and consume products, and re-defining what is possible through recycling and re-use' (www.WRAP.org.uk).

INDEX

NB: chapter conclusions, chapter notes and references are indexed as such page numbers in *italic* indicate figures or tables

3PLs (third-party logistics) (and)   164, 194–96 *see also* third-party logistics in construction
   access to resources   201
   definition of   184
   future roles of   196
   network collaboration   201
   transactional cost savings   200–01
4PLs (fourth-party logistics)   184, 187
   and Norbert Dentressangle   146
   operators   203

Abdelhamid, T S   214
Abdullah, S   209
AbouRizk, S M   206
Abu Hassan, S   63
Advanced Panel System (APS)   150
Agapiou, A   206, 212, 215
Aggregate Industries   146, 148, 203
aggregates   35, 37–40
   customers for   39–40
   key suppliers of   37
   supply and sourcing of   38–39
aggregating global products for JIT delivery (and)   25–34
   commercial and risk issues   33–34
   delivery of aggregation and lean delivery capability   32–33, *33*
   environmental legislation, quality and good waste management   28–29
   global sourcing   26–27
   investment in procurement and centralized decision making   27–28
   lean supply onto site with plot-picked delivery   29, 31–32, *30*
   other considerations for   31–32
Ahuja, H N   206
Al-Hejji, S   215
Amazon   28, 32, 34
Anderson, S   227, 240
Ashdown Agreement, targets of   145
asphalt   35, 40–42
   customers for   41–42
   key suppliers of   40
   and supply/supply challenges   40–41
Assaf, S M   215
Azmin, S M   209

B&Q   *see* case studies: third-party logistics operators in construction
Baccarini, D   92 *see also* project complexity
Ballal, T   63
Ballard, H G   92, 114
Ballard, R   6
Bargstädt, J H   208, 213
Barthorpe, S   63, 65, 68, 74, 75, 180, 227, 235, 237
Basily, S Y   215
Beaumont, W   5
Beliveau, J Y   209
Bennett, J   86
Biddy, P   205
big data   5, 102–08, 110–11, 117
   challenges of   105–06
   in construction   106, 108, *107*, *109*
   definitions of   102
   examples of   106
   key characteristics of   103–05, *104*
   and smart citizens, cities and governments   110–11
   value proposition of   103
Billington, C   97
BIM   *see* building information modelling (BIM)
Birmingham New Hospital Joint Venture   153
Bock, T   19
Bodin, L   215
Bowen, P A   215
Braithwaite, A   11
BREEAM excellent rating   149
Brown, A   1
Brown, B   106–07
Browne, M   4
Brundtland, G H   124
Brynjolfsson, E   103, 105
Bubholz, M   5
builders' merchants   4, 26, 32, 37, 54, 194, 200 *see also* Jewson; Travis Perkins *and* Wolseley
Builders Profile   82
Builders Research Establishment Environmental Assessment Method (BREEAM)   125, 142–43
   and BREEAM excellent rating   149

Index

building information management (NIM) systems   251
building information modelling (BIM) (and)   4–5, 22, 91–92, 95–97, *96*, 113, 117, 143, 202
  Digital Built Britain level three strategy   92, 97, 108, 110
  level two   108, 111
  value proposition of/data-driven management   97, *98–101*
Building Regulations   142
  and 'The Code for Sustainable Homes'   142
BuildingConfidence   82
Built Environment Commitment   140
  as strategic priority of Construction 2025   140
bulk materials, supply of (and)   35–61
  aggregates; asphalt; cement; ready-mixed concrete   *see individual subject entries*
  logistics, customers and bulk materials   35–43
  logistics models in construction bulk materials   43–55 *see also subject entry*
  supply chain maturity   55–60
  see also subject entry
Business Innovation & Skills, Department for   187
business to business (B2B) space   34
business to consumer (B2C)   34

Caledonian Building Systems   150
Caragliu, A   110
case studies (for)   134–37
  construction supply chain management strategy
    Mace Business School   85–86
  delivery management systems
    M1 motorway widening   254–55, *255*
    Media City UK, Salford   253–54, *253*
    MidKent College   256, *256*
    Royal Adelaide Hospital   252–53, *252*
  London 2012 Olympics   199–200
  Material Logistics Planning, Central St Giles   232 *see also* Lundesjö, G
  off-site manufacture
    Jocelyn Park   150–51
    Ropemaker   149
  role of logistics in achieving sustainable construction
    Triangeln (the Triangle) – Malmö, Sweden   135–37
    'University Hospital of the future' (Linköping, Sweden)   134–35

third-party logistics operators in construction
  Aircraft Carrier Alliance (ACA) and Wincanton   190–90, *190, 191*
  B&Q and Wincanton   192–93, *192, 193*
  London 2012 Olympics   199–200 *see also subject entry and* Wincanton
CCC(s)   *see* construction consolidation centres (CCCs)
CEEQUAL   142
cement   35, 36–37
  bagged   37
  bulk   36–37
  customers for   37
  key suppliers of   36
  supply and production of   36
challenge of construction logistics (and)   9–24
  challenges of the urban environment   21–22
  definitions and importance of logistics   9–11
  diversity of the construction industry   12–13
  factors that influence logistics activities   13–16 *see also* logistics activities
  logistics and the supply chain   11–12
  role of logistics management within construction   16–21 *see also* logistics management
chapter conclusion (for)
  aggregating global products for JIT delivery   34
  challenge of construction logistics   22–23
  consolidation centres in construction logistics   240–41
  construction logistics   61
  construction supply chain management strategy   87
  data management for integrated supply chains in construction   117–18
  delivery management systems   256–67
  effective management of a construction supply chain   74–75
  managing construction logistics for confined sites, urban areas   218–20, *218, 219, 220*
  resource efficiency benefits of effective construction logistics   155–57
  role of construction logistics manager   181–82
  role of logistics in achieving sustainable construction   137–38
  third-party logistics operators in construction   203

Index

chapter notes (for)
    challenge of construction logistics 23
    resource efficiency benefits of effective construction logistics 156–57
Chartered Institute of Building (CIOB) 182
Chartered Institute of Logistics and Transport 182
    Supply Chain Forum 169
China 26, 29
    increasing labour rates in 27
Chiu, Y C 209, 210, 216
Christian, J 213
Christofides, N 215
Chui, M 106–07
Clausen, L E 215
CLOCS/CLOCS campaign 174, 181
COBie construction operations building information exchange 111
Colin, J 10
collaborative planning 50
common data environment (CDE) 111, 113
Competition and Markets Authority 195
Considerate Constructor Scheme 66, 67
consolidation centres in construction logistics (and) 225–42, *226 see also* construction consolidation centres (CCCs)
    benefits of using a CCC 233–37, *236 see also* London; Stockholm *and* Waste and Resources Action Programme (WRAP)
    resources, functionality and operation 227–33
        delivery of materials 231
        ordering materials 228–29, *229*
        output of materials 231
        receiving materials 230
        resources and facilities 228
        storage of materials 230
        value-added processes 232–33
        warehouse management systems 231–32
Construction 2025 – industrial strategy for construction 140
construction consolidation centres (CCCs) 6, 21, 25, 68, 70, 71, 72, 74, 75, 84, 144, 151–52, *152*, 196, 219–20
    benefits of using 233–37 *236*
    hidden, single user, shared consolidation, virtual consolidation 238
    locating 239–40
    projects: Hammarby Sjöstad (Stockholm); Heathrow Consolidation Centre (HCC) *and* London Construction Consolidation Centre (LCCC) 227, 235–36
    types of 237–39
construction and demolition (C&D) waste 140
construction, demolition and excavation (CD&E) 140 *see also* waste
construction logistics (and) 64–67, *65 see also* construction supply chain
    consequences of failing to manage 17–18
    plans (CLPs) *see* construction logistics plans (CLPs)
    role of manager *see* role of the construction logistics manager
    supply of bulk materials *see* bulk materials, supply of
    sustainable 126, 128, *126–27*, *129 see also*
Construction Logistics and Cyclist Safety (CLOCS) 22, 174, 181
construction logistics plan (CLP) 5, 19–20, 66, 68, 71, 155, 161
    best practice (2018) 70
    creating a 174, *175–80*
    definition of 225
    implementation of 75
construction logistics strategies: influence on resource efficiency (and) 144–54
    construction consolidation centres (CCCs) 152, *152*
    delivery management systems 154
    demand smoothing 151
    just-in-time delivery 151
    off-site manufacturing 148–50
    on-site logistics specialist 151–52
    packaging 148
    reverse logistics 145–46
    transport: 4PL, transport types and driver training 146–47
    waste management and reprocessing logistics opportunities 153, *153 see also* waste management
Construction Management Strategies: A theory of construction management 86
Construction Manager 169
construction operations building information exchange (COBie) 111
Construction Products Association 185
construction projects
    2012 Olympic Games, London 19
    see also London
    airport development in Berlin 19
    Terminal 5 at Heathrow Airport 19
    see also Heathrow
Construction Research and Innovation 169
construction supply chain *see* effective management of a construction project supply chain

Construction Supply Chain Forum (CILT)   174, 181
  Focus magazine   169
construction supply chain management strategy (and)   77–87
  case study: Mace Business School *see* case studies
  concept of supply chain management   77–78
  framework agreements   84
  logistics in construction   84–85
    see also case studies
  supply chain risks   79–84
    see also subject entry
Constructionline   82
corporate social responsibility (CSR) compliance   29, 173
Crossrail   84, 187–89, 243, *244*, 255

data
  analysing   116
  visualization   116–17
data management for integrated supply chains in construction (and)   91–119
  big data and construction   102–08, *104, 107, 109,* 110–11 *see also* big data
  data and the integrated supply chain/management systems   111, 113–14, *112*
  enterprise-level integration (and)   115–17
    continuous improvement   115–16
    data visualization   116–17
  information management in construction   *see subject entry*
Dawood, N   211, 214, 215
DB Schenker   19, 45
Deepen, J   184
definitions (of)
  3PL   184
  big data   102
  logistics   10–11
  project complexity   92
  sustainability   124
  system   244–45
Del Bo, C   110
deliveries, out-of-hours   50
delivery management systems (and)   6, 243–57, *244 see also* case studies
  benefits of proper management   247–50
    and measurements to drive improvement   249
  definition of   244–45
  features/key features of computerised delivery management   245, 246–47
  the future for   251–52

  users of   250–51
  Zone Manager   154
Design for Resource Efficiency   143, 156
Deutsch, R   101
DHL   32, 195, 239
Digital Built Britain   108, *109*
  level three BIM strategy   92, 110
distribution centres (DCs)   12, 15, 34, 68, 189, 190, 194–95, 196, 202, 226
  regional (RDC)   16
DIY retailers   192, 194
Donnelly, I A   110
Donyavi, S   210
Dozzi, S P   206
driver training   143, 157
  and coached driving styles   147
Dumbill, E   102
Dun & Bradstreet   81

Eastman, C   92
EC Harris   199
Edmun-Fotwe, F   214, 216
effective management of a construction project supply chain (and)   62–76
  best practice – 2018   70
  construction logistics   64–67
    see also subject entry
  defining   67–70
    emphasis on control   68–69
    logistics management and current best practice   67–68
    prefabrication and off-site production   69–70
  improvement strategy: CCC as sustainable proposition   71–72, 74, *72, 73*
  typical construction project supply chain   63–64
Eilon, S   214
Einarsson, C   5
EJ Berry & Sons/Recycling Solutions Ltd: collection service   146
Ekholm, A   209
Elbeltagi, E   212
Eldsouky, A   212
emerging web-based retailers   32
Emmerson, Sir H   91
Enshassi, A   215
enterprise resource planning (ERP)   60, 111
Eschemuller, J   208
European Union (EU)   80
  goal of achieving virtually CO_2-free city logistics by 2030   23
Everett, J G   214
expanding role of logistics in construction   1–2, *3*
  'construction is logistics'   2

Index

Fabbe-Costes, N 10
Fallon, K 95
Fang, Y S 214, 215
Fernando, T 216
figures
   big data, key characteristics of *104*
   British Land ropemaker site *150*
   building a block wall *3*
   causal loop diagram: issues with material management on confined construction sites *207*
   construction consolidation centre (CCC) *152*
   construction logistics plan (CLP) – best practice format *175–80*
   Crossrail construction site *244*
   Digital Built Britain operational model strategy *109*
   ease of capturing big data's value and magnitude of its potential across various sectors: US economy *107*
   function of 'logistics' within the 'supply chain' *65*
   graph comparing number of deliveries made to site with a CCC versus traditional deliveries to site *220*
   high-level theoretical framework to address concepts related to material flow within context of confined construction sites in congested cities *217*
   illustration of the principles of consolidation *226*
   integrated workflow *112*
   logistics strategy for a construction project – a systematic approach *129*
   major projects considered in central London, 2000–14 (sample of) *72*
   modern contractual structure *94*
   project complexity *93*
   project durations *73*
   relationships process utilizing BIM and integrated teams *96*
   resource efficiency in the built environment – the case for action *141*
   simplified view of construction supply chain by materials types, highlighting typical characteristics and 3PL roles *186*
   theoretical model utilized to develop a logistics model *218*
   traditional contractual structure *93*
   traditional relationship process *95*
   variation of materials stored in the construction consolidation centre *221*
   wood waste to be converted to compost *155*
Flanagan, R 208
Flinders, P 6
Focus (CILT) 169
Fong, D 214
Formoso, C T 213
Franklin, M 4
freight-operating companies (FOCs) 53
Fridqvist, S 209

Gannon, D B 110
Georgy, E M 209
Georgy, M 215
Glaskowsky, N A Jr 10
Global Reporting Initiative (GRI) 125
Gosling, J 86
Green Construction Board 141
Guo, S 210

Hamzeh, F R 216
Hanafi, H M 209
Harris, F 214, 216
Harris, F C 211
Harrison, C 110
health and safety 145, 147
   assessment criteria: CHAS, Exor and Safemark 82
Heathrow 19, 25, 34, 187
   Consolidation Centre 227, 235
Hegazy, T 212
Hendrickson, C 215
Heskett, J L 10
high-profile construction projects 149, 187, 203
Hinze, J 213
Hoare, N 6
Hobbs 201
Holt, G D 211
Horman, M J 209, 2142
Howell, G 92
Howell, G A 210
Huang, X 2153
Hui, M 208
Huovila, P 111

Ibrahim, E M 209
ICT, importance of 110
Industry Strategy for Construction 194
information management in construction (and) 92–97, 101–02
   building information modelling (BIM) 95–97, *96 see also* subject entry

information distribution   94, 95
project complexity   92–94, 93, 94
synchronization and concurrent workflows   101–02
value proposition of BIM and data-driven management   97, 98–101
Institute of Civil Engineers (ICE)   182
internet of things   97, 110, 115
Ivie, R M   10

Japan, prefabrication industry in   19
Jewson   26, 32
Jones, D T   92
Josephson, P   215
just-in-time (JIT)   14, 226, 234
  delivery   25, 33, 128, 130, 131, 132, 151, 209
  pull system   231

Kaisler, S   102, 103, 105–06
kanban/*Kanban*   28, 113–14
Kooragamage, R   6
Koskela, L   111, 213
KPIs   11, 56–57, 59, 143, 156, 171, 236
  internal   60
  scorecard   82
Kurt Salmon Associates   113

Lafarge Tarmac   26, 37, 40, 42, 57
Laing O'Rourke   2, 239
Lambeck, R   208
Larsson, B   215
Larus, J R   110
Latham, M   64, 66, 68
Lautanala, M   111
Leadership in Energy and Environmental Design (LEED)   125
lean   117
  aggregated supply chain model characteristics   29, 30
  construction   113
Lee, H   97
legislation (UK)
  Building Regulations   142
    see also standards
  Competition Law   83
Li, H   215
Lieb, K   187
Lieb, R   189
Lieb, R C   186
Linner, T   19
logistics activities (and)   13–16
  control of the supply chain   16
  key transport and storage considerations for products   15–16
  special characteristics   14

time issues   14
value to weight ratio   13–14
volume to weight ratio   13
logistics management (and)   16–21
  see also report(s)
  consequences of failing to manage construction logistics   17–18
logistics models in construction bulk materials   43–55
  aggregates and asphalt   47–53
    planning (aggregate replenishment work)   50
    planning (asphalt and general market aggregates)   48–49
    transport operations (aggregate replenishment work)   51–52
    transport operations (asphalt and general market aggregates)   50–51
    transport operations (rail)   52–53
  cement: planning and transport operations   53–55
  concrete: planning and transport operations   45–47
London
  2012 Olympic and Paralympic Games   19, 78, 84 *see also* case studies
  Construction Consolidation Centre (LCCC)   25, 227, 235–36, 236
  Crossrail project   243, 244
  Olympic Stadium   243
Loosemore, M   208, 214
Lu, M   213
Lundesjö, G   6, 228, 232, 237, 238, 240

McAfee, A   103, 105
McCaffer, R   214, 216
Mace Business School   77, 85–87 *see also* case studies
  and Building Magazine Supply Chain Management of the Year Award (2010)   86
Mahdjoubi, L   211, 216
Mallasi, Z   214
Managing Construction Logistics   180, 227, 235, 237
managing construction logistics for confined sites in urban areas (by)   205–24, 218, 219, 220
  developing a theoretical framework (through)   211–18
    challenges involved with material coordination and programme   212
    contractor's materials spatial requirements exceeding available space   211–12

managing construction logistics for confined sites in urban areas (by)   (*continued*)
   developing a theoretical framework (through)   (*continued*)
      difficult to coordinate storage requirements of subcontractors   213–14
      difficult-to-store materials on site for lack of space   212–13
      effect of spatial time collision on health, safety and productivity   214
      location of site entrance impacts delivery of materials   212
      managing material flow routing in congested cities   214–15
      material flow and material routing management   211
      material routing and path planning in confined construction site   216
      theoretical approach to address material flow   216–18, *217*
   identifying current challenges in   206, 208–10, *207*
      identifying a suitable definition for confined construction site   208–09
      spatial congestion on-site   209–10, *210*
Mangan, J   12
Manyika, J   106–07
Marasini, R   211, 215
material logistics plan (MLP)   154–55
Messner, J I   213
models
   3D real-time   111
   4D   251
   5D   251
   data visualization   116
   logistics   43–45, 71
   simulation   110–11, 219, 220
   sustainability   123, 137–38
modern methods of construction (MMC)   64
Moone, B   5
Mossman, A   63, 66, 68, 69
Mulholland, B   213
multichannel aggregators   28
multichannel providers   32

Naoum, S   214
national delivery centre (NDC)   33
Nepal, M P   211, 213
Network Rail: redevelopment of Reading train station   150
Ng, T   214, 215
Nijkamp, P   110
Norbert Dentresangle   146, 201
Norman, G   206
North, S   213

O'Byrne, R   200
off-site manufacturing (OSM)   27, 113, 148–50, 150, 183, 189, 203
Oglesby, C H   210
Olomolaiye, P O   211
Olympic Park   187, 188
Olympic Stadium (London)   242
Olympics   25, 197 *see also* case studies
Omar, B   63
Osman, M H   209
Ottoson, M   227, 234
'Our Common Future': Report of the World Commission on Environment and Development, (UN Commission, 1987)   124

Palmer, M   95
Park, M   211, 213
Parker, H W   210
perspectives and opinions   4
Pheng, L   208
Peter Brett Associates for TfL   240
planning
   collaborative   50
   pull   114, 116
Premier Waste UK PLC   154
prequalification questionnaire (PQQ)   79–81
product areas   35 *see also* aggregates; asphalt; cement *and* ready-mixed concrete
production, last planner system of   114
project complexity   92, *93*

radio frequency identification (RFID) tags   251
Radosavljevic, M   86
rail freight   53, 55
Rana Plaza building collapse (Bangladesh 2013)   29
ready-mixed concrete   35, 42–43
   customers for   43
   key suppliers of   42
   supply of   42–43
Reed, D A   110
references (for)
   challenge of construction logistics   23–24
   consolidation centres in construction logistics   242

construction logistics – supply of bulk materials 61
data management for integrated supply chains in construction 118–19
effective management of a construction project supply chain 75–76
managing construction logistics for confined sites in urban areas 221–24
third-party logistics operators in construction 203–04
regional distribution centres (RDCs) 16
report(s) (on)
'Accelerating Change' (Strategic Forum for Construction, 2002) 17
Freight Best Practice (Department for Transport, 2007) 236, *236*
'Impact on the climate from the construction process (2014) 124
management of construction logistics (BIS 2013) 18
'Our Common Future' (World Commission on Environment and Development, 1987) 124
Rethinking Construction (Construction Task Force, DETR, 1998) 63
'Supply Chain Analysis into the Construction Industry' (EC Harris, 2013) 194
research (on)
construction projects (BIS, 2013) 94
critical factors in managing materials/material flow (Spillane *et al*, 2011) 206
impact of Mace Business School (Gosling, Cardiff Business School) 86
urban and rural population growth (UN, 2008) 205
use of big data analytics as part of strategic planning (BARC, 2013) 101
resource efficiency benefits of effective construction logistics (and) 139–58
benefits to supply chain 155–57
construction logistics strategies: influence on resource efficiency *see subject entry*
construction sustainability impact 140–42, *141*
legislation and standards 142 *see also* legislation *and* standards
material logistics planning 154–55

supply chain influence on sustainable construction logistics 143–44
clients 143
contractors 144
design 143
suppliers 144
Waste and Resources Action Programme (WRAP) *see subject entry*
Riley, D R 213
Robbins, S 2, 5, 63, 64, 65, 66, 67, 68, 69, 71, 74, 75, 180, 227, 235, 237
Roberts, P W 205
Roe, P 195
role of the construction logistics manager (and/as) 161–82
construction logistics managers (and) 169–74
beneficial qualifications 174
desirable qualities 173–74
desirable skills and competencies 173
responsibilities 169–74
consulting logistics professional (engaged in) 165–66, *167–69*
authority permissions 166
project commencement 165
project definition stage 165–66
project delivery 166
creating a construction logistics plan (CLP) 174, 180–81, *175–80*
logistics professional and service sourcing (via) 163–65
agency staff 164
consultancy staff 163–64
in-house professionals 163
logistics package contractors 164
third-party logistics companies 164–65
training required 180–81
role of logistics in achieving sustainable construction 123–38 *see also* sustainability *and* sustainable construction (Swedish perspective)
Royal School of Military Engineering 150
Russom, P 103

Safety Schemes in Procurement (SSIP) 82
sales and operations planning (S&OP) 44, 48, 49, 53, 57, 58, 59, 60
Sanders, S R 213, 214
Sanvido, V E 213, 214
Sawacha, E 214
Shakantu, W M 215
Sidler, B 195
Sikka, S 211, 215
Site Managers Safety Training Scheme 181

Skyes, H   205
SmartLIFE project   150
Soltani, A R   216
Son, B   211, 213
South Somerset Homes Housing Association   150
  and Jocelyn Park   150
Spillane, J P   206, 208, 211, 212, 214
Sporre, L-G   5
standards
  Builders Research Establishment Environmental Assessment Method   142–43
  CEEQUAL   142
  Code for Sustainable Homes   142
Steele, S   67
Stockholm   235
  and Hammarby Sjöstad logistics centre   234–35, 238
storage issues   145
studies (on)
  big data: 20 sectors in US economy (2011)   106–07, *107*
  interactions between BIM and lean (Sacks *et al*, 2010)   113
  Unilever House (WRAP, 2007)   237
  vehicles delivering to construction sites 233 (WRAP 2012a)   233
Sullivan, G   63, 64, 65, 68, 74, 75, 180, 227, 235, 237
suppliers of
  asphalt   40
  bulk materials for construction   57
  cement   36
  ready-mixed concrete   42
supply chain
  complicated and 'unstructured'   185
  of DIY retailers   194–95
supply chain maturity (and)   55–60
  coordinating across the external supply chain   60
  current (for)   57–59
    aggregates and asphalt   58
    cement   58–59
    ready-mixed concrete   58
  integrating and aligning supply chain functions   60
  need to increase   59
  stages of   56–57
supply chain risks (and)   79–84
  assessing
    capability risk of new supply chain companies   83
    capacity risk   83
    compliance   80–81
    financial risk   81
    performance risk   82
    the risk   80
    second- and third-tier risk   83–84
    third-party accreditation   82
  understanding the company: the prequalification questionnaire (PQQ)   79–81
survey(s) of/on
  CEOs (PwC 2014)   22
  global supply chain (PwC, 2013)   55
  top European 3PL CEOs   187
sustainability (and)
  'The Code for Sustainable Homes'   142
  concept of   124–25 *see also* report(s)
  construction logistics   5
  model (Sweco)   123
  standards for   125
sustainable construction (and)   123–38
  case studies   134–37 *see also subject entry*
  considerations for efficient logistics   130–33
    administrative system support   133
    deliveries   131
    deliveries to/from site   133
    finance   133
    labelling of materials   132
    the logistics centre   131–32
    packaging design   132
    planning   130–31
    the team   131
  logistics   126, *126–27*
  for a construction project   128, *129*
Sweden   *see also* sustainability *and* sustainable construction
  Sweco and 'sustainability industry' approach (2013)   125

tables
  analysis of general merchants vs emerging web retailers   *33*
  classifying main types of spatial conflicts with safety, damage and site applicable to spatial congestion on-site   *210*
  common supply chain problems and data solutions   *98–101*
  comparison between lean and conventional processes   *30*
  investigating various parameters using the proposed framework   *217*
  key construction logistics elements to consider when developing a project plan   *167–69*
  large and small resources   *229*

number of vehicles and cost of congestion charges 236
prices of fuels purchased by manufacturing industry 187
summary of driving factors as to why the construction industry makes better use of 3PLs 198
sustainable industry concept: dimensions, content and examples relating to logistics 126–27
tarmac/tarmacadam *see* asphalt
Thabet, W Y 209, 210
third-party logistics operators/company (3PLs) 6, 184, 230
third-party logistics operators in construction (and) 183–204
 3PL definition 184
 complicated and 'unstructured' supply chain 185
 the construction industry and use of 3PL services 197, *198 see also* case studies
 evolution of the 3PL role: phases 200–01
  access to resources 201
  network collaboration 201
  transactional cost savings 200–01
 final mile logistics 196 *see also* construction consolidation centres
 impact of downturn 185, 187–88, *186*, *187*
 international construction supply chains 195–96
 omni-channel 194
 primary and secondary distribution networks 194–95
 supply chains with a dominant entity 188–93 *see also* case studies
 trigger for momentum of 3PL role in construction logistics 202–03
Thomas, A 63, 64, 67, 68, 71
Thomas, H R 213, 215
Thomas, R H 209, 212
Thomsen, C 101
Thornton, G M 205
three Rs – right material, right location, right time 130
Tookey, E 215
tools
 CaliBRE 149
 SMARTWaste 149
Toyota 187
 Production System (TPS) principles 113
track-and-trace systems 46, 49

Transport for London (TfL) 200, 233
 CLP Guidance documents 174
 construction logistics plans (CLPs) 66–67, 155
 and Stanhope plc, Bovis Lend Lease and Wilson James 227
transport management system (TMS) 49, 54, 60
Travis Perkins 26, 32, 33

Uher, T E 208, 214
Underwood, J 5
Unilever 56, 237
United Kingdom (UK) 26
 Contractors Group ((UKCG) 62, 140
 Environment Group 140
 government construction strategy (2011) 91
 government information economy strategy 97
 Government PAS91 questionnaire 81
 transformation of the construction industry 107
United Nations (UN)
 definition of sustainability (1987) 124
 research on urban and rural population growth 205
urbanization 4, 6, 21–22, 110, 209

value chain 50, 62, 114, 215
value stream mapping 114
van Rijmenam, M 108
vendor-managed inventory (VMI) 50, 59
Voigtmann, J 208, 213

Waddell, M 5
warehouse management system (WMS) 228, 230
 technology 231–32
waste 9, 11, 16, 17, 19, 26–27, 38–39, 63, 92, 95, 97, 128, 136, 139, 155
 construction and demolition (C&D) 140
 management 28–29, 64, 68, 70, 144–46, 153, *153*, 162, 170, 173
Waste and Resources Action Programme (WRAP) (and) 140, 196, 237
 Green Construction Board 141
 Halving Waste to Landfill 140
 Efficient Construction Logistics (2007) 199
 reports on Barts Hospital and Central St Giles 239
 study of Unilever House 237
 waste arising across CD&E in England 140

Waste and Resources Action Programme
(WRAP) (and) (*continued*)
website, guidance and reporting tools
on   144
Watkins, M   210
Watson-Gandy, C   214
Wegelius-Lehtonen,   215
Williams, T M   92
Williamson   200
Wilson James construction specialist   32, 218
Wincanton (and)   196, 199–00 *see also* case studies

Aircraft Carrier Alliance (ACA)
190–91, *190*, *191*
B&Q   192–93, *192*
Kingfisher plc   192
Winch, G M   94, 213
Wolseley   26, 32
Womack, J P   92
Wong, E T   206
Woodcock, M   4
Wu, I C   209, 210, 216

Yang, L J   211, 216